PENGUIN BOOKS

ON THE TRAIL OF THE SERPENT

Richard Neville was an Australian writer and commentator who first came to prominence as the editor of the counterculture magazine *OZ*. Having travelled the 'pot trail' throughout the 1960s and '70s, Neville was commissioned by Random House to write the story of con man and serial killer Charles Sobhraj. The result, *The Life and Crimes of Charles Sobhraj*, was a global bestseller. His books include *Playpower*; *Hippie, Hippie, Shake*; *Out of My Mind*; and *Amerika Psycho*. Richard Neville died in September 2016.

Julie Clarke trained as a journalist on the *Sydney Telegraph* before joining ABC television. She later became a New York correspondent for Australian Consolidated Press and worked as a TV producer. Along with her partner Richard Neville she wrote *The Life and Crimes of Charles Sobhraj*, an endeavour that took the pair all over the world for two years.

RICHARD NEVILLE
and
JULIE CLARKE

On the Trail of the Serpent

The Epic Hunt for the Bikini Killer

REVISED AND UPDATED BY
Julie Clarke

Previously Published as
The Life and Crimes of Charles Sobhraj

PENGUIN BOOKS

PENGUIN BOOKS
An imprint of Penguin Random House LLC
penguinrandomhouse.com

First published in Great Britain by Jonathan Cape 1979
First published in the United States of America as
Charles Sobhraj by Pocket Books 1979
This revised and updated edition first published in Great Britain by Vintage UK,
a division of Penguin Random House Ltd, 2020
Published in Penguin Books 2021

LIBRARY OF CONGRESS CATALOGING-IN-PUBLICATION DATA
Names: Neville, Richard, 1941–2016, author. | Clarke, Julie, 1952– author.
Title: On the trail of the serpent : the epic hunt for the bikini killer /
Richard Neville, Julie Clarke.
Other titles: Life and crimes of Charles Sobhra.
Description: 1st Edition. | New York : Penguin Books, 2021. |
Revised and updated by Julie Clarke.
Identifiers: LCCN 2020052861 (print) | LCCN 2020052862 (ebook) |
ISBN 9780143136859 (paperback) | ISBN 9780525508359 (ebook)
Subjects: LCSH: Sobhraj, Charles. | Murderers—Biography. |
Murder—Asia—Case studies.
Classification: LCC HV6248.S6136 N48 2021 (print) |
LCC HV6248.S6136 (ebook) | DDC 364.152/32092—dc23
LC record available at https://lccn.loc.gov/2020052861
LC ebook record available at https://lccn.loc.gov/2020052862

Printed in the United States of America
1   3   5   7   9   10   8   6   4   2

Set in Dante MT Std

Contents

Preface

More than forty years have passed since this book began for us. In 1977 Richard Neville and I were journalists living and working in New York City, I as a correspondent for an Australian media company and Richard as a well-connected freelancer.

Our relationship was in its early days. We'd rented a loft in Chinatown, tucked between two methadone maintenance clinics and a kung-fu studio, furnished with only a double bed and a ping-pong table. The loft was always perfumed with the scent of ducks, rubbed with anise and roasting on spits, wafting up from the restaurant beneath us.

Then came the call that ambitious young writers dream of. Random House was asking if Richard could leave immediately for Delhi. A notorious and charming young criminal named Charles Sobhraj had just been arrested in India. Of Vietnamese-Indian heritage, he had been raised in France and had impersonated many nationalities as a con man and poisoner in the five-star hotels and casinos of the world. Now he was implicated in a string of gruesome murders and druggings of tourists in Asia. It had been a highly publicized manhunt. Currently jailed in Delhi awaiting trial, the enterprising Sobhraj had sold his story to a Thailand-based American entrepreneur. Random House had purchased the rights. Richard was offered a contract to write his life story, quickly.

We were the opposite of hard-nosed news-hounds. Having made a name for himself as the publisher and editor of a frisky but radical underground magazine called OZ (today it's literally a museum piece in the Victoria and Albert Museum in London), Richard was known as an articulate spokesperson for the counterculture. A natural maverick, with a dislike for authority that stemmed from being sent to boarding school too young, Richard loved to taunt the Establishment. He could talk his way into and out of any situation and was so funny and charming that some people became addicted to him. I suppose I was one of them.

In 1965, with his best friend, the psychedelic artist Martin Sharp, Richard had travelled from Sydney to London via a route that was only just opening up and was soon to become known as the 'pot trail', and later wrote of his experiences in his first book, *Playpower*.

By the early sixties, the young avant-garde had discovered that there was a big space on the map of the world between Australia and Europe: Asia. Nothing seemed to have changed there for hundreds of years, or since the British Raj. It was amazingly cheap, and thrillingly exotic, with cannabis and all sorts of drugs freely available. Time was different then too. Unlike the 'weekends away' and 'city breaks' of today, it was not uncommon, after finishing university and/or saving up for a year after high school, to take two or three years to float across the world, maybe doing some buying and selling along the way to keep the finances in shape.

From all quarters of the Earth students began flocking to Asia; it was the original magical mystery tour, like walking into history and geography books from other centuries on LSD, like trekking into the pages of *National Geographic* on ayahuasca. Unchanged cultures, the Himalayas, sensational cheap food, endless pristine beaches, $1-a-night hotels, crumbling Raj piles for $5 a night, and 50-cents-a-night guesthouses built of bamboo teetering beside green rivers. For shopaholics and budding traders there were exotic embroideries and costumes, gemstones and antiques, not to mention all sorts of drugs, sold for a fraction of the price in the West.

There were no guidebooks in 1965 when Richard left on that journey. In fact, he checked into a brothel (the Thai Son Kit) in Bangkok and stayed there for a week believing it was a hotel. Or so he claimed.

When I left on the same journey ten years later, the soon-to-be founders of Lonely Planet had printed a modest pamphlet called *Across Asia On the Cheap*.

The authors' well-thumbed copy of *Across Asia on the Cheap*, the first guide published by what would become Lonely Planet.

I have a beautiful girlfriend whose mother, when she was seventeen, packed her suitcase for her across-Asia adventure; it contained ball gowns, Chanel type suits and kitten-heels. By the time she arrived at the other end, having, among many experiences, lived for three months with a family in Afghanistan, she had a Kalimantan basket containing antique sarongs, museum-quality lace blouses from India, and a heavily embroidered Afghani wedding dress. And not only had her wardrobe changed. She had taken LSD and had profound realizations that changed the course of her life – in a good way, I believe.

Not all the stories were so happy. I heard of another girl from my university who was skinny-dipping in a river in Afghanistan and was shot dead by an outraged Pathan tribesman who had seen her from a hilltop.

My own journey began at the start of 1975 in Bali, which was then close to how one could imagine Heaven. On our first night in Kuta Beach, a tiny village without electricity and at the end of a muddy track, a local teenager sold us LSD, which inspired us to go body-surfing in the giant waves at the beach until dawn, enjoying the light show and sound effects of the violent thunderstorms. Quite unaware of our good fortune in having survived, we then ordered magic mushroom omelettes at Poppies café. And so our aptly named 'pot trail' journey began.

By May, having already been robbed twice and with one travelling companion ill enough to go to hospital, we had checked into the Hotel Malaysia in Bangkok to recover in what seemed at the time to be luxury. The Malaysia had plumbing. It had sheets! And there was a swimming pool. It was *the* place for student travellers to stay in Bangkok. The lobby was a meeting place for everyone on the road, and travellers of all nationalities met and exchanged advice.

It was for this very reason that just three weeks after we had moved on, the Malaysia became one of the headquarters for Charles Sobhraj and his 'befriend, drug and rob' operations. Which quickly, and mysteriously, became 'befriend, drug and murder'.

Unaware of what was about to unfold at our favourite luxury hotel, we all set off on the next stage of our trip: across India, into Pakistan, then Afghanistan, Iran and Turkey, which we undertook with a Bedford van and a block of government-certified hash the size of a brick which had cost a few dollars at a market in, I think, Pakistan.

I cannot exaggerate our naivety and I mention this to cast light on the culture in which Sobhraj was able to operate. We had no idea what country came next. Most of us had only recently left homes where the toilet paper was decorated with floral motifs and our mothers daily vacuumed the wall-to-wall carpet. Now we were learning to squat in third-world lavatorial situations and pour water over our bottoms with teapots.

Oh, how we rejected the consumer society. Thanks to new translations of their sacred texts, Buddhism and Hinduism had recently become on-trend. Incense was inescapable. Meditation in caves with gurus at ashrams in India and retreats with Tibetan lamas in Nepal were à la mode. Kids were hunting down the meaning of life and the promise of enlightenment like American big-game hunters on the scent of a white rhino. Reality was a moveable feast as hash and marijuana were everywhere, and basically legal in most of Asia. There was heroin too, which was also everywhere. Heroin belonged in a dark underworld we found repugnant, but it played a role in the culture of the road, and nothing but tragedy ever came of it.

Five years later, when Richard and I began researching this story, privileged youngsters from a privileged country, the dark side was unknown territory. I had been a feature writer mainly for women's magazines. To Richard, it seemed to me, 'crime' was something daring and romantic he imagined from reading Rimbaud and Verlaine.

The pot trail was risky, there were the inevitable minor problems of diarrhoea and petty thievery, but mainly (apart from avalanches) that was because of the ignorance and irresponsibility of we who undertook this initiation.

Now, it seemed, a hypnotically dangerous stranger, like a serpent in a garden, had entered the scene and betrayed the trust of travellers, a group we would always identify with.

It was because Richard and I were steeped in the enriching culture of the overland trail that we found the Charles Sobhraj story so shocking and fascinating, and made the irresponsible but adventurous decision to get the story.

Julie Clarke

2020

Author's Note

This book is a work of journalism which uses some of the techniques of the novel. The conversations between people are based on what they remembered they said at the time, or are derived from official reports, police statements or private letters. As for Charles, little reliance was placed on information he gave which could not be corroborated by historical records or reliable witnesses. These were in excessive supply.

The thoughts and feelings which Charles Sobhraj claimed to have experienced at certain times have been included when they 'rang true' and seemed compatible with known facts. There were some episodes which, by their very nature, could not be checked against records and where the only participants, other than Charles, had died, were still at large, or could not be contacted. Such scenes have been attributed to Charles.

The people in this book are real and all the events are true to the best of our knowledge and belief. The identities of those who make a brief appearance in this story and are referred to only by their first names have been changed. To spare additional grief and embarrassment to members of Charles' family, their names have also been altered, as have those of his mentor Alain Benard; the Belgian diplomat Gilles de Giverney; the house-guest in Bangkok, François Dubily; Marie-Andrée's friend Jules Dupont; Chantal's parents, the Lemaîtres; and Albert Goyot, the antiques dealer.

On the Trail of the Serpent

Prologue

In Bangkok, behind a high wall on Wireless Road, at the end of a long asphalt driveway lined with flowering shrubs, stood a grand white mansion which had once been the residence of a member of the Thai royal family. Now it housed the Royal Netherlands Embassy.

Herman Knippenberg sat at his desk in the new L-shaped wing behind the mansion where a staff of seven diplomats had their offices. It was his first foreign posting. At only thirty-one, tall and well dressed in a light-grey suit, he was the third secretary and acting head of the consular section. He was reading the mail that had just arrived in the embassy pouch from The Hague. It was 6 February 1976.

The Ministry of Foreign Affairs had asked him to trace the whereabouts of two Dutch travellers, Henk Bintanja and Cocky Hemker, but their photographs, supposedly enclosed with the package, were missing and the letter from the worried family was incomplete.

'Damned dilettantes,' Herman muttered, his pleasing but serious face quickly becoming animated as his brain computed the lack of vital evidence. He had double his usual workload due to understaffing and felt he could do without such sloppy deskwork from his colleagues.

In the past year, 30,000 Dutch tourists had come to Thailand, twice the number of previous years, and requests for help from the embassy like the one Herman had just opened were not unusual. Missing travellers were generally located – meditating in a cave in a forest monastery or smoking pot in a beach paradise. And yet this letter disturbed Herman with its tone of methodical urgency. He read it again:

In their last letter of 8 December 1975, Cocky and Henk told us that they planned to leave Hong Kong by plane on Wednesday 10 December at 11 p.m. to Bangkok. They wanted to stay about one week to renew passports and apply for visas. Afterwards they planned to go to Chiang Mai for about two weeks and then travel to South India and Ceylon, and they asked us to send their letters addressed to Poste Restante Chiang Mai. To this address we sent four or five letters.

In their letter they also wrote that they had met a Frenchman, a dealer in precious stones between Bangkok and Hong Kong. Cocky and Henk were invited several times by this Frenchman to his hotel, the Hyatt Regency. The Frenchman planned to leave on 8 December for Bangkok where he and his wife lived in an apartment.

Cocky and Henk were also invited to go to this apartment, and they had to tell him when exactly they were arriving in Bangkok so that the Frenchman's secretary could meet them at the airport. He also promised he would take them to the gem mines.

Putting down the letter, Herman made some notes and asked a Thai-speaking secretary to contact the post office at Chiang Mai to see if the Dutch couple's mail had been collected. He told an aide to check the embassy register to see if their passports had been renewed and he dictated a wire to The Hague requesting the mislaid photographs and the missing page of the letter. Then he went on with his correspondence.

After a brilliant academic career in Europe, Herman had completed his post-graduate work in international relations at Johns Hopkins School of Advanced International Studies in Washington, D.C., where he met his wife, Angela, a German-born graduate of Bryn Mawr. With a cool gaze and chiselled features, she was more than an intellectual match for Herman and they made an impressive couple. They had arrived in Bangkok seven months earlier, and despite her own qualifications Angela supported Herman as a diplomat's wife. Herman's duties at the embassy were varied. He processed papers for Dutch couples wishing to adopt Thai babies; he helped administer financial aid to neighbouring Laos; and he prepared reports for the Ministry of Foreign Affairs on the Southeast Asian political scene. Heroin was not the only contraband bound for Amsterdam. Another of his more banal tasks was to screen Thai applicants for visas to the Netherlands and weed out any sex workers.

The office intercom buzzed: Cocky's and Henk's passports had not been renewed; and at the Chiang Mai post office there was still mail waiting for them. Herman wondered where they were.

He lit a cigarette and stared through the window at the swimming pool, where the suntanned ambassador was churning through the water doing his laps. Herman could do nothing more until the photos arrived. In his student days he had backpacked around Europe and the Middle East, and he knew first-hand the eagerness of travellers to pick up their mail from home. The family had good reason to be anxious, he thought.

In San Pedro, California, on the morning after Herman Knippenberg first heard the names of the missing Dutch couple, Emma Knowlton called on a neighbour who had a typewriter to help her compose a letter to President Gerald Ford.

'I am in desperate need of your help,' she began dictating as the tears ran down her face. She had not heard from her granddaughter Teresa since she had arrived in Hong Kong on 5 October, and now Christmas had come and gone without even a postcard. Emma had not been reassured by the optimism of a letter from a lama at Kopan Monastery in Kathmandu where Teresa had been headed, suggesting that it was probable her granddaughter had made some friends and was having a nice time in Hong Kong.

Emma had already written to the US State Department, the Hong Kong Police and immigration departments, and the US consulate in Hong Kong for news.

'I have heard nothing from any of these departments,' she wrote.

Mr President, surely it can't take this long to find out if she left Hong Kong and what her destination was to be? My granddaughter always wrote to me where she would be going and where I would next hear from her. I am very alarmed, and, as an American, I should have information on what the State Department is doing to locate Teresa. I want to know if she is well and has not met with foul play.

Sincerely, Emma Knowlton.

Other families from the US, France, Turkey and Canada were writing similar letters to their consulates in Bangkok and Kathmandu in search of their children who had disappeared on Asia's hippie trail.

PART I

Bad Justice

April 1944 – June 1970

1

The Face of an Angel

Late on a sultry afternoon in Paris in July 1976, a middle-aged man strolled from his office and into the rush-hour crowds. He wore horn-rimmed glasses and carried a battered briefcase. Alain Benard, a lawyer, had been a corporate executive for fifteen years but looked more like an academic.

Billboards of bronzed girls in bikinis smiled down on Benard as he jostled his way towards the Metro. It was nearing the time of year when millions of Parisians would leave the city for their annual summer holidays.

Benard sidestepped an elderly man bent over a pile of magazines. The man was cutting the twine from the bundle and stacking the copies of *Paris Match* on the racks of the news stand. Benard's eyes followed the recognizable bright red logo. Then, having glimpsed the cover photo, he froze. The dark eyes glowering from the familiar face had stopped him in his tracks. A cold, arrogant but handsome face. There was no mistake. It was Charles Sobhraj. The headline read 'Death Rides the Road to Kathmandu'.

Benard hurriedly bought a copy of the magazine, sat down at a pavement café and contemplated the cover. Charles was pictured in a pose Benard knew well, one hand on his hip and the other on a table scattered with dollars. Next to Charles was a dark-haired young woman wearing sunglasses and leaning forward in a low-cut T-shirt. She looked more attractive than Benard remembered her.

'Police have embarked on a massive manhunt for three brutal killers,' read the photo caption. 'They slay young hitchhikers on the holiday road – a dozen victims have so far been found.'

Horrified, he quickly opened the magazine, where his eye was caught by a lurid comic strip. It showed his friend Charles with two young travellers on a palm-fringed beach. Charles' girlfriend Marie-Andrée was silhouetted against the tropical moon, holding up a syringe. Next, two bodies were pictured lying on the sand, Charles bent over one of them. His girlfriend knelt next to the body of a man in shorts. Then the body was on fire, and Marie-Andrée was smiling as flames soared into the air. In the last frame, the young couple peered demoniacally from the page as smoke billowed behind them.

Benard felt sick. Surely, he told himself, it was impossible, it was absurd. And who was their accomplice? An Indian national, apparently, a young man called 'Ajay' whom Benard was sure he had never met.

He turned the page and found a photograph of a girl in a bikini, her arms outstretched and her eyes closed. 'An 18-year-old American found dead in Pattaya,' the caption read. 'Another victim of the fiendish trio?' Almost against his will, his eyes skimmed the story: charred corpses in Kathmandu covered with stab wounds, throats cut, necks broken, druggings and drownings, teenagers burned alive in Bangkok ... All the work of a mysterious 'Alain Gautier', now one of the most wanted men in the world.

Could Charles have committed those crimes? It was still a mystery to him how his own life, that of an orderly and respectable bachelor, had become intertwined with this wounded young man – an incorrigible criminal whose career was now sending the world's press into paroxysms of grisly prose.

Looking up at the blue sky, his thoughts travelled back to that day ten years earlier when a sudden impulse to do good for the world had drawn him into close proximity with this terrible darkness.

Benard remembered he had been taking a Sunday afternoon stroll through the park near his home. It was 1966. He was thirty-eight, prosperous but bored. The air was sweet with the

smell of freshly cut grass and flowers but the ease of his cultivated life seemed sterile and cloying. He was trapped in a ghetto
of privilege.

Above the swaying green of the poplars he noticed, not for the
first time, the high grey watchtowers of Poissy Jail. Behind those
walls, he knew, lived those for whom there could be no fastidious
savouring of doubts on a Sunday stroll.

It was at this moment, Benard still remembered so clearly, that he
had made a fateful decision. His father, a commodities broker, had
been a volunteer prison visitor many years before. Alain decided to
follow his example. This could be a fair exchange. He could use his
legal training to help others and he would gain a passport to another
milieu. The next day Benard applied to become an official prison
visitor at Poissy Jail.

At first his part-time duties were simple: he advised Yugoslav construction workers who had overstayed their visas; he patched up
domestic affairs for Corsican burglars; and on some weekends he
would visit as many as fifteen inmates, who were happy just to have
someone to talk to.

Then one day, the prison priest approached him about a special case.

'I thought of you, Benard,' said the older man, 'because this case
needs an intellectual with a lot of patience. It's a young boy, very
bright, in fact exceptionally so, and a rebel. He seems to live in a
world of his own and refuses to come to terms with reality. But if he
had a friend to connect with him, and help him, I'm sure he could go
a long way. Are you interested?'

In fact it had seemed like the perfect project, one he embraced
with alacrity.

The following weekend, on a wet October afternoon, he found
himself walking through the heavy iron gates of the jail and waiting
patiently for the guards to examine his pass and unlock the second
set of doors. He followed the grey-haired social worker into the
reception area.

'Five months ago,' she said, turning to him, lowering her voice,
'Charles broke out of Haguenau. Did you read about it?'

Benard nodded. Last May three prisoners from the psychiatric jail had jumped over the wall after knocking out a guard and tying him to a radiator.

'They caught him and transferred him here,' she confided as she started to walk along the grey cement corridor. Benard followed.

'It was a self-destructive act,' she went on. 'Another month in Haguenau and he probably would have got parole. Now he refuses to work and will have nothing to do with his cellmates. He wrote to the warden here accusing him of degrading the prisoners. Then he went on a hunger strike for forty-five days.'

She opened the door into the empty visitors' room, with its ugly green linoleum. Benard was well accustomed to the place.

'Don't let me give you the impression that his is a hopeless case,' she whispered urgently as they sat down. 'As you must have gathered by now, we believe that there is no such thing. No case is lost! And the fact that Charles is so young and his crimes relatively minor, well, there's reason to hope.'

'And his background? What do we know?' Benard enquired politely.

'He was born in Saigon to a Vietnamese mother, but his father is Indian. His stepfather is French, an army man. A casualty of the mess we created in Indo-China,' she sighed.

It was twelve years since the French army had been routed by the Viet Minh at the Battle of Dien Bien Phu, yet Benard was well aware of the consequences of his country's foreign policy in Indo-China, where almost 80,000 French soldiers had died. The Vietnam War, some people believed, had begun in Paris in 1858 when the politicians first ordered gunboats to sail up the Saigon River and establish a garrison. For ninety-two years the French had profited from the country's raw materials – raising revenue to administer the colony by monopolizing opium sales to the Vietnamese.

The woman touched his arm, growing more serious.

'I suggest that if you agree to accept this case, Mr Benard, you should do so on one condition only, a condition that we would ask you to regard as inviolable.' She paused. 'If you decide you want to help Charles, you would have to stay his friend throughout.'

'Throughout what?'

'Throughout his life. Up to now he's been shunted back and forth between parents and continents. It's made it hard for him to form attachments. On top of that, he had to live through the war. If you come into this boy's life as a friend and then disappear, it would be much worse than doing nothing. Everyone has judged him, this whole system.' She gestured at the small barred windows, the fluorescent light, the ubiquitous ugliness. 'He needs a strong father-figure. Firm, but not judgmental. He needs just one person to stand by him.'

They heard the harsh voices of the guards herding prisoners along the corridor to the visiting rooms and the social worker got up to leave. She nodded and said, 'We'll talk again later. Good luck.'

Benard walked into the empty room, sat down and waited.

A few minutes later a twenty-two-year-old swaggered into the room. Of medium height, slim but muscular, Charles Sobhraj was strikingly handsome. He had high cheekbones, and the black eyes in his sallow face seemed to notice and analyse Benard's every physical detail. His mouth indicated an unusual sensitivity, even sensuality. He shook hands and sat down facing Benard across the desk, comfortably in control of the situation.

'So, Charles,' said Benard gently, 'you've had some bad luck in life?'

'I'd call it bad justice,' the young man said. His voice was intimate, rich and low.

'It must always seem that way inside a place like this.'

'I've already learned to live above external circumstances in life,' Charles said, leaning back against the chair with his arms folded, staring.

'That's a stoical attitude,' said Benard, intrigued by the young man's intensity.

'Yes, the Stoics are my favourites, actually. Their ideas are much more useful in my situation than those of the priests.'

'From what I understand of the Stoics,' said Benard slowly, 'they teach the importance of mastering desires. But you're here because you succumbed to yours.'

'I stole out of necessity,' Charles said. 'The authorities had ordered me out of France, and I had no money. So, to drive across the border, I stole a car.'

It was said with such self-assurance that the action sounded reasonable.

'But if you admit you stole, where's the injustice?' asked Benard.

'Copping four years for trying to obey an order to leave France.'

'You could have worked for the fare, perhaps?' suggested Benard with a smile.

'Without proper papers? I tried that. Peeling potatoes for four francs an hour.'

'What about your family?'

'I went to Marseilles to ask my mother for help. She just ignored me. She was too busy with her new boyfriend. In the end she gave me forty francs. Forty francs to leave France!'

'So, you and your mother don't get along?'

'My mother is dead to me. I've cut her out of my life. I expect nothing from her.'

'But where will you go when you leave here, Charles?'

'I'll go back home.'

'To Vietnam?'

'Yes. My mother brought me here – to this wonderful country where I'm treated like shit – when I was nine. You know, Mr Benard, the last time I was in Saigon I was drafted, and yet I'd still rather go back and fight than stay in France.'

'So, you're Vietnamese?'

'Officially, no. My father was born in Bombay, but even the Indians refuse to issue me a passport. Anyway, as the Stoics say, it is better to be a citizen of the world than of Rome. And when I get out of jail I will be kicked out of France because I don't have a passport.'

'So, it's because of all this that you've got into trouble with the warden?'

'No. It's because they won't leave me alone to study. They stick me in this hole, so I should at least make the best of it. I try to deepen myself. Every day, you know, I exercise because however the circumstances change, I always have my body. Sometimes they put me in solitary which, of course, I don't mind. They cut off tobacco. So what? I don't smoke. They ban me from the cinema. I haven't seen a film for nine months.'

The list of adversities seemed to cheer him.

'Is such self-discipline a Vietnamese trait?' Benard asked, polishing his glasses.

'It's not French,' Charles said with a chilly smile. There was an impatient rattle of keys.

'It's a problematic situation, a man having no nationality. I'll look into it,' Benard offered quietly.

'You're under no obligation to do anything for me,' the young man said, 'and you know, Alain, maybe you're a prisoner too – of your own guilt. Why else would you hang around jails?'

Benard was amused by Charles' insolence. 'Convicted prisoners are driven by unconscious forces too, especially the ones who keep coming back.'

'Yes. Clack! Clack! Clack! Since I was eighteen. This is my third French jail.'

As the guard opened the door the two men stood up.

'I'll see you again next week,' said Benard. 'We'll have more time to talk.'

'Please yourself, but remember, I'm used to being lonely, Mr Benard —' He lowered his voice dramatically '— and that is how I shall always be.'

'Is there anything I can bring you?'

'I need nothing except books, thank you,' said Charles, and he was led away.

In the weeks that followed, Benard visited Charles Sobhraj every Saturday afternoon and picked over his library to feed the prisoner's ravenous appetite for psychology, philosophy, law, and executive training manuals. Sometimes he boasted to Benard that he sat at his desk in the cell for nineteen hours a day, poring over books. He hardly noticed the other prisoners.

It seemed that Charles sought not only self-improvement, but an intellectual armoury – he wanted the weapons, conventional and otherwise, to cut through the jungle outside, to carve his path to the top. Socially, Charles was on the bottom rung, without wealth, nationality or education, and jail had added a five-year handicap. But he had inherited one gift, the gift of charisma, of power over people. Charles had decided to build on this and to learn all he could about clues to the human character; the better, he thought, one day to mould them to his will. Palmistry, handwriting analysis and characterology would help him penetrate other minds and would offer short cuts in social relations.

As his friendship with Benard grew, so did Charles' requests. Benard was relieved when the young man who had only wanted books also admitted to simpler human needs for chocolate, stationery and socks.

The young Vietnamese prisoner had become a permanent fixture in Benard's ordered life. Now he began to investigate how to solve the problem of Charles' nationality.

Each Saturday they would meet, and he would carefully explain to Charles how his research was progressing. He wanted to show his ward that he was taking his case seriously.

'There's nothing different about you. You're entitled to a nationality like everyone else. I've written to the Indian embassy.'

'They will say no too,' Charles said. 'Each country will close its doors.'

'In that case I need to be armed for the fight. I need to know more about you, Charles, your past: documents, dates, where you were brought up. I'd like to write to your family, if you'll allow me?'

Charles was silent for a minute, affecting the melodramatic gesture of someone thinking deeply. It was a pose that Benard was becoming used to. 'I prefer not to look back,' he said, 'but you can write to my stepfather Roussel in Marseilles, although you won't get much sense out of him. He's doped up on tranquillizers.'

'Can I write to your mother then?'

'No.' Charles banged his fist on the table. 'I've told you. She no longer exists for me.'

They argued for some time without result and then Benard suggested that he could write to Charles' father in Saigon.

'Before I met you, Alain,' Charles said angrily, working up towards an impassioned diatribe, 'I must tell you that I was often close to suicide in my cell. I stopped eating. I couldn't sleep. I was always depressed. That's why they transferred me to Haguenau. After many nights without sleep, I asked myself, "Why die now? Go to the source of your misfortune and see who's responsible."

'I did that, and it was my father. And you know something, Alain? With this idea, I felt better. I swore to myself to have a new life, a pure life, and to have revenge on my father. That's when I wrote him this letter.'

Turning to a sheaf of papers which Charles habitually brought with him to the visitors' room, he handed Benard the letter he had written. Benard took it eagerly. Usually these papers were comprised of lists of books or a scribbled page of introspection or poetry. This was different. With mounting disquiet he read and then reread the words written in Charles' distinctive cursive style:

It is really unfortunate that you are my father. Why? Because a father has a duty to help his son build a future. You pray to God at the temple, but your conscience is heavy. You bore a son, but you ignore him. You abandon him worse than a dog, worse than for the lowest beast!!! From you I will carry only the name you gave me. The faithful love I had for you, I have still, unfortunately. But I will fight it. You are no more my father. I disown you. Live in your abundance, enjoy it as much as you can. For myself, I have as my only treasure, bread and water. But it's precious treasure because it fortifies me every day and gives me the strength and will to hold me on only one target.

I will consume you. I will make you suffer. I will make you
regret that you have missed your father's duty. The fortune, I
will get without you. And I will use it to crush you.

Benard put the letter down. There was a pause. He didn't know what
to say.

'I also have a poem I wrote with it,' said Charles, watching Benard
intently. 'It's very short. Do you want to hear?'

Benard nodded.

Charles began:

> 'In the sunny country where you walk
> My abandoned self could also go
> If my body had wings to fly
> Like my spirit has.'

For a moment Benard remained speechless. Then he asked quietly,
'Don't you think a life based on revenge is self-defeating?'

'Maybe it's my Asian upbringing,' said Charles, 'but I can't accept
this Christian forgiveness.'

'And so you become obsessed with revenge,' Benard countered
quickly. 'When you do that ... don't you see, you let him get the
upper hand. You allow him to twist your very soul.'

Charles looked up, was silent for a moment and then said, 'OK, I
agree. You can write to my father. Don't say anything about where I
am now. He is very conventional, a rich businessman. And you
should use your company's letterhead when you write, that will
impress him.'

Finally, Benard thought, I am making a breakthrough.

The next time Benard visited Charles it was Christmas. On his way
through the courtyard of Poissy Jail he passed by three prisoners
who were decorating a small Christmas tree. His old friend the social
worker was helping them. She noticed that Benard was carrying a
present.

'Is that for Charles?' she called out. 'So, I see you've taken the case to heart. You've made the commitment?'

'Yes, I am committed,' he replied, taking a worn sheet of paper from his wallet. 'Do you want to see the first letter I received from Charles?'

Benard handed it to her. Their eyes met. She nodded and quickly opened it. He watched her read:

Dear Alain,

I am a being who has cried out, 'O Lord, my God, why have you made me what I am? You know, O Lord, that I only ask to love, to live. Why don't you grant this? In order to prepare me for my destiny? But what is my destiny, O my Lord? Tell me, give me a signal. Why was I born a being that the whole world despises, one who could die without anyone shedding a tear? O Lord, I have had only misfortune. Send me some happiness. You, who know the secret of my soul, guide me, tell me what must be done. I don't know any more what to do.' For a long time, nothing, there was no answer. Then I knew He had heard my cry, Alain, the scream of a drowning man. He sent you.

Returning the letter, she lowered her eyes and half smiled.

'You've got yourself in deep,' she said.

'Yes. I wasn't quite prepared for this,' he admitted. 'He's no longer bitter and suicidal, at least, but who knows how it will end?'

They parted and Benard went through to the visitors' room with the gift. He hoped he had chosen appropriately.

When Charles unwrapped it, he was silent for a moment.

'Alain, I will have these framed,' he said, holding out the two drawings – one of Jesus and one of St John. 'What can I give in return? All I can offer you is my brotherhood, but, I promise, that will be deep and eternal.'

Benard was embarrassed but touched by this declaration. Now he had to tell Charles that the Indian embassy had turned down his request for nationality.

'I'm sorry,' he said. 'They say you have not lived in India long enough.'

'Who wants to be Indian, anyway?' said Charles, brushing the news aside. 'Did you hear from my father?'

'Yes, he was glad to hear news of you.'

'Next time you write, Alain, could you ask him to send me some suits? You know, he's in business as a tailor.'

'Yes, and his letter was very warm towards you.' That was not exactly true but Benard hoped to heal the father–son relationship.

'OK, Alain, even if he hasn't given me the love of a father, I suppose I must pray that I can give him the love of a son.'

Benard didn't quite know what to make of this sudden onrush of filial piety, but Charles now seemed filled with anguish and began pacing around the room.

'What a waste my years in jail have been,' he said. 'If I hadn't met you I would have lost myself. Now I want to make up for those wasted years. The warden has given me permission to study a course in law at the University of Paris. Can you get all the enrolment forms and textbooks for me?'

Benard was thrilled to see academic ambition unfolding. 'Of course I can, Charles. It's good that you're looking ahead to the day you come out. But we still have to sort out your nationality. Your mother has all the papers. Please, you must let me see her.'

Charles said nothing. He looked away, but Benard decided to keep pushing.

'You know it's the only way,' he said tactfully and firmly.

There were tears in Charles' eyes when he finally agreed.

The tall masts of the yachts bobbed in the Old Port of Marseilles, and oil tankers on the horizon plodded towards Saudi Arabia. From the deck of the incoming ferry from Tunisia, passengers were waving scarves and shouting. It was a cold December afternoon as Benard drove his Triumph Herald up the wide, bustling La Canebière. This was where he had grown up.

He was curious to meet Noi Roussel, Charles' Vietnamese mother, who lived twenty minutes away in a seaside suburb. He had prepared for his visit by arranging for a local social worker attached to the prison in Marseilles to visit Noi. Her report had painted Noi as an 'iron butterfly'. He parked beside the densely packed, modest houses lining one of the steep alleys that criss-crossed the Mediterranean hillside.

A high wooden fence surrounded Villa La Roche. He pressed the bell on the gate. Through a crack between the palings he watched a small boy who looked remarkably similar to Charles run down the garden path, chased by a large Labrador. With its steeply terraced garden and walled-in veranda, Villa La Roche suggested a suburban fortress. A craggy headland blocked the view of the sea. Opening the gate, the boy grinned self-consciously.

Noi Roussel was standing on the top step of the porch. Her black Chinese trousers and turquoise high-necked silk jacket matched her beaded slippers. She looked young enough to be Charles' older sister. Her black hair was swept up from her face in a lacquered beehive. She had fine skin and a trim figure.

'It's so nice of you to come all this way, Mr Benard. Do excuse the garden. Without a man around the house, things run away with themselves, don't they? This is Guy, my son.'

She led Benard into a small, neat room dominated by the television set and decorated with oriental bric-a-brac. On an upright piano stood one of the brass three-tiered family shrines Benard had seen before in Vietnamese homes.

'Guy, run off and play,' Noi called out. The boy ran from the room, followed by the dog. Noi Roussel placed a tray of tea on the table.

'I must say I'm relieved that Charles is locked up,' she said calmly as she poured green tea into a glass cup and offered Benard a plate of cakes and biscuits. 'Last time he was here, he was so rough. He even threatened me. He wanted money.'

'Ah, yes. He told me about it. He said he needed the money to leave France.' Benard spoke casually. He looked around at the case of tiny glass animals in the corner, not a speck of dust anywhere.

'As I told him then, not that he ever listens, I needed the money to feed my family. I have to feed seven children on my husband's disability pension.'

Noi nibbled on a biscuit. Her long manicured fingernails were lacquered crimson.

'How is your husband, Mrs Roussel?'

'He's been in a psychiatric hospital for six years now, and I bring him food every day. Sometimes he's allowed to come home, but it's no good. Jacques hears strange voices, and they tell him to kill me. Last time he was here he attacked me with a kitchen knife, and I locked myself in the bedroom.'

'That is so sad,' Benard said, his eyes wandering to the mother-of-pearl flamingos on the wall. 'And how difficult it must be bringing up children without a father in the house. I don't suppose Charles was much help?' he added.

'Ha! He helped my hair go grey,' she said.

Benard, looking at the scrupulously coiffured black beehive, thought that no, not even Charles could do that.

'He'll be coming out in six months,' he said, 'and, perhaps, you and I should talk about what's to be done. He says he wants to go back to Vietnam.'

'Charles always wants to be where he isn't,' she sighed.

'Perhaps because he doesn't know where he belongs,' Benard said. 'Perhaps the first thing to do is to give him a country.'

'Yes, I wanted to give him France, at least a good French education. That's why I brought him here.'

'So, why wasn't he formally adopted and granted French citizenship?'

Noi explained that at one point her husband had made the necessary application to the French adoption agency but had heard nothing more.

'It got lost in a file or something, and then my husband was posted to Dakar and then he got sick.'

'Mrs Roussel, if I'm to be of any help to Charles, I need to get a sense of his family history. I'd like to see any documents relating to your son – if you still have any.'

'Oh, Mr Benard,' she said, smiling her hard, glittering smile, 'I have every one of them, every scrap of official paper. Has he convinced you I don't love him? I love him best of all. When I had to leave him behind in Saigon to come here the first time, I used to walk up and down the Vieux Port, always thinking of him.'

She took a green photo album from a shelf under the TV set and showed him childhood snapshots of her children. 'See, he has the face of an angel,' she said, pointing to a photograph of Charles in a chef's hat, 'but somewhere I think a devil crept into his soul.'

She briefly left the room, returning a few seconds later with a white plastic shopping bag stuffed with documents and papers. She put it on the floor and found inside it a tiny woollen cardigan which she began stroking against her face. 'This was the first little jacket I ever bought him,' she said, her eyes filling with tears, 'and sometimes I sleep with it under my pillow.'

As Benard was leaving, the light from the corrugated plastic that walled in the veranda bathed both their faces in a green light.

'You don't like the view?' he asked curiously.

'We had the screens put up to stop the neighbours staring.'

As she walked with Benard down the path to the gate, Noi said something quickly to Guy who ran back to the house.

'Monsieur Benard, I can see you're really concerned for my son,' she said.

'Oh, I just offer a helping hand.'

'I think you can do more for him than I have been able to.'

Guy arrived at the door with the paper-filled bag, and Noi handed it to Benard.

'Mr Benard,' she said dramatically, 'I give to you my son.'

2

The Fruit of War

Back in his own spacious apartment in Marseilles, Benard began unscrambling the mass of papers which, in addition to official documents, included personal letters, newspaper clippings, fiercely worded bills from shipping companies, police charge-sheets, school records, and, in answer to follow-up enquiries from a Paris hospital where he had been treated for bed-wetting, a weary biography of Charles by his stepfather, Jacques Roussel.

Benard sorted these into neatly labelled manila folders and stacked them into the green box files on his bookcase. He resumed his weekly visits to Charles, and over the following months Charles began to speak about his tumultuous childhood.

From these sources, as well as his own understanding of France's involvement in Southeast Asia, Benard was able to form a picture of the history of the lonely young man now marooned without a nationality in Poissy Jail.

During the Second World War, when Charles' mother, Noi, was an alluring teenager, her parents died and she left the rubber plantations of her village to come to Saigon, 'the Paris of the Orient'. The war had not dulled the city's renowned glamour. The Japanese victory in Southeast Asia had reassured its residents that the white races could be repelled. From Saigon Cathedral, a nineteenth-century building in the Romanesque style, the bells rang out across the opium dens, dance halls, brothels and casinos of the former fishing village which buzzed with Renault taxis and the armoured cars of occupying troops. The women, in their white silk trousers and long, coloured tunics slit to the waist, cycled along the wide boulevards lined with cafés.

Noi found a job as a shop-girl in a smart men's outfitters off the Rue Catinat and was quickly promoted to cashier. One evening as she was leaving work she noticed her employer, a handsome, light-skinned Indian, standing in the doorway talking with a Japanese officer in his own language. Her boss was stocky, and in his flashy Western clothes exuded an air of confidence and prosperity. Hotchand Sobhraj invited her to join him that evening at the casino.

Indians were unpopular in Saigon because so many of them had made fortunes as moneylenders to the Vietnamese. Hotchand Sobhraj was a leader among the expatriate Indian community, and in the tradition of his forefathers, who came from the valley of Sindh, he too was a moneylender. Sobhraj also owned two tailor's shops in the prosperous quarter of Saigon and above one of these, at 80 Ngo Duc Ke, he lived in a large apartment with four servants. Noi became his mistress and moved in with him. Soon she became pregnant.

On 6 April 1944 Noi went into labour, and as her contractions intensified so did the steady rumble of the bombs, shaking the hospital. The Viet Minh were relaunching their guerrilla campaign against the Japanese occupation forces. Noi was growing accustomed to the sound, and it was an easy birth. She was twenty years old.

She gave her new son an Indian name, Gurmukh, and he took his father's surname, Sobhraj – but in the years that followed he was to have countless names. As a young boy he was christened Charles after the hero of the times, President de Gaulle.

One day when Charles was one year old, his mother was walking with her son in her arms past the food stalls that lined the river. Suddenly, before she had time to scream, two men sprang from behind a rickshaw and threw mother and baby into a motorized sampan that disappeared into the maze of waterways. The crowds went on with their business – such abductions were common. It was safer not to ask questions. Within hours Hotchand Sobhraj received the ransom demand. Noi and Charles had been spirited off to the Rung Sat Swamp, a time-honoured hideout for pirates and bandits known locally as the Forest of the Assassins. One of these gangs, the Binh

Xuyen, had temporarily allied itself with the Viet Minh and kidnapping was its standard method of fundraising. A shrewd merchant who spoke eight languages, Hotchand had been careful to make the right social connections. Now he sought help from the Japanese army. When the Binh Xuyen came to collect the ransom, they were ambushed by Japanese soldiers. Noi and the baby were rescued.

On 15 August 1945, the Japanese surrendered to the Allies. Ten days later, to the sounds of carousing in the streets, fireworks and a nine-hour victory parade celebrating the end of colonization, the Viet Minh installed themselves as the government of Saigon. For the Sobhraj family and other residents there followed a short period of unaccustomed tranquillity until, three weeks later, the British arrived. Backed by Indian Gurkhas and Gaullist French, they cleared the city of Viet Minh, conducting a ruthless door-to-door search for its leaders. From Marseilles the troop ships steamed east, then up the Saigon River, and soldiers reoccupied the city as the capital of Cochin-China, a colony of France. After bloody street-fighting the Viet Minh were smashed back into the Forest of Assassins, and the French officers, whom Hotchand Sobhraj had already begun to cultivate, celebrated their victory at the House of Five Hundred Girls.

That same night the Sobhraj household was awakened by the sound of gunfire and explosions. The Viet Minh had left assassination squads to carry on the resistance. Flames illuminated the night sky, bombs shook the house, and Charles woke up crying. Noi wrapped him up in a blanket and slid the screaming bundle beneath a heavy wardrobe, where he was left until dawn when the squads' reign was over until the sun set again. Terror became part of the city's nightlife and, whenever the bombs came close, the baby Charles was hidden away in the hot stuffy darkness under the wardrobe.

When Charles was three and Noi was pregnant again, Hotchand returned from a visit to his home in Poona, India, and announced that he had married an Indian girl.

'It was all arranged by my family,' he explained to Noi. 'It makes no difference. You can still live here.' Noi shouted and wept and packed her bags, storming out of the apartment with her little boy under her arm.

Soon she was to meet Jacques Roussel, a shy, sensitive adjutant-sergeant from Bordeaux, who fell in love with Noi and agreed to accept Charles as his son. They were married in September 1948, after the birth of Noi's second child by Hotchand. She was named Nicole, after Roussel's mother, and was formally adopted at the wedding ceremony.

After being taken from his father, four-year-old Charles became difficult. His new home, three rooms in the French barracks, seemed depressing and ugly after the luxury he had known at his father's. He refused to call Roussel 'Papa' and ran away whenever the young French soldier tried to take him in his arms. 'I want Hotchand,' he kept yelling at his mother, who was only too well aware of the drop in material circumstances. When Jacques was posted back to Marseilles, she decided to leave Charles with his natural father, since his future seemed secure in the prosperous household. She wept as she kissed him goodbye, expecting never to see her handsome little boy again.

In Paris, government geographers redrew their maps of Southeast Asia, and the colony of Cochin-China was added to the Protectorates of Annam and Tonkin to form the country of Vietnam. The French sank deeper into the morass of a colonial war and by 1951, when Jacques Roussel was sent back to the front, the government was spending a billion dollars a year, with half their army committed to the battle. The French were losing more officers annually than graduated from Saint-Cyr, France's top military academy.

Noi was now pregnant with her fourth child and, with three-year-old Nicole and two-year-old Jean-Daniel, who had been born in Marseilles, she sailed with Jacques Roussel back to her war-torn homeland.

Saigon now bristled with barbed wire and machine guns. Watchtowers stood at kilometre intervals along the main road, and police stopped cars, bicycles and trishaws (which had replaced the hand-drawn rickshaws) to search for bombs. After the cloistered domesticity of life in Marseilles, Noi was back in a land that lived its life on the pavements, where dentists extracted teeth under the tamarind trees, egged on by jostling passers-by.

'So you are his mother?' the headmaster said. Noi had left her other children at the French barracks and rushed to the school. 'You will find your son in the yard looking after the pigs. He's being punished for unruliness and insolence and disrupting the lessons of the other children.'

Clutching her handbag, Noi picked her way through the muddy ground in her high heels, looking for the pig-sty, where she embraced the boy she had missed so much.

Hotchand had now installed his Indian wife, Geeta, in the apartment above the shop and, perhaps not wishing to be reminded of her husband's former relations with Noi, Geeta had left Charles to look after himself. He had learnt to survive with the other street kids, absorbed in the back-alley hustle of a booming war town. The children of Saigon were ingenious and versatile, grinding out sugar-cane juice from portable hand mills to sell to patrons of battery-powered peepshows, taking bets from French soldiers on directions the crickets might jump, and running messages for the Viet Minh. While the seven-year-old seemed to have thrived on domestic anarchy, Noi was appalled, and with Hotchand's agreement she registered her rights of maternity at Saigon Town Hall and took Charles back into the Roussel family.

If the city was Vietnam by day, by night it was Viet Minh. In the quarter which housed the families of French soldiers, the guerrillas stalked the rooftops, looking for ways to break into the bedrooms and cut the throats of their sleeping enemies. In the Roussel home the doors and windows were barricaded. The family went to bed frightened, their ears alert for suspicious noises. When the alarm sounded Noi roused her children and hurried them out under the floodlights of the compound with the other families to wait for the security police.

One afternoon Noi took the seven-year-old Charles to the cinema. The two were queuing on Rue Catinat when suddenly Charles changed his mind about the film he wanted to see and begged to be taken to another cinema across the street. To avoid one of his recurrent tantrums, his mother acquiesced. After the show they passed the first cinema and saw dozens of bodies being carried out on stretchers to ambulances, victims of a Viet Minh bomb attack.

'Charlie – look! You saved us!'

Noi hugged him tightly and saw in his black eyes an expression of pride. The ambulance sirens followed them as they walked home together holding hands, and Charles realized that he was someone special, immune to violence. He was protected. Others would suffer – he accepted that already – but his own fate was to be different.

As the months passed the violence escalated. When he had just turned eight, Charles was walking home from school along the steamy streets, where French priests in black cassocks jostled with Chinese merchants, French Legionnaires and, by now, the occasional American official. The explosion that blew the street apart did not touch him. It was a thundering crash, a sheet of white light, and then silence and dust.

Bodies lay scattered on the ground. The boy saw something moving where an old stone wall had been. The noodle-stall proprietor lay crushed under his stand. His head had been blown off his shoulders. Charles saw the skull nearby. It had been split open by the blast. People screamed and bodies writhed in pools of blood. The sirens soared and Charles Sobhraj ran home to his mother.

Although he was indulged more than the younger children, Charles did not like the struggling atmosphere of the Roussels' quarters, where his mother was now nursing her fourth child, Guy. He did not respect his stepfather, who seemed dull and subservient. Jacques had been trained for administrative duties and was overwhelmed by the everyday carnage of guerrilla warfare.

Charles still missed Hotchand, and one night when the Roussel family met for dinner, the boy had disappeared. Noi became hysterical, fearing another kidnapping. Later that night, servants from the house of Hotchand Sobhraj returned Charles to his mother. He had been found hiding under his father's bed. Next time he was left alone Charles ran away again, ducking through the police checkpoints and navigating the maze of back streets until he reached his father's home. Noi was mortified – her son's disobedience caused her to 'lose face' in the eyes of the Sobhraj household. From then on she locked him in the bathroom when she went out, to prevent him from escaping. No matter how tightly she secured the door and windows, he would invariably find a way out and back to his father's. Noi began tying her son to the bed, from which he also broke loose. When he was returned, she bound him more securely and, to teach him a lesson, left him tied to the bed for several days.

In 1953 Jacques Roussel was granted home leave. When Charles heard his mother discussing preparations for the voyage to France, he decided to run away from the house the night before departure and hide near the river until he saw their ship sail. Instead, on the crucial night, he fell asleep. In the morning Jacques Roussel carried the child aboard the troop ship, where Charles woke up in time to watch Vietnam disappear into the haze above the South China Sea. He felt abducted from his homeland, and although he knew he would never forgive his mother, he was even angrier with himself for his own weakness.

Under the leadership of Ho Chi Minh, the Viet Minh were gaining ground in the mountainous north, and the French amassed their forces for a decisive campaign upon which their future in Vietnam would depend. A few months after he had landed in France, Jacques was ordered back to the beleaguered colony. Noi, who had recently had her fifth child, would accompany Jacques back to Vietnam with her three youngest children, leaving Charles and the seven-year-old Nicole in boarding schools.

The nine-year-old boy found himself in a suburb of Paris walking with his mother through the austere lobby of a Catholic boarding school. He had never worn a tie before, or a jacket. The uniform didn't fit, and the grey flannel pricked his thin legs.

'But Mama, I hate this country,' he pleaded, clinging to her skirt. 'Take me back with you.'

'You'll soon get used to it, little one,' she said in her rapid high-pitched Vietnamese. 'Be brave. It won't be for long.'

'But why won't you take me?' His eyes were full of tears.

'We want the best for you. This is an expensive school. It's time for you to learn French and start your education. You're a big boy now, Charles, and you're very lucky to have this chance to grow up French,' she told the boy. 'There's no future in Vietnam.'

Charles did not adapt to this new country. Far from forgetting about Vietnam and his father, he had built them up into a fantasy of material bliss and parental affection. For Noi the most annoying symptom of her son's discontent was his bed-wetting. She had taken him to several doctors without success, and he had been admitted for exhaustive tests at the Armand Trousseau Hospital in Paris. The problem was not physiological, Dr Male explained, and it would disappear of its own accord when the boy had overcome his feelings of insecurity, surely understandable, given the sudden shifts between two parents and two countries. Disappointed in the failure of Western science, Noi resorted to a more practical remedy for her son's enuresis. When she put Charles to bed at night, she knotted a piece of string round his penis.

Watching his slim, beautiful mother waving goodbye from the taxi as it disappeared along the school's gravel driveway, Charles felt betrayed. He looked around at the priests and his grey-uniformed schoolmates saying their formal goodbyes in a language he did not understand. He was so overcome by feelings of abandonment and isolation that he ran to the dormitory, where the pictures of French saints stared down at him, threw himself on his bed and wept.

At first the other boys ignored him, but as the term went on, he became the outcast and the butt of their racist jokes. To catch up on his studies, he had been placed in a class of boys three years younger than himself. That was reason enough for them to sneer at him even if he had been able to keep it secret that he was a member of the race against which France was at war, and that he wet his bed.

Charles spent his free time writing long desperate letters to his mother begging her to take him back home to Saigon. Noi had given birth to her sixth child, a boy she christened Jacques after her husband. The letters Charles waited for never came. Now he was sure his family had forgotten all about him. No one had thought to arrange for visits between him and his sister Nicole, who was faring better in her girls' school because she had grown up speaking French. He didn't care, he told himself. He had decided he would never forgive Nicole, the daughter of Hotchand Sobhraj, for accepting the French soldier as her father. In his dreams his mother came to him, and swept him back to Saigon and the apartment above the tailor's shop.

At the end of term Charles had nowhere to go. He stayed on at school, the only boy in the deserted playgrounds, taking his meals with an elderly teacher and sleeping alone in the empty dormitory. When the other boys returned full of stories of their holidays, they laughed at the Vietnamese urchin who skulked alone in the quadrangle, abandoned, despised, and obviously loved by nobody.

After a year at school Charles was called out of class one day. His heart sank. Was he going to be punished for his failure in the examinations? No, the attendant told him there was someone to see him. In the lobby he saw a fashionably dressed young Vietnamese woman. It was his mother! He ran, almost slipping on the highly polished floor, and threw himself into her arms, his eyes filling with tears of happiness. But when she spoke, his face clouded over.

'Mama, I don't understand you,' he cried. 'Speak in French!' With a cold, dislocating shock he realized that he had forgotten the language of his homeland. It was terrible, as though he had lost one of his senses. Now, how would he be able to talk to his friends in Saigon?

In her basic French, Noi told her son that the family had left Vietnam for ever and that he could come home and live with her and his brothers and sisters.

'What about Papa?' he asked. 'Did he give you any message for me?'

'He's sick,' she said. 'The war was lost. Many soldiers died in the battle. Jacques was lucky, but now we must all be very kind to him.'

'No, not Jacques,' Charles said impatiently. 'My real Papa. I want to go back to him.'

'You can't go back to Hotchand any more, my darling,' she told him. 'He's dead.'

Battle-weary after Vietnam, Jacques Roussel had been given an administrative posting in the sleepy French protectorate of Senegal in West Africa. In 1957, when Charles was thirteen, he sailed from Marseilles with the Roussel family to the capital city, Dakar. His mother was nursing her new-born daughter, Martine, her seventh child. The wide boulevards of the port, crowded with traffic and lined with pavement cafés and shiny new shops and hotels, gave the town an unexpectedly cosmopolitan air. The family stayed temporarily in a hotel, and while Noi was caught up with her baby and arrangements for their new quarters, Charles was free to run off and explore the streets of this strange new city.

Following the back streets, he soon crossed into the Médina, where he heard the throb of drums and saw Senegalese in bright cotton robes living on the street while food was fried in truncated kerosene tins and witch doctors mixed mysterious potions. He saw snake-men, musicians, conjurors and the ragged children, wild and friendly, so unlike his cruel, priggish schoolmates in France. At the end of the day Charles left the frenzy of the Médina and returned to the family's hotel suite with its trappings of luxury, reminiscent of the life he believed he had lost in Saigon.

The next day, the family piled into two taxis and were driven along a road lined with packing-case shanties and cement igloos to the military barracks in the Point E area, row after row of tin-roofed bungalows planted on the dry desert sand, shaded by date palms. Charles was disappointed. This was to be his home for the next two and a half years. It was dark inside the bungalow. The blinds kept the harsh sun from penetrating. The incense from Noi's brass altar infused the house with the musky smell that reminded Charles of life in the house of Hotchand Sobhraj, who, he had begun to suspect from his mother's evasive answers, was still alive.

The three-tiered altar with its pagoda roofs mystified the other children, but Charles understood its symbols. The photographs of ancestors were to be worshipped, the candlesticks shaped like storks symbolized longevity, and the brass turtles on which they stood embodied the virtue of hard work. A picture of the Buddha stood on top, and around the altar were bowls of sweets left as an offering. If the children touched them Noi would whip them savagely, sometimes ordering them to cut their own switches from the garden or steal them from next door.

The younger children sensed that there was something different in their parents' attitude towards Charles, although they were not yet aware he was a half-brother. He was their hero. At night when Jacques blocked out his nightmares of Vietnam with sleeping pills and Noi disappeared to gambling soirées with her friends, Charles would lead his brothers and sisters in games of blind man's bluff, turning out all the lights and terrifying them until they begged him to stop.

'Let's go and clean out old Mamoudia's shop,' he said to his oldest brother and sister after one of these games. What an adventure! They all liked Mamoudia, the gentle seven-foot Senegalese who sold them Carumbas, their favourite caramel sweets. In the darkness Jean-Daniel and Nicole watched as their big brother opened the wooden latch with his pocket knife and slipped inside. In the bright moonlight they could see him stuffing packets of Carumba into his satchel. Then they froze, hearing the crunching footsteps of the patrolling watchman. The man shone his flashlight across the bamboo porch. Through the crack in the door, still slightly ajar, they saw Charles in his grey school shorts stop so still that he seemed not to be there. A few seconds later the watchman continued his rounds. Charles had already realized that people only see what they expect to see. Back in their brother's bedroom the children gathered as he distributed Carumbas to each of them. 'OK, now leave for a few minutes,' he said, 'while I hide the rest.'

The following night Jean-Daniel and Nicole raided Mamoudia's store on their own. At breakfast there was a knock on the door. Mamoudia himself appeared, looking sad, and he showed Noi a trail of sweet wrappers that led from their door to his shop. In a rage, ignoring the visiting neighbours, Noi whipped Jean-Daniel and Nicole mercilessly, teaching them, unwittingly, that it was not safe to steal unless Charles was there to lead them.

Mamoudia's shop with its few jars of sweets, bolts of fabric and groceries quickly became small-time for Charles, who had now mysteriously acquired a transistor radio. The children realized that if they pointed out a toy they liked in the supermarket of the Point E area, there was a good chance that Charles would present it to them a few days later. On their birthdays, previously threadbare occasions, he gave them expensive presents which they had to keep secret from their parents, although they sensed that Noi, who sometimes shared their chocolates and pastries without asking where they came from, would not be as hostile as Jacques to their brother's acquisitiveness.

Charles had been enrolled in the Orientation College in Dakar which he attended as little as possible, often forging his father's signature on explanatory absence notes. His school report for 1959, when he was fifteen and still in the class with the twelve-year-olds, was consistent: Geography, 2 (out of 20), 'No serious work'; Science, 1, 'Bad pupil'; Manual work, 1½, 'Undisciplined, lazy, unwilling'; and so on through all the subjects, escalating to a massive 7½ in sport for which the teacher recorded, 'Not very courageous, must awake.'

Jacques decided to discontinue the farce of his stepson's education and found him a job as an apprentice mechanic in the garage of a friend. A few days later he was sent home.

'May I ask why you gave Charles the sack?' Jacques asked his friend.

'He reversed the wires on the electrical transformer and almost burned the building down,' said the astounded owner. 'Why would anyone do that? You understand that I can't keep him on.'

'Yes,' said Jacques, 'I understand.'

Jacques tried to be firm with the children, but already he was looking frail and stooped and was losing grip of his sanity. At night the children heard him screaming in his sleep as the grenades of the Viet Minh landed around him. Charles despised the Frenchman because he failed to maintain the family at the level of prosperity he had known in Saigon with Hotchand. In addition, Noi had started to be unfaithful, and Charles took Jacques' dignity and tolerance in the face of this for weakness.

Noi had developed a habit of going off on long walks on a path around the headland above the beach. One day Charles followed her on his bicycle. Waiting on a lonely bench he saw a French officer and watched as his mother embraced the man. He picked up a handful of gravel and tossed it at the couple. 'You dirty whore!' he screamed, as he pedalled off.

That night, when the rest of the family were asleep, Charles went to the refrigerator and emptied its contents into a knapsack. He tip-toed into his parents' bedroom, took money from his mother's purse, and left a note on the kitchen table. 'I cannot believe my father is really dead. I'm going to Vietnam.' For a few kilometres he walked along the moonlit road towards the town before curling up to sleep in a field. In the morning he was awakened by the blazing sun. After a few bites of cold chicken he continued his journey. Reaching the docks of the crowded port, he discovered that a ship was sailing for Marseilles the next day. From Marseilles, he knew, boats left every day for Saigon. Overjoyed, he stared for hours at the huge vessel which symbolized all his dreams of returning home. The next day he would slip on board with the other passengers.

He spent the rest of the afternoon at his favourite beach, where he made a fork from a stick and some rusty nails and caught crabs. That night under the stars, cooking the crabs over a fire in a tin can, he imagined he was already in Saigon with his father. He would have his own car. Hotchand would dress him in suits and take him to the casinos. His father would love him even more because he had refused, all these years, to believe he was dead.

In the morning after a swim, he went back to the dock. He walked towards the gateway and noticed two turbaned Senegalese police-men checking each young passenger against a photograph. Jacques had reported him missing. The police were after him. Hopelessly, he returned to his beach where he spent the next three days living off crabs and sea urchins. 'I'll build a raft,' he said to himself, 'and float back to Saigon.' He began to collect driftwood but soon gave up. Depressed and rebellious, he walked back to town still determined not to return to his parents. As he was sitting on the pavement in the twilight, he heard footsteps behind him.

'Come on, let's go home,' Jacques said, smiling and taking his stepson by the hand.

'No. I don't want to. My home is in Vietnam!'

'Come on, Charles. Do you think we don't love you? We love you like all the others.'

Ashamed, the fifteen-year-old returned to the barracks. A few days later Jacques found Charles a job as assistant chef in a restaurant. He was pleased, even though he knew the owner was one of his mother's lovers, because it meant he would be out of the house all day, earning money he could use to get back to Vietnam. A few weeks later he heard that his stepfather would soon be posted back to France. He walked out of his job the same day. How could he work when he was so happy? He passed the time at the beach spearfishing. When his parents packed, they were surprised to find Charles in a good mood, dutifully helping everyone.

Back in France, Jacques Roussel tried again to further his stepson's education. Since he was worried by Charles' influence on the rest of the family, he decided to send him to boarding school. At fifteen, Charles was still wetting his bed and after several schools declined to enrol him, he was sent to an agricultural college at Miramar, 190 kilometres from Marseilles.

This time Charles made friends easily with his French schoolmates, who were awed by his worldliness and his tales of Senegal. For a while he applied himself to his studies with the aid of a teacher who was convinced, as he assured Noi, that his pupil had 'a unique form of intelligence'. The teacher was sympathetic to the boy's story of losing both his country and his father and wrote to Jacques Roussel requesting Hotchand Sobhraj's address so that Charles could begin a correspondence to 'heal the dislocations of his past'.

Noi and Jacques' efforts to convince Charles that his father was dead were faltering. Noi's lie had been an easy one, but behind it lay another kind of truth: Hotchand cared little for Charles any more. Noi had only been trying to protect her son and help him build a new life. Yet here was a teacher encouraging otherwise. Noi responded to his letter with a brusque request for him not to intervene in family affairs.

On Charles' sixteenth birthday, Jacques received a letter from the headmaster informing him that his stepson had broken out in a wild burst of unruliness, disrupting classes and smashing school property. 'The most likely cause of this rash of pranks,' the headmaster wrote, 'is the arrival of puberty, always a difficult time.' A few weeks later the Roussels received a telegram saying that Charles had run away.

Jacques left his modest cubicle in Paris where he served as an administrator in the army and rushed to Marseilles. He found Charles in the backyard of a former neighbour's house.

'Everyone has lied to me,' he scowled. 'You say Hotchand is dead, but I don't believe you. I want to go and find him.'

'It was for your own good, my son,' Jacques said quietly. He had never shouted at his children and he was saddened now, convinced that it had been a mistake to lie to the boy about Hotchand. 'Your mother didn't want you to depend on him. He has two families now, six children in Poona with Geeta and three more in Saigon with Chu. Remember your nurse? He married her. So you see, his time is taken up with them.'

'So now you tell me that instead of being dead he has nine children.' Charles smiled bitterly. 'Well, it makes no difference. I still want to go back to Saigon.'

Jacques found Charles a position as a kitchen hand at La Coupole, an iconic brasserie in Montparnasse. He was popular with the staff and reported punctually for work, but in July 1960, as Jacques began gathering the rest of the family from their various schools for a holiday at their summer cottage in Marseilles, he was told that Charles had, once again, disappeared. Unable to find him anywhere in Paris, the Roussels proceeded to the villa, where neighbours told them that

Charles had arrived a few days before and had borrowed thirty francs. He had asked for the key to the cottage, taken tinned food from the cupboard and vanished.

One of Charles' young friends, Michel, was also missing from home. The radio broadcast an emergency bulletin, and a local newspaper published a missing persons' report. Jacques contacted the Messageries Maritimes shipping line and was told that no boats had recently sailed for Saigon. This made Charles' disappearance even more mysterious. Noi, Jacques and the six other children began their summer holiday at their Villa La Roche in a mood of nervous expectancy, waiting for news of Charles.

'Do you want to go on an adventure?' Charles had asked his fourteen-year-old companion Michel when he had met him in the local park after running away from La Coupole. Charles convinced him that an exciting time awaited them both in Saigon. They took a bus to the docks of Marseilles, where they studied the departure lists of ships bound for Vietnam. In two days *La Bourdonnais* was sailing to Djibouti, a port in north-east Africa on the Red Sea, part of French Somaliland. Ten days later another ship would dock at Djibouti bound for Saigon. Charles and Michel climbed the tall wire fence surrounding the dock and dodged swiftly between the maze of crates until they saw *La Bourdonnais* standing huge and splendid against the night sky.

'Oh, Michel, isn't she beautiful!?' cried Charles, putting his arm around the boy's shoulder. 'She's going to take us to another world.'

The boys clambered up a stay rope and hid in a lifeboat. The next day as sailors swabbed the decks, the boys delved into the emergency rations of milk and salt beef which they warmed over matches. At dawn the engines rumbled to life and Charles peered through the canvas to see the cliffs of Marseilles recede in the distance.

'Stay here,' he said to his shivering friend. 'I'll check things out.'

Charles slipped from the lifeboat, dusted his suit, straightened his tie, and taking a comb from his back pocket, smoothed his short black hair. Sauntering to the bar, he ordered a Coke. He had soon made friends with a group of teenagers who, like himself, sat giggling at the sedate foxtrot in progress on the dance floor. 'Let's go and play shuffleboard in the games room,' he suggested.

Charles spent the night in a deck-chair. In the morning he found the first-class dining room where he sat down at a table and nervously reached for a croissant. The tall African waiter leaned over his shoulder and said politely, 'Good morning, sir. Tea or coffee?'

'Coffee, thank you,' Charles said, scanning the breakfast menu ravenously and buttering his croissant while trying to appear at ease. The waiter filled his cup and asked for his order. When he had left, Charles leaned back, smiling. The tinkle of china and silver and the modulated conversation of the first-class passengers pleased him. He was back in the world where he really belonged, Charles thought, and nobody guessed that he was a stowaway. If you sat at a first-class table, Charles deduced, you became a first-class passenger. All that mattered was the appearance of things – people were easy to fool. Charles straightened his tie and nodded graciously at the waiter who had arrived with his breakfast.

'Where in hell have you been?' Michel demanded from beneath the tarpaulin when he returned. 'I've been awake all night. I thought you'd been caught.'

Charles told him of his adventures, and Michel demanded to join him. 'No. You're not old enough to carry it off. Do as I say, and everything will be OK.'

He walked away and rejoined his new friends from the night before. Over the next few days he maintained the masquerade, showering in economy class and sleeping on different decks every night so as not to be noticed. Occasionally he returned to the lifeboat with scraps of food for Michel.

When the ship docked at Djibouti, a French possession where no passports were required, the boys walked down the gangway saluted by two Somali policemen.

Charles discovered that there were many Vietnamese businesses in the small garrison town. At a photographic studio run by a family from Saigon, he poured out his story. The sympathetic owner drove

Charles and Michel to the beach and promised to return that night with food. The boys swam in the Red Sea and dozed under coconut palms until the proprietor, laden with Vietnamese delicacies, arrived with his wife and four children, all of whom were eager to meet the brave runaways to Saigon.

Inspired by the example of his older companion, Michel wandered into town the next day and confided his story to the proprietor of a restaurant. The Frenchman promptly called the police.

'Where do you come from?' the gruff commissioner asked Charles at the police station.

'Saigon,' Charles said. He decided that if he stuck to his story, the police would believe him in the end.

'Liar!' The policeman slapped him hard across the face and waved a piece of paper in front of him. It was a cable from Marseilles with details of the missing boys. 'That must be someone else,' Charles said, hoping that it was still possible to convince them. Another slap stung his face and he was told he would be sent back to France on the same ship that had brought him to Djibouti. Charles realized that the game was up. But he had almost made it, and if it hadn't been for Michel, disobeying his orders, the plan would have worked.

His new Vietnamese friends stood sadly on the dock as Michel and Charles waved from the deck of *La Bourdonnais*, now making the return journey to Marseilles. The liner heaved through the Red Sea past the Bab-el-Mandeb – the Gate of Sorrow – and Charles promised himself that next time he would make it to Vietnam.

When Charles saw Jacques and his mother on the dock at Marseilles, he did not return their friendly waves, although he smiled at his favourite teacher, who had also come to welcome him home.

'You'll never stop me from running away to my father,' he told Jacques in the taxi to Villa La Roche – and refused to answer Noi's questions about his recent adventures.

'Would you like me to write to Hotchand and see if he will agree to take you back?' Jacques asked, finally defeated, his haggard face looking older than his forty-two years.

'Of course,' Charles said. 'That's all I've ever wanted.'

'But if he refuses,' Jacques said, 'if he wants you to remain here, will you accept it? Will you go back to college and apply yourself?'

'It's a deal,' Charles said, still ignoring his mother, 'but I want to watch you write the letter, and when you post it, I'm going with you.'

At the end of the summer the family returned to Paris, and Charles found work at another restaurant while he waited for his father to reply. Finally it came, a short, friendly note on stationery emblazoned with the letterhead 'Hotchand Sobhraj – Textiles. Imports and Exports' and the cable address 'Activity Saigon'. His son's future was too complicated a question to be decided by post, Hotchand wrote, but as it happened he would be coming to Paris in January. He would settle the matter when he arrived.

On 6 January 1961, the day Hotchand Sobhraj was to arrive in Paris, Charles woke his stepfather at dawn and by 6 a.m., hours early, they were waiting at Orly Airport. It had been almost ten years since Charles had seen his father, and when the stocky, impeccably dressed Indian walked through the immigration barrier wheeling a cart loaded with expensive luggage, he was almost knocked over by his son's embrace. Charles took charge of the bags with a proprietorial air, and in the taxi on the way back to the Roussels' small apartment on the outskirts of the city, Charles besieged his father with questions about Vietnam.

'Can I go back and live with you, Papa? Can I please? I could help you in your business. I learn very fast.'

'What are you doing with yourself here? I must say I've heard some bad reports from your mother,' Hotchand said indulgently. He bore a striking resemblance to Georges Pompidou as he leaned back, smiling expansively and lighting a cigarette.

'I'm the chief under-assistant to the chef at La Saladiere. That means I peel potatoes, chop onions ... that sort of thing.'

The smile left the Indian's face.

'A son of mine? In the kitchen? That's no good.'

'He's lucky to have a job,' Jacques said mildly. 'His school record is not the best.'

'It's not appropriate for the son of a Sindhi to work in such a capacity. It is not done.'

'It's not, I know, Papa. I hate it. But what can I do? Unless you take me back to the country that I love, where I belong.'

'Maybe it could be arranged, but I expect hard work and obedience. You'd start at the bottom of the ladder . . .'

'And very soon I'll get to the top. Just give me one chance, and I'll prove myself.'

Jacques Roussel kept a distance during the reunion of Charles' parents. Noi agreed that Charles should go back to Saigon with his father and learn the family business. 'What good can I do for him, with six others to raise and no money?' she asked her former lover. 'It's about time you did something, with all your shops and your servants and your cars.'

'I'll go to the ministry to make arrangements to get him a passport,' Jacques said, heading off the impending argument.

'OK, Jacques. It's agreed. You fix up his passport, and I'll take him back when I leave at the end of the month,' promised the elder Sobhraj.

Hotchand booked into the luxurious Georges V Hotel, and Charles, who had stopped going to work at the restaurant in accordance with Hotchand's wishes, spent all his time with him, happily discussing the journey he had been dreaming of making since the age of nine. But by the time Hotchand's visit had come to an end, the passport had not been issued. The morning Hotchand was to catch his plane they had breakfast together in the hotel's cedar and gilt dining room. Charles was morose.

'Come on, it makes no difference. I'll send you a ticket and you can come as soon as the documents are ready.'

'How do I know you will really send the ticket?' Charles said darkly.

'Don't talk with your mouth full. The way your mother has raised you is shocking.'

Charles swallowed and said angrily, 'I'm used to these promises. When Noi left me in boarding school she said, "Just for a little while, I'll soon be back to get you." She took a year to come back. Always people promise they will do this or that. Nothing ever happens. No one cares about me. You won't send the ticket.'

'Your mother is a very flighty woman. More a woman than a mother. I am a businessman. And how does business work? On trust. My word is law. You will learn that, Charles.' Hotchand glanced at his gold watch.

'Now I must leave; I'll be seeing you very soon. In the meantime, be good. Don't give any trouble. You promise?'

'I promise, Papa.'

As his father's limousine disappeared into the traffic, Charles watched with his hands thrust into the pockets of his coat, wondering if his chance had passed him by again.

After his father left Paris, Charles spent his days at home, leaving his room only when he heard the postman. All he lived for was the day his passport and ticket would arrive, and it was as though, as his mother said sarcastically, he had already left the family. The atmosphere in the crowded apartment was tense, reflecting their resentment at Charles' impatience to leave them.

He passed his time reading magazines and books and indulging in fantasies about Saigon. With his European experience he would soon rise to the top in the business. Charles imagined his own car, a house, a Vietnamese wife. He hoped that his humiliating experiences in France would be forgotten. Perhaps he would join the army and fight in the jungles. This seemed a romantic idea, and he could see himself driving a tank.

Then, one day, there was a knock on the door and Jacques entered.

'Charles, I have a surprise for you.' He handed him a manila envelope.

Inside was his new French passport – the thin blue book that gave him his freedom. He opened it and looked at his name, neatly lettered, and his photograph on the first page.

This put him in a good mood for days, but then the old doubts began gnawing. Had his father forgotten him? Hotchand had returned to Saigon a month ago and the ticket had still not arrived.

I'll pay my own passage, he thought, but I need money. Where can I get it? Go back to work? But, no, that takes too long. My mother? Impossible. She cares only for gambling and wouldn't help. I could steal. But how to begin?

He lay on the bed trying to think of a plan. He rushed down to the letterbox. There was still no ticket. Flicking through the evening newspaper, he read a report about housewives being robbed at home in the daytime. He felt his heart thumping. Why not something of that sort? He rushed back up to his room to be alone. No, I'll never do it, he said to himself, shivering.

With the last of his savings he went to the sports counter of the Bazar de l'Hotel de Ville, a Parisian department store, and bought a gun. The clerk handed him the package and, running his hands over it in his pocket, he felt strong and exhilarated. Charles walked down the Rue de Rivoli towards the Metro, indifferent to the cold. When he got home he went to his bedroom, locked the door and stared at the grey pistol. Now I can do it, he thought.

In the morning he took the local train to a suburb near Choisy-le-Roi and wandered towards the area of cheap, government-built blocks of apartments. Choosing a building surrounded by a shabby lawn, he looked at the letterboxes and saw that most of the residents were couples. He felt nervous and had almost decided to forget the plan.

But if I don't do it this time, I'll never do it. I'll never get to Saigon, he said to himself. He walked up the stairs and listened at the first door on the landing. He heard nothing. Feeling relieved, then angry at himself for this feeling, he listened at the next door, then another, and still he heard no sounds. He went up to the third floor. He reached the fourth door on the landing before he heard the sound of a woman's voice talking to a child.

Charles trembled. I can't do it, he thought and walked quickly back to the stairs and sat halfway down the steps, trying to overcome his fear by thinking of the wonderful life he would lead in his father's house in Saigon.

No, I won't run away, he thought, turning around and going back up to the door where he had heard the woman's baby-talk. He felt the gun in his pocket. What will I say? He wanted to leave again, and so, to stop himself, he pressed the buzzer.

'Yes,' the woman said, opening the door and putting her hand to the scarf on her head.

'Good morning, Madame,' he said, looking serious and respectable in his suit. 'Sorry to disturb you, but I must check the meter.'

'Come in,' she said and closed the door behind her. When she turned around, Charles was facing her with a gun.

'Don't move,' he said, 'and don't scream.'

The woman froze and she let out a terrified shriek.

Charles dropped the gun, jumped on her, and put his hands over her mouth. 'Shut up! Don't shout! I won't hurt you.'

'Oh God,' she said, 'be careful, I'm pregnant.'

Charles felt ashamed and wanted to go, but he heard himself saying, 'I won't harm you, Madame. Just give me your money.' He followed her into the kitchen, half planning to ask her forgiveness and disappear.

The woman picked up her handbag from the kitchen table and gave it to Charles. 'It's in the purse,' she said. He stuffed the notes into the pocket of his jacket.

'I'm sorry, but I must tie you up.'

'Please, can you do it in the bedroom? My baby's there.'

'Of course,' he said, following her. 'I'm only doing this to give myself time to escape,' he apologized.

Without a word the woman sat down on a chair near the crib as Charles took two towels from the bathroom and tied her hands and feet to the chair. 'Please don't gag me,' she said.

'All right, but you must promise to give me thirty minutes before you shout for help.'

'Yes, I promise.'

Charles left and took the train back home. Disappointed with the seventy francs, he put the gun back in its hiding place and fell asleep until Jacques woke him for dinner.

Two days later Charles repeated the crime, this time throwing his coat over the young housewife when she screamed. Her six-year-old son ran out of the apartment to the landing, crying, and Charles fled downstairs to the basement. There was a long corridor with a series of gates on each side. Charles squeezed himself into one of the storage rooms and lay on a heap of coal behind two crates of wine.

It was twenty minutes before he heard the voices.

'Look! A pair of feet. Can't you see? Let's get him.' Charles wanted to faint. In a few seconds he was blinking into the glare of a flashlight. A fist hit his face. He fell down and was kicked in the stomach. Two gendarmes pushed through the crowd and hurried him upstairs where more tenants rushed towards him, trying to attack him. Police formed a cordon and dragged him to the van.

At the prefecture, the police took down his name and address and put him in a cell. Charles sat on the bunk, sobbing. Later he was taken into an office where he saw Jacques, his mother and the woman he had just tried to rob. He stared at the floor and said nothing.

'What have you done?' Noi asked bitterly. 'Why have you done this?' Charles still could not speak.

'Don't you think you should beg this lady to forgive you?' she said.

Jacques looked dazed, with a sad faraway expression in his eyes, lost for words. Charles made an impassioned plea to the woman and asked her forgiveness.

She smiled and said to the station sergeant, 'I withdraw my complaint.'

The police drove the Roussel family home, with Charles staring at the floor in silence and Jacques trying to stop Noi's angry denunciations.

'Go to your room and sleep, Charles. You look tired,' Jacques said. 'We'll talk about it later.'

In the morning Jacques took his stepson with him on the Metro. 'I understand that you do not wish to accept me as your father, Charles,' he said to the boy, 'and I don't wish to hold you back from going to Vietnam. Be patient. Hotchand will send the ticket. You must try to realize from this experience what a dreadful mistake you have made. Until the ticket arrives, I must ask you to come with me to the office every day.'

A few days later a call came from the police station asking Jacques to bring his son in for further questioning.

'Have you done anything else, Charles?'

'No, nothing,' he answered.

Several hours passed before he was brought in front of the judge of the juvenile court and arrested for the offence committed against the woman in the first apartment he had entered.

'Why, Charles, oh, why have you done this?' Jacques was almost weeping. 'If you wanted to go so badly, I would have paid for the ticket.'

Charles was taken into a cell and ordered to strip naked. His clothes and his body were closely searched. When he was dressed, he was put in a cell with two other prisoners whom he ignored. Curling up on a bunk he faced the wall and drifted off to sleep. All the next morning he remained there, trying not to wake.

When Jacques and Noi came to see him that afternoon, Charles refused to talk to them, or even look up. Noi wept, and Jacques, grim and depressed, sat in silence with his arm around her shoulder. Thoughts spun in Charles' head. Is this really happening? Is it possible that I'm in jail? That I robbed a woman? Back again in the cell he curled up on the bunk and tried to fall asleep and convince himself that the situation was just a dream.

Two days later Noi returned alone to visit him.

'Where's Jacques?' he asked. 'Where's my father?'

'He's in the hospital with a nervous breakdown,' she replied. 'He doesn't recognize me any more. That's what you have done. Are you pleased?'

Charles rushed from the visitors' room back to the cell, tears streaming down his face. He sat on his bed crying, indifferent to the jeers of his two cellmates. When Noi returned to the juvenile detention centre two days later, she told her son that Jacques Roussel's condition had worsened.

'He's completely insane, now,' she said. 'He'll be in the hospital for the rest of his life.'

'Oh, God, Mother, get me out of here. It's my fault. I'll never be bad again. Only let me see him.' He had realized at last that Jacques cared for him, and he hated himself for what he had done.

A few days later Charles was called before the examining magistrate. His mother was in court and so was his first victim, the pregnant woman.

'Mother, I want to apologize to the woman immediately,' he said and asked the policeman to let him talk to her.

The woman looked at him, surprised. Charles said nothing. His face swelled up with tears again, and he could find no way to put his remorse into words. She looked at him encouragingly.

'Please forgive me,' he blurted out,' I don't deserve it, but I beg your forgiveness.'

'You must have hurt your parents very much,' she said, her eyes softening. 'You must promise never to do such things again.'

Noi introduced herself to the young couple, and they talked until the case was called. The woman told the court that she wished to withdraw her complaint. Her request was accepted, but the magistrate explained that Charles would have to appear before a special juvenile court in a few days. Then Charles was sentenced to six months' imprisonment, suspended under the First Offender's Act.

His mother took him home on the bus, weeping quietly. All the way back to the apartment neither of them spoke, until they were inside and Charles' brothers and sisters were hugging him. 'Don't think you weren't punished,' Noi said. 'While you were in jail the police came and took away your passport.'

'Why? Because of ... what happened?'

'No. They said it was a mistake that you got it. They said that you aren't a French citizen.'

'But I have to go to Saigon ...' he said, and his face was stricken with panic.

'Jacques has arranged for you to get a *laissez-passer* instead of a passport. It's for one journey only. It was the last thing Jacques did before he fell ill.'

The following day Charles went to visit Jacques in the military psychiatric hospital. His stepfather looked old and very small in the white bed. He smiled weakly as Charles came into the room.

'Oh, Papa, forgive me,' he said as Jacques embraced him.

'The most important thing is that you are out of prison.'

'And there's more good news. Guess what arrived in the post this morning – my ticket to Saigon!'

'I'm glad for you, boy. I hope Vietnam is all that you dream it is. For me it was a nightmare.' Jacques' eyes closed and he seemed to have gone to sleep. Charles tiptoed out, relieved at the brevity of the visit.

Charles' *laissez-passer* was stamped with a temporary visa to South Vietnam, and under the heading 'Nationality' the issuing official had written the words: 'To be determined'.

On a crisp and clear day in March 1961, the gaily coloured streamers snapped and blew in the breeze as Charles waved goodbye to his mother, who was crying, and to his old teacher from Miramar, who had unexpectedly turned up to see him off. The now familiar sight of the cliffs of Marseilles filled him with euphoria. This time, nothing could go wrong. His room in the house of Hotchand Sobhraj was waiting for him.

Three weeks later the passenger liner docked by the banks of the Saigon River and Charles saw his father and three of his daughters, Shibani, Madhu and Rajni, waving their bright scarves on the wharf.

'You'll find so many things changed here now,' his father said, beaming as Charles was bundled into the waiting taxi, 'and the first thing you must learn is how to speak English.'

Charles had remembered Saigon as a city of bicycles – now the streets buzzed with Vespas and Lambrettas. Crewcut men in Hawaiian shirts drove Chevrolets bearing red, white and blue stickers on their bumpers depicting an American–Vietnamese handshake. 'The Yanks, burning their dollars,' Hotchand explained as he waved to an American officer in a passing Jeep.

Hotchand Sobhraj was an impressive figure. He was handsome and had a reassuring air of prosperity. Charles enjoyed the way so many people waved and nodded to him as they drove through the city, past the tanks and barbed-wire barricades.

The wide, tree-lined boulevard which Charles remembered as Rue Catinat was now called Tu Do Street, and with its pavement cafés and flower stalls it still looked French, although the graffiti on the white concrete walls of all the new buildings were now scrawled in English: *Support Only President Diem ... Don't Give Information to the Vietcong*. Twice, Hotchand's car was stopped and searched by police.

The car turned off Tu Do Street into Ngo Duc Ke and pulled up at number 80. It was a two-storey cement building, with the drapery shop downstairs and the six-room apartment on the second floor. The family's four servants lined up to welcome him, and Chu, who had been his nursemaid and was now his father's wife, greeted him coolly. Her fingers glittered with gems.

Hotchand's decision to marry the Vietnamese servant when she became pregnant had outraged the Indian community in Saigon. The conventional practice was to send the woman away with a small pension. Instead, as mother of his three daughters and now pregnant with a fourth child which Hotchand hoped would be a boy, she was mistress of the comfortable apartment.

Charles was given his own room, and his three half-sisters giggled and showed him round. Behind the shopfront was a big garden shaded by plane trees, and in the living room, in pride of place, was a record player and a collection of records. Although luxury in Saigon was nothing by European standards, Charles was delighted by his new status as the son of an important and wealthy merchant.

For the first two weeks after his arrival, Charles got up eagerly, and dressed in the new clothes his father had given him. It was Charles who was downstairs first to open the shop at 7.30 a.m. Business began early to avoid the midday heat and the downpours of the rainy season. Rattling his keys with self-importance, giving orders to the staff and serving customers with the charm of a born salesman, he was absorbed by the novelty of his new life and imagined the day the sign-painter would come to change the title above the door to *Hotchand Sobhraj and Son.*

In the warm evenings he left the shop and strolled down Tu Do Street to the American–Vietnamese Friendship Association School, where he was enrolled in English classes and a commercial business course. Typing and shorthand failed to hold his attention for long. Instead he had discovered karate.

The Vietnamese passion for karate was a legacy of the Japanese occupation during the Second World War. In the cavernous hall hung with prayer flags, incense burners and paintings of Buddha and Confucius, among the hundreds of men and boys in traditional white pyjamas, Charles felt he had rediscovered his Asian identity as he practised the graceful movements of the ancient martial art. The philosophy of self-discipline and emotional restraint appealed to him, but more important was the new sense of physical power as his body became lithe and strong, and he developed new and lethal skills.

The daily routine of the shop soon began to bore Charles. In a city that lived under the constant threat of bombs and whose whole economy depended on shady deals, punctuality and accounting ledgers seemed irrelevant. He began skipping classes and missing work and instead met his friends in the cafés of Tu Do Street to discuss the business deals he dreamed up. He discovered gambling and girls, both passions which required more money than his father gave him.

His first scheme was a smuggling operation. A hairdresser who worked on the ocean liners that berthed in the Saigon River agreed to provide him with duty-free perfume and cigarettes. There was a black market that controlled the retail life of the city and it would buy whatever Charles could supply. In order to start his 'business' Charles stole from his father.

When Charles' visa expired, he was called up before the military board of Saigon. His nationality was still undetermined. He was told that since his mother was Vietnamese and he had been born in Saigon, he had to join the Vietnamese army. Hotchand would have none of it. Charles thought half-heartedly that he wanted to fight for his homeland but he went along with his father's plan to arrange Indian nationality for him. This would exclude him from the draft. An official explained that to be naturalized Indian, Charles would have to live in India for at least a year, learn a dialect, and acquire an understanding of Indian culture.

Three weeks after putting his son on the boat to Bombay, Hotchand Sobhraj came home to find Charles at the table wolfing down beef and noodles. He looked up, and without swallowing, launched into an angry diatribe.

'Why did you send me there? I was hungry all the time. They are vegetarians. I couldn't speak the language and I hate India.'

'How did you get back here?' his father demanded.

'I stowed away and climbed over a fence here when it got dark,' he said, proud of his resourcefulness. Although he had disobeyed his father, Charles had been sure that Hotchand would be happy to see him back again. But his father was furious.

'Why did you come back? Do you think I want you here? To steal my money, to behave recklessly, to set a shocking example to my children? You had your chance. Now go back to India. Learn the ways of our forefathers and stop thinking you're too good for them. Do you want to stay here and get killed or maimed for a lost cause?'

'Yes! That's what I want. To fight. To do something. To know that I belong somewhere!'

Their shouting had awakened the baby. Chu had given birth to a son. Despite his brave words, Charles realized that he couldn't stay in Vietnam. He passed the next few days in a state of misery as his father made arrangements for his departure.

When Hotchand saw him off at the dock his parting words were firm: 'You're not wanted here. Remember that.'

Charles stayed up on deck, watching the dusk fall and the coast of Vietnam recede. The thought of the hidebound household in Poona, with its traditional Indian values, made him shudder. He was French, after all. How could his father expect him to sleep on a straw pallet on a mud floor in a house without plumbing?

'Where does the ship go after Bombay?' he asked a sailor.

'We go on to Marseilles. Then we come back.'

He would refuse to leave the boat in Bombay, he decided. When he arrived in France his mother would be forced to pay for his passage. She would have no other choice.

3

Freedom Now!

Late one night in early 1968, Benard sat at his desk, going once again through the documents that Noi had given him. Charles' life had been so complicated and unhappy, Benard wondered if the boy had had any chance at all. Now that he understood the whole story he was convinced that Charles' statelessness had contributed to his feeling of dislocation and his criminal record.

Charles had been eighteen years old when he arrived back in Marseilles after his disastrous trip to Saigon. When French immigration authorities gave him only a temporary visitor's permit and refused him permission to work, a pattern of petty crime was established – mainly stealing cars – for which he was punished with ever-increasing jail terms and a deportation order.

Once Charles' current jail term was completed he would face deportation from France again. But to what country? India? Vietnam? The problems would only repeat themselves. Benard got up and walked out into the night air, on his way to the library, where he had already spent months poring over history books and legal records relating to France and Cochin-China.

He thought that there must be a solution to the problem, and since current legal opinion was ambiguous, he had been searching for forgotten laws that might still have effect. At the end of the evening he found one: a law of 1898 which proclaimed that people born in Saigon automatically had the right of French citizenship.

On Saturday 6 April 1968, Charles turned twenty-four. He spent the entire day in solitary waiting for Benard to arrive for his usual visit.

Finally Benard entered the visitors' room wielding a large brown paper parcel.

'See if they fit,' he said, watching Charles' face as he removed the wrapping eagerly. Inside was a crisp new shirt, a jacket, trousers and a shoe box. As the lid came off to reveal a pair of shiny leather shoes, he was pleased he'd been able to follow Charles' instructions. He'd been careful to avoid a pointed toe.

'Thank you, Alain. I'm so happy today. I don't even care that they put me back in solitary. They expect me to work. But I refuse! How can I work with only eleven more days to freedom?'

'I've never seen you look so healthy,' said Benard, feeling content.

'I sleep well, eat well, do yoga, and pray every day. But what about the suit?'

'Hotchand has sent you some clothes,' said Benard. 'They should be here by the time you're free.'

He hadn't told Charles that when he'd first written to his father he'd received a frankly despairing account of Charles' visit to Saigon. It concluded with this admission: 'When Charles left, I decided I must forget him for ever.'

Fortunately, in the ensuing eighteen months, the father's attitude had softened and Hotchand had sent a measuring chart to Charles so that he could make him some suits. He even offered to have his son back and to make him manager of one of his stores.

'If he behaves nicely,' he wrote to Benard, 'some day he will be rich.'

Noi had also kept in touch. 'Thank you very much for all the things you do for my son,' she wrote to Benard soon after their first meeting. 'Tell him I've forgotten the past, and I think of him always.'

Starting to enjoy his birthday for the first time that day, Charles couldn't contain his excitement.

'It's been five years now, Alain, five years in jail! What a waste. And now, thanks to you, it won't happen again. It will never happen again. I feel so different, like a new man, Alain. And when I look back at my past, it fills me with horror.'

'It's not about what you did, Charles,' said Benard quickly, 'it's more what was done to you.'

'But everything changed the day you gave me a country, Alain. You came through that door and handed me a future.'

'I didn't give you a nationality, Charles. You are legally entitled to that.'

'But before you, nobody cared,' he said, carefully buttoning up his new white shirt. He stood before Benard in his new outfit. 'So, how do I look?' he asked expectantly.

'Like a business executive on his way to the top,' Benard said, impressed by Charles' transformation.

Even in his prison clothes Charles had always looked stylish. He was meticulous about his personal appearance. Now, in the black trousers, white shirt and sports jacket, he radiated a commanding presence.

'You look ready for your new life. And I have news. You start with the fire-equipment company selling fire extinguishers two weeks after you're out, and in three months they'll give you a car.'

'A country, a job. You are even letting me stay in your apartment. Without you, what would I do?'

Having finished preening, Charles walked over to the table and sat down opposite Benard. For a moment, he put his head in his hands, and then as if in a trance, he began to talk. Later Benard realized what a startling confession he had made.

'I know I've been impulsive in the past, Alain,' he said, 'but that's all over now. You can trust me. I understand myself better now. I know that inside me there are two natures at war with each other. On one side is my logic and intelligence, even my spirituality. And on the other, there is my weaker side, my emotions. It is this side which made me fixate on wanting to be with my father. It was an obsession that drove me back to Vietnam and to disaster. And so when I ended up in jail, I decided to kill this side of myself. That's why I went on the hunger strikes, Alain. And the first few days were torture. I wanted to give up. "This is crazy," I said to myself. "It's too hard. Forget it." But I answered myself. "No, don't give up! Resist! Suffer! And then you can anchor this suffering inside."'

Charles thumped his stomach with his fists, proud of his muscled torso.

'If my feelings ever get swept away again, I have this inner core I can cling to now. That's how I lasted forty-five days without food.'

Although accustomed to his young friend's intensity, Benard was alarmed. And yet he was deeply moved too.

'If you eliminate your feelings, Charles,' he said gently, 'you'll turn yourself into a monster.'

'I still have feelings,' he said calmly. 'But I'm in control. Remember the day you came and told me that you had seen my mother? She had given you all the papers relating to me and told you, "Here is my son. Take him. I give him to you." I had been completely numb until that moment, and then a strange sensation came into my heart. So many times you have come into this room, bringing me the things I have needed so desperately. My citizenship papers. Remember? It was you who gave me a fatherland. All this you did for me and more, much more.'

Benard nodded. He had done everything he possibly could for his troubled friend.

'And then one Saturday you didn't come,' Charles continued. 'All day I waited in the cell, expecting them to call my name. It got dark, and still I waited. Where were you? Why weren't you here? When at last I realized you wouldn't come, that same strange sensation flowed into my heart, stronger than before. It took me back to my child-hood. I smelled the soup stalls near the river in Saigon.'

Charles looked up, straight into the older man's eyes, and smiled.

'I analysed this feeling, Alain. And then I realized what it was. It was the emptiness in my heart when Noi took me away from my father.'

He jumped up and began pacing the cell.

'It was a yearning, an ache, like my emotions for Hotchand,' he explained. 'It made me laugh, Alain. I laughed, and then I wept. I had gone all around the world searching for my father until I landed in Poissy Jail and then here, deep in the dungeons, my father comes to me, my true father.'

Benard stared at the handsome young man. He felt the mesmeric pull of Charles' eyes.

'Do you realize, Alain?' said Charles, coming over to him, clamping both hands on the man's shoulders and staring into his eyes with a sort of joy. 'You have become my father.'

At this moment they heard the rattle of keys, and a guard pushed open the door. Charles' hands dropped to his sides. He stepped away from his friend, and Benard stood up quickly, aware that the guard was listening.

'Do you need anything else before the seventeenth?' he asked, attempting to keep the emotion from his voice.

'Just a belt, thanks, Alain,' said Charles nonchalantly. 'The trousers are a bit loose.'

At dawn, eleven days later, Alain Benard drove through the forest of St-Germain-en-Laye to Poissy Jail. At home, the boy's room was ready, and the suits which had arrived from his father in Saigon were hanging in the cupboard. Now, he wanted to be there, waiting for Charles when he came through the gate. But as he turned the corner out of the forest, he saw him sitting on a suitcase under the streetlamp in front of the tall iron gates. As he pulled up beside him, Charles leapt up, grinning broadly.

'They couldn't wait to get rid of me!' he exclaimed.

The very next evening, Benard surprised his charge with an invitation to a dinner party. He had not been able to resist the opportunity to introduce his young friend to an educated fraternity of his peers and knew their hosts' tastefully appointed home would impress Charles.

Everything began propitiously. The murmur of pre-dinner conversation rose and fell. The silver candelabra blazed on the sideboard. Three bottles of burgundy were uncorked and the hostess ladled gazpacho into pink china bowls. Benard, sitting at her right, passed the bowls to the rest of the dinner guests, discreetly keeping an eye on Charles, who was clearly at ease despite the great contrast with his recent circumstances. Rather than feeling like a fish out of water, which Benard had feared, he seemed to be enjoying himself.

Also seated at the table, opposite Charles, was an exquisite young woman. She had captured Charles' attention immediately, but her response to his glances was not what he hoped. In fact her mind was quite elsewhere. Just that morning, her boyfriend, a fellow student at the Sorbonne, had told her that he wanted to end their relationship. When she did notice that Charles was staring at her, she felt slightly annoyed. She was in no mood for unsolicited male attention. When her soup arrived, she was relieved to find a distraction, turning to the guest on her right.

With the arrival of the duck, the host stood up and began to slice the meat. His young niece stood next to him pouring from the sauce boat. Conversation lulled as the plates were passed along the table. Charles, who attached little importance to food, was secretly bemused by the formality of the proceedings and the glow of entitlement enveloping the scene. He glanced again at the luminous young woman at the other side of the table. This time he caught and held her eyes. A shiver went through her.

Why does that handsome young man keep staring at me? she asked herself, aware that the intensity of his gaze was making her feel uncomfortable. She averted her eyes. When she glanced up again, he was smiling and talking to the people around him. With his high cheekbones and sensual mouth, he was unlike anyone she had ever seen before. He seemed so composed, so in his element, and yet there was something electric about him that singled him out.

Benard had noticed this covert exchange, and the way Charles was attempting to mask his interest in the young woman. He decided to keep an eye on the pair. When dessert arrived he began to pass bowls of lemon sorbet down the table. He was so proud of the boy. Watching him, so at home in his new suit and tie, talking urbanely with this group of intellectuals, he became convinced that Charles was going to make it. With his brains and charm, how could he fail?

After the meal, the guests dispersed to the library for coffee. The young woman chose a seat by the window.

'Forgive me, Mademoiselle,' said Charles, taking the opportunity to approach her. 'Perhaps you caught me glancing at you a few times.

I admit, I couldn't help but notice your beautiful hands. Tell me, has anyone ever read them?'

For years he'd been studying the pseudo-science of reading palms. The lines on his own hands indicated a long life. He drew a chair close up beside her. She extended her fingers, which tingled as her skin made contact with his.

'Do you believe in palmistry?' she asked, uncertainly. He bent his head over her hands.

'I can see a journey across two cultures,' he murmured.

'I was born in Morocco,' she said, taken aback.

'Maybe that's it,' he replied slowly, 'although I was looking at the path of the future.'

'I don't understand how it could work,' she said, drawing back from the sudden intimacy. 'I've always assumed it was like people being obsessed with astrology.'

'It goes against my love of logic too,' he replied, reassuring her.

'Cognac, Cointreau, Calvados?' asked their host, as he wheeled a cart past tinkling with bottles of liqueur.

'No thank you,' said Charles, letting go of her hands and sliding back into his chair. An awkward silence followed and the young woman was relieved when Benard arrived to join in the conversation.

'Do you work together?' she asked Charles politely.

'No. I'm Alain's guest at the moment while I finish my studies,' he replied quickly.

'Allow me to introduce my friend Charles Sobhraj, Mademoiselle,' said Benard. 'Charles, this is Chantal Lemaître.'

She smiled, producing a cigarette from her handbag and lighting it.

'What are you studying?' she enquired.

'Law,' he answered, looking shyly at Benard, who remained silent. 'But mostly I travel and do business in different parts of the world.'

She sensed his evasiveness, but just then several of the other guests decided to join them, and the moment was lost.

*

Charles was up early the next morning and dressed in one of his new Saigon suits, tailored to his detailed specifications: single-breasted, high-buttoned, with narrow lapels and tapered trousers. He splashed himself with Benard's Eau Sauvage and lightly oiled his glossy black hair.

'Alain, is it possible for you to advance me a few francs on my future salary?'

Hovering anxiously as he watched the former inmate transform himself into an impeccable young gentleman, Benard readily agreed. Although a court order forbade Charles from entering the inner-city arrondissements, he guessed the boy was headed for the centre of Paris. Let him enjoy his first day of real freedom.

From the Metro, Charles joined the crowds walking along the Boulevard St-Michel. Tourists sat in cafés, watching the elegant Parisians from behind copies of the *International Herald Tribune*. A man played a flute, and there was laughter in the air as couples strolled arm-in-arm towards the Luxembourg Gardens. For a moment Charles was caught up in the easy atmosphere of a Parisian spring. He had his whole life ahead of him, safely anchored to the community as a citizen of France. He was ready to seek his fortune – preferably an enormous one – to make up for the five years of captivity.

Finding a café in the Place de la Sorbonne, he took a seat at a table where he could watch the students surging through the stone archway of the university. He found himself enthralled by commonplace sights, and savoured the passing parade for an hour or so. It was still hard to believe he was free.

Then Charles saw her. In a short tartan skirt and a silk blouse with a satchel slung over her shoulder, Chantal was walking towards him, caught in the stream of the lunchtime crowds.

'Chantal, hello,' he called, rising from his chair, trying to look casual. 'I've been doing some research in the library. What a lucky coincidence! How about lunch?'

'Why not?' she agreed, and sat down. In contrast to the nervousness of the previous evening, they now found each other to be completely relaxed.

From that day and over the ensuing weeks he pursued her relentlessly, driving her to her classes in Benard's Triumph Herald, surprising her with expensive gifts, narrating selected episodes from his past, and being altogether attentive, serious and devoted. Around them, seemingly without warning, the protests of May '68 unfolded as the students of Paris stormed the streets. They burned cars, built barricades, and draped red flags over the statues of Victor Hugo and Louis Pasteur. *It is forbidden to forbid*, proclaimed the graffiti. *We are inventing a new world!*

So it seemed. The Sorbonne itself was occupied, and a lecture hall renamed 'Che Guevara'. A jazz band played day and night in the courtyard. The riotous mood spread. Factories and schools closed, and at one point all of France shut down for a twenty-four-hour general strike. In support of the students, half a million men, women and children marched forty abreast from the Place de la Republique through the Latin Quarter to the Place Denfert-Rochereau, chanting, 'De Gaulle – Assassin!'

A sign was hung from the Sorbonne declaring: 'Ten days of happiness already.'

One afternoon in the middle of May, Charles and Chantal wove their way, in an almost dreamlike state, through the disarray of barricades to the blossoming cherry trees on the banks of the Seine. Oblivious to the crackle of tear gas and the echoing chants of 'Freedom now!' Charles took her hand and asked Chantal to marry him.

From this time on, Chantal began to stay quite often with Charles in his room at Benard's apartment. An only child, she had always lived at home with her elderly parents at Châtenay-Malabry, a town on the outskirts of Paris. Now the new arrangement led to bitter arguments with her parents.

Benard, too, made her feel uncomfortable.

'Doesn't your father mind you staying here?' he asked her one morning as she was pouring a coffee.

'Yes, Alain, he does,' she had answered serenely, 'but I remind him that I am twenty-one now and getting married soon.'

A lukewarm smile was all Benard had to offer before he disappeared behind the pages of *Le Monde*. She didn't understand him. He was never rude to her, and yet he kept her at a distance, avoiding friendship. Was he jealous, she wondered? In any case, she would be glad to get away from this apartment.

One day Charles suggested that a trip to Deauville would give them a chance to spend time alone. Wouldn't it be romantic to visit the lavish casino for dinner? She readily agreed. She had no interest in gambling, she'd never been to a casino before, but the chance to have Charles to herself was irresistible.

In Deauville the summer people had left for the warmth of Cannes and Monte Carlo. Chantal had selected a blue silk dress for the evening and was proudly wearing the diamond necklace her mother had given her. But they never made it to the dining room. Instead, in the lavish, half-empty casino she found herself one of a small crowd which gathered, as if hypnotized, to watch Charles play chemin de fer. No one noticed her beauty, the blue silk dress, or the necklace glittering in the light from the chandeliers. She watched Charles commanding the cards with the cool poise of a professional. He seemed incapable of losing. Within three hours his handful of chips had become a cluster of tall towers. All around her, people were looking on with awe. This was the man she was going to spend the rest of her life with. She loved everything about him. His strangely sculptured face was so unique and compelling that she never wanted to take her eyes from him.

Yet she soon became aware of the press of men with cigars and cognac trying to push past her to watch Charles play. At one moment he smiled and lightly brushed her cheek with his hand, before turning back to the table. As the croupier pushed another mound of chips towards Charles, the crowd closed in front of her. She lost sight of him, and could suddenly bear the tension of the gambling throng no longer. Claustrophobic, drenched with perspiration, she escaped outside to the terrace, glancing impatiently at her watch.

Why didn't he quit? she asked herself, her heart thumping, her throat contracting with fear. Surely he had won enough already.

If he stopped playing now, his winnings would mean they didn't need to wait to get married. Perhaps they could even afford a car and he would stop borrowing other people's. Lately, this had worried her. Charles didn't have a licence and she didn't really know why people let him use their cars. Charles seemed to be doing well at his job, and he would soon be promoted and given a car of his own. But she was afraid he would lose this chance if he were caught driving illegally. Already she was dreading the return trip to Paris. The Ford sedan that Charles had magically acquired was jammed in second gear, the windscreen wipers were broken and only one headlight worked.

She looked up at the dark-grey skies of the resort town. Even these anxieties could not dampen her joy at their forthcoming wedding. She knew that with their combined intelligence and beauty, she and Charles would go far. Up to a few months ago, her whole life had been given over to 'culture', to art, music, ballet and poetry. Now she thought of these occupations as adolescent. Real life, a shared adventure with Charles Sobhraj, was to replace them. At night after her classes, she typed out the lists of his prospective customers and ironed his shirts. She would do anything for him.

Chantal's only sadness lay in the coldness with which her parents had greeted the engagement. Mr Lemaître was a conservative civil servant, and he had learned that Charles was a man with a criminal past. But she strenuously defended her fiancé. 'Given his wretched upbringing,' she insisted, 'it would be surprising if Charles had not got himself in trouble!'

She had never pressed her fiancé about his past convictions, nor did he like to talk about them. She believed her love was the antidote to the insecurity which must have sparked his criminal behaviour. And, in the end, she knew she would win even her father over.

Now she saw Charles coming towards her. In her heart, she knew already what had happened.

'Everything?' she asked, as he came up and took her hands.

'Everything. More than everything,' he replied without emotion.

'Oh, Charles! You talk so much about self-control. Why didn't you just stop?'

He looked up at the sky above her head before answering.

'You know, I kept thinking, just a little bit more, and we can own our own house. And then, what about a new car? Of course then I thought we will have children one day. I want the best schools. Today my luck is running high.

'I guess my dreams ran away with logic and I couldn't stop playing. I started to lose. Then I thought, I'll get it back and then, little by little ...' He shrugged. 'Darling, forgive me.'

How could he tell her what he was feeling? That he resented having to work each day for so little. He would never regain the years stolen from him by France. Five lost years! He wanted to win them back. Chantal did not know the extent of his criminal past, so how could she gauge the bitterness he felt? Even to himself, Charles couldn't admit that his gambling was a compulsion.

'Of course I forgive you, Charles,' she said immediately. 'You lost a lot, but remember, you started out with very little.'

He stepped away from her, glancing back at the casino, bright with lights.

'Actually,' he said soberly, 'I need to settle some things with the management before we can leave here. I'll need to borrow your necklace.'

'Charles, what do you mean?' she said, confused, her hand automatically moving to the necklace she had been so proud and excited to wear.

'I'll pawn it. We can get it back later.'

'But it's from my mother, and her mother gave it to her. It's a family heirloom.'

'I know, darling, that's why we will get it back,' he said as he moved around behind her, caressing her neck as he unclasped the necklace.

As they set off for Paris less than an hour later, it began to pour with rain. Visibility was bad. Charles avoided the Normandy Autoroute and took secondary roads. Near Lisieux they picked up a hitchhiker. By the time they reached the village of Thiberville, Charles was ignoring the speed limit. Sirens began to wail and two motorcyclists began to chase them.

'I must ask you to excuse me,' Charles said politely, turning to the hitchhiker, who was cowering in the back seat, 'I just don't have time tonight to stop for the police.'

Despite her fear, Chantal was about to giggle when the car crashed into a pole and she lost consciousness. The three of them were rushed to nearby Bernay Hospital for observation. Chantal was given eight stitches in her chin, and the hitchhiker was discharged. Charles, however, disappeared as he was waiting to be X-rayed. Chantal could not understand why until the police explained that he had been driving a stolen car. The following day he was found, arrested and sent to Évreux Jail.

Alain Benard looked up at the Christmas tinsel hanging from the ceiling of the prison hospital. With a heavy heart he waited outside the emergency ward. Why had Charles been rushed here? Had he done something desperate? Was the shock of yesterday's court sentence too much for him? Charles had often said that if he lost Chantal, he would kill himself. Had the revelations of his criminal background finally broken his spell over her?

Benard had watched the whirlwind courtship unfold with alarm. Chantal was an innocent, adoring child, convent-educated in Morocco until she was eighteen. She'd grown up in the sheltered community of middle-class colonists. Her love for Charles made her easy prey to his grand delusions. Often Benard had wanted to warn her. Many times he had debated telling her that Charles had spent five years of his life in prison, that legally he was not even supposed to enter the metropolitan area of Paris, that some nights he came back to St-Germain with young girls who later phoned Benard complaining that Charles had tricked them into giving him money. He had wanted to warn her, but he had vowed to remain a neutral ally of Charles. It was not his role to be the bell around a leper's neck, and the boy was already handicapped enough by his past. So, in the end, Benard had said nothing. Yet whenever Chantal had stayed the night at St-Germain, he could never fully disguise his embarrassment at her ignorance.

He looked up as he heard a light step approaching. It was Chantal. She was looking pale, and there was a scar on her chin. Usually, by mutual agreement, they had visited Charles in jail on different days.

'How is he?' Benard asked. 'What's happened?'

'You'll be amused,' she said. 'They've taken him off to operate. You'll never guess what he did ...' Her eyes shone. 'He swallowed a spoon.'

'My God! What was he trying to do – kill himself?'

'No. It was so they would transfer him from Évreux Jail to here. The visiting hours are longer. I've just been with him for three hours.'

Benard decided to postpone his own visit and offered to drive Chantal back to Paris. For most of the way their conversation skirted the subject of Charles, but as he neared Chantal's parents' home, he said, 'So you finally found out.'

'Yes. The first time I went to see him in Évreux he told me everything. And he told me about you too, Alain. He owes you a lot.'

Benard would like to have said that Charles owed him nothing, that he received 'grace' for what he did, but instead he asked, 'Will you still marry him?'

'Of course, Alain. I tell you honestly; I love him now more than ever. I know what you're thinking, and it's true. Until the crash I was blind, a stupid, love-crazed schoolgirl. But I was knocked out and a light went on.'

She laughed at the phrase.

'Now I can see the little boy inside the man, and he knows it. And he also knows that I'll stand by him. That will help him adjust to reality, don't you think?'

Benard sighed. 'Another six months in jail could have a bad effect. He'll be bitter. He won't reform overnight.'

'Nor will I abandon him overnight,' she said, passionately. 'Do you expect me to drop him because he's not a model fiancé? It will take time, Alain, of course, but it's worth it. You already know that. He's a special person, isn't he? Unique, gifted, more intelligent and real than those revolutionaries who used to hang around the Sorbonne. I love him, Alain. I'm committed. He's dropped into the abyss, and if I do nothing else in this life, I just want to help one human being climb out of his own despair.'

'But when you're his wife, Chantal, you'll be dependent on him. He's strong, he'll overpower you.' Benard shook his head. 'He needs treatment.'

'I'm strong too, Alain. I can give him what no psychiatrist can. Love.'

'He already had your love when he stole the car.'

'He was miserable in other ways. Next time he tells me he's borrowed a car from a friend, do you think I'll believe it?'

Benard pulled up outside her house. 'It's more complicated than just giving him love or security. The court psychiatrist said there were problems.'

'What problems?'

Benard explained that he had been told that Charles was compulsively rebellious, and perhaps incapable of learning from his past experience. He might be unable to sympathize or identify with others; he could even show a lack of remorse at harming others.

'And did this psychiatrist say anything positive?' Her voice was trembling.

Benard wondered if he had gone too far. He had only wanted her to see that Charles had a black side to him.

'Yes. He said his adjustment to society is possible, with treatment, and that he isn't dangerous.'

'Of course he isn't!' she cried out. 'There's such gentleness inside him, such spiritual awareness. He is really searching for something deeper from life. But I don't need to explain that to you, do I? Otherwise you wouldn't have bothered with him. He's not just another petty crook, is he?'

Forced to respond, Benard said what he had often thought: 'No, Chantal, he is not a gangster in his soul.'

Chantal kissed him and got out of the car.

★

A few days later Benard received a letter from Charles. In it, he thanked him for all he had done. But he wasn't finished. The letter went on in thick black ink: 'You no longer have any power over me. Get out of my life. And lay off Chantal.'

In a way, Benard had expected this, and he sent a copy of the letter to Chantal with a note: 'I knew Charles would not pardon me for warning you. Take courage, Chantal. It will be sad if you become the victim of your own generosity. This letter from Charles is like the last chapter of a book. Please don't ask me to open it again.'

It was over. Benard asked her to get the key to his apartment from Charles and post it to him. She never forgot the last line he wrote.

'How shocking is this tragic destiny I see unfurling.'

4

A Last Chance

Until the day of sentencing after the car accident with Chantal, Charles had been hopeful. Benard had prepared a sympathetic biography for the court. The court psychiatrist had seemed understanding. After all, he had only wanted the car for one night to take his fiancé on a romantic day trip. He was overpowered by temptation, surely understandable given his family history. Yet the judge had ordered that he remain in jail until June 1969. Six months!

While he waited out his sentence, Charles decided that Benard's God wasn't giving him the results he felt entitled to, and devoted his time to books on comparative religion. Confucius was too authoritarian; the Koran too much like the Bible. In the end he chose Buddhism for its offer of freedom from the fetters of the mundane world via the practice of non-attachment. It also addressed his suffering rather than his sin. From now on, he would rely on himself alone. He returned the Bible Benard had given him in Poissy by post. He had not forgiven his old friend for his attempt to alienate the affections of Chantal. Charles was finding that jail was even more intolerable now that he was separated from someone he loved.

Replacing prayer with meditation, Charles also resumed his studies in psychology, concentrating on the peculiarly French tradition of characterology – a system of personality study. This was the antithesis of psychology as expounded by Freud, Jung and their descendants, who sought to understand human behaviour from within. Instead, characterology was an attempt to categorize people. It promised to enable its practitioners to predict and manipulate the behaviour of those they encountered.

From the books of a Sorbonne professor, René Le Senne (*Lying and Character, A Treatise on Characterology*), and a later popularizer, Gaston Berger (*Character and Personality*), Charles was able to absorb a system for classifying people. Using three basic divisions of character, Le Senne had formulated eight fundamental types. Fit your subject into one of these types, it was argued, and their tendencies become clear and predictable. Charles tested the system on himself.

Regarding the first division ('Emotive' or 'Non-emotive'), he knew that he was emotional, judging from the frequency and intensity of his feelings, no matter how hard he tried to suppress them. For the second ('Active' or 'Non-active'), he was a type who took pleasure in action, not one to sit around brooding. With regard to the third ('Primary' or 'Secondary'), Charles believed that he was not a Primary, like a mirror to experience, where all is recorded but nothing remains, but recognized himself as Secondary, a type purported to react after rather than during the event, a prisoner of his own past. According to Le Senne, that put him in the same category as Napoleon.

That's me, Charles thought. He delved deeper into Le Senne, expanding his understanding of the other seven types, which he tested on fellow prisoners. At that time many French people used characterology, along with graphology, the study of handwriting, to observe and construct their everyday relationships. For Charles, these bourgeois occupations would become a lethal tool in the outside world. With this system, he believed he could play people like pawns in a game of chess.

Each morning Charles stripped to his shorts in his cell and began stretching exercises, building up his ability to stand and relax into martial arts poses: knees bent, feet apart, fists clenched at his waist. He began to study kung fu, his 'meditation in motion', a personalized ballet poised between a fight and a slow-motion dance, with spins, pirouettes, twists and a graceful routine of circular jump kicks.

This time when Charles was released from jail, in June 1969, it was Chantal – not Benard – who was waiting outside for him. They were married five months later, in the town of Châtenay-Malabry. A small reception was held at the home of the bride's unhappy parents. Alain Benard was there, having responded to Charles' renewed overtures of friendship. Sipping champagne, he endured the rage of Chantal's father with his usual discretion.

'Sobhraj will ruin my daughter for ever,' mourned Mr Lemaître. 'The boy's a public danger. What are they waiting for to arrest him once and for all? This will keep happening. And what will become of Chantal if he is arrested while they are abroad?'

The only member of the bridegroom's family to attend was his mother, Noi. Looking dainty, manicured and much younger than her forty-six years, she made polite small talk with Mrs Lemaître while the father of the bride stood near the wedding cake, scowling.

After the marriage, Charles worked as a waiter in the early months of 1970, then as a salesman for personalized matchboxes. Because of his criminal record, the court again exiled him from metropolitan Paris, and again Benard successfully appealed for the prohibition to be lifted. In return, Charles was ordered to report to the police once a week.

Within four months of married life Charles had become thoroughly demoralized by the grind of steady work and his compulsory visits to the police station. He was free, but not completely. He fantasized about starting a new life with his wife in Asia. All he needed, he thought, was capital. He knew his only full-blood relative, his sister Nicole, was well off. She managed the Moules Farcies, a Parisian restaurant owned by her wealthy boyfriend. If only he could borrow some cash for a few hours, multiply it, and return it with interest ...

On the morning of Tuesday, 17 March 1970, Charles rushed into the Moules Farcies.

'Nicole,' he cried out, 'you need to come quickly! Your son's been hurt, crushed by a truck.'

Charles drove her at speed to his studio apartment at Rue des Ursulines, a half-hour from the centre of Paris. When Nicole rushed inside, Charles locked the door behind her. Her son was still at school, quite safe.

He drove back to the restaurant.

'It's an emergency!' he told the cook. 'My sister asked me to bring her handbag and the receipts from the cash register.'

Charles forged Nicole's signature on her cheque book, withdrew 6,000 francs from her bank, and rushed to a casino. Although his name had been officially listed, at his own request, as banned from every casino in France, it failed to prevent him from reaching the chemin de fer table at Enghien. He then lost every sou.

Chantal did not waste words scolding him. She rushed to see Nicole, returning her cheque book and the customers' receipts from the cash register. She said she would repay all the money in instalments as fast as she could and offered to sign a binding legal agreement. Nicole refused.

'Charles' behaviour is impossible to forgive,' she told her sister-in-law.

'But this is inhuman, Nicole,' Chantal argued.

They ended up quarrelling until Nicole phoned the police.

Charles was arrested and put in La Santé Prison, but the judge deemed the whole episode a family affair and stated he could be released if Nicole withdrew her complaint. The rest of the family tried to persuade her. Every day Chantal wrote desperate letters to Benard, who was away in the Middle East on a business trip. When she visited Charles in jail, she had never seen him more wretched. He was broken. 'I will die if I am sentenced again,' he told her. She tried to cheer him up with the news that she was pregnant, but this only made him more desperate for freedom. Charles decided to write to Benard again.

'Save me, Alain, my life is in your hands.'

After ten days in jail, Benard returned from abroad and spoke to Nicole. At his request she finally agreed to withdraw the charges, and Charles was released from jail. When he got home, he found a letter from Saigon waiting for him. Hotchand Sobhraj wrote that he would soon be coming to Paris.

*

Every few years Hotchand Sobhraj took a trip round the world. He would do some business, look up his black-market contacts, visit the major sights, and buy presents for his families in Poona and Saigon. As he walked through the arrivals gate at Orly Airport on 24 June 1970, he did not recognize the stylish young man waving to him. It had been eight years since he had last seen his son, disconsolately huddled over the rails of the SS *Laos* as it edged down the Saigon River.

Charles rushed up to embrace his father. He was in good spirits and brimming with confidence as he drove Hotchand to Alain Benard's apartment in St-Germain-en-Laye, where he and Chantal were staying while their friend was abroad on business. At last his father had returned to Paris and, this time, Charles could play host.

On the Saturday morning Charles took Hotchand on a shopping tour of Paris. He was driving Benard's Triumph which he was in the process of buying. Hotchand followed his son into an expensive jeweller on the Place Vendome and watched admiringly as Charles negotiated the purchase of a $500 gold wristwatch. Charles waved aside the assistant's reluctance to accept a cheque by paying a portion in cash. His air of self-confidence allayed any objections.

Charles turned to his father. 'Would you do me the favour of presenting this watch as a gift from you to Chantal? She would love you for that.'

Hotchand was impressed. His son might only be twenty-six but he was already making his way in the world. All Charles had needed was a chance, some encouragement, and he could conquer Paris just like his father had conquered Saigon.

'Come, Papa, choose something now for your wife.'

That afternoon, the three of them dined together at a restaurant in St-Germain-en-Laye. Chantal giggled as her Indian father-in-law related Charles' childhood pranks in Saigon. Charles was calmly drinking Coca-Cola as he poured his father champagne.

'I'm thinking of going East soon, Papa,' he said, handsome in a new hand-tailored blue suit. 'I want to branch out, to launch an import-export business.'

Chantal was unsurprised by this announcement. Ever since her husband had got out of jail he had talked of going back to Saigon and starting a new life. Charles began to tell his father his plans of returning to Vietnam and opening a chain of retail stores, maybe to sell precious stones to the tourists. Chantal smiled at the two men as she listened to them talk. She had liked Hotchand Sobhraj on their first meeting. He had the same ease of manner as her husband, the same grace and style; a nobility of bearing and an engaging smile. His effect on Charles was to make him deferential and respectful. And he really did look like Mr Pompidou!

'If you plan to sell gems in Saigon, my son, you'd better hurry up,' Hotchand said. 'The rich are beginning to leave and there's fear in the air. The Yanks have got themselves in a bloody mess.'

Saigon was on the brink of bankruptcy, the good times were over. Luckily, because of Hotchand's dealings on the currency black market and his contacts at the major money exchanges all over the world, he was still doing fine. But for how much longer?

'But Papa, Asia is where I belong. I'm an outcast in France. I want to go home!'

Charles' mind was racing. The cheques he had been cashing all morning were drawn on an account he had opened the day before with a token deposit. On Monday the fraud would be discovered. He had spent thousands of dollars. How could he save himself between now and then? It was madness, he knew that, but he owed nothing to France. To his father, however, he had a duty to hold up his head, to be proud and dignified.

Hotchand began to tell the couple about his stopovers in New York and Los Angeles.

'Everywhere I went the young people were misbehaving and up to no good. It was shocking,' he said disapprovingly. 'Some of them tried to burn down the Bank of America. In Central Park they were smoking marijuana, and the boys looked like girls.'

'Oh, Hotchand, it's the same everywhere,' said Chantal, who was enjoying herself, believing that with Hotchand's help she and Charles might be able to start again. 'The Maoists are rioting in the Latin Quarter, and everyone is predicting a repeat of 1968.'

Charles sat quietly, thinking. He could make a run for it. First, he would go to their studio a few doors down the street from Alain Benard and clear out the desk and pick up the passports. There was no point in staying there again. The bank would give that address to the police. He was now impatient to get out.

'Excuse me, Father. You two finish your meal,' he said, standing up and handing some cash to Chantal. 'I've got a business appointment. I'll meet you back at Alain's in an hour or so.'

When he had gone Hotchand confided in his radiant young daughter-in-law.

'Charles was such a scoundrel when he was a boy. Thank goodness he seems to have come to his senses. You know, my dear, he was always a devil with the ladies. I'm glad he seems to be settling down, especially now he has met someone as beautiful as you.'

Chantal was pleased. She could see from whom Charles had inherited his charm. Hotchand took a small parcel wrapped in tissue paper from his pocket and presented it to her.

'Father, it's beautiful! You shouldn't have done this!' she said, holding the thin gold watch in the palm of her hand. She leaned over the table and kissed him.

'You deserve it,' he said, 'especially as I hear you are going to present me with a grandson?'

'I hope so, Papa. The baby's due in November. That's why we've been working so hard.'

'Well, it seems to have paid off,' he said. 'Charles was spending money like water today.'

'He was?' Immediately Chantal panicked. Ever since she had told Charles she was pregnant, he had seemed a changed man, working hard, applying himself. But what was her husband up to now?

'Oh yes,' Hotchand continued. 'Charles told me this morning that he had five thousand dollars in the bank.'

She didn't know what to say.

After lunch they returned to Benard's apartment, where Chantal prepared a silver tray of coffee and liqueurs and brought it into the study, where her father-in-law was looking at the family portraits on the wall.

'I'm sorry not to have met Mr Benard. He seems to have done a lot for my son, and now I'm staying in his apartment!'

'Perhaps on your next trip?' she suggested as she poured the coffee.

As they sipped it, Hotchand quizzed her about her life in Morocco, but she found it hard to concentrate. What was Charles doing? Where was he?

At last the door opened and Charles walked in carrying a suitcase.

'Father, how would you like a lift to Geneva tomorrow?'

Chantal tersely motioned him into the bedroom. She shut the door, leaving Hotchand to spread out his itinerary on the table.

'Your father says you were writing cheques for huge amounts this morning.'

Charles said nothing, and she knew it was true.

'Are you mad? You'll be arrested.'

'No I won't. We've got twenty-four hours to get out of the country.'

'Darling, no!' she cried, truly frightened. But Charles was unperturbed.

'It was only a bank, Chantal, a lousy French bank. No one gets hurt. It's all paid for by insurance. Can't you see there's no other way? I don't belong here. Your family hates me. I can't get a decent job. Every time a Vietnamese commits a crime, the police come looking for me. We need a chance. Well, today I got it, six thousand dollars. It's enough to begin. It's worth ten times that in Asia. We'll go to Saigon and be near my family. I can start a business.'

'But Charles, I've got to go to work on Monday. I can't just drop everything and go to Saigon. It's halfway round the world. What about our baby?' Her eyes filled with tears.

'I have to get out of here or it's jail,' he said flatly. 'Just pack a few things and come to Geneva. You can fly back tomorrow if you want and still go to work.'

She didn't know what to do. If she didn't go with him, would she ever see him again?

'Listen, darling,' he continued, taking her in his arms, 'the world is changing. Students are burning banks. People are beginning to wake up about the state and the system. The French kept me behind bars for five years. I had nothing before that except liberty – and they took that away. I was forced to live like a pirate. It was my fate and the deed is now done. This is our break. Let me work hard for a few years, and I'll turn this into a million. And then we can stop. In the end you can pay it back if you like. Take our chance now while we're young and free. For our baby.'

With tears streaming down her face, Chantal packed her suitcase. Charles went into the living room, where Hotchand was tactfully absorbed in examining Benard's collection of records.

'This Benard must be a very cultured man. I see he even has some Vietnamese music.'

'He bought it especially for me,' Charles said, walking over to his father.

From the bedroom as she hurriedly packed her bags, Chantal could hear the haunting, high-pitched voice of the Vietnamese singer. Then she heard another voice, a voice she knew, but with so much depth of feeling that she forgot her anger and came out into the room. Hotchand was sitting on the couch with a glass of whisky watching his son with tears in his eyes. Charles stood beside the turntable singing along with the music, his voice faltering at first over some of the words. But as he persevered, his voice grew louder until it overwhelmed the recorded voice. He held them both in a trance, oblivious to their surroundings, lost in the music of Vietnam.

One hour later, at 2.30 a.m. on Sunday 28 June, the three of them piled into the old Triumph and drove east, reaching Geneva by 10.30 in the morning. At the bar of the Grand Hotel, Charles and Chantal kissed Hotchand goodbye as he set off on his grand Alpine tour.

'It's only eight thousand kilometres to Saigon,' Charles said, turning to his wife, 'and Papa will be so happy to see us there.'

PART II

On the Run

August 1970 – July 1975

5

An Impossible Husband

Saigon
29 August 1970

Dear Chantal,

I have received your letter dated 5 August from Iran. You have made a great mistake to come this way by car. The roads are very bad and mountainous and you find different kinds of people in every place. The roads to Afghanistan are very dangerous – besides, you are pregnant, and it is hard to go such a long way by car.

I have received a letter from your father. He says you and Charles disappeared from Paris on 27 June and never said a word. He and your mother are worried about you. In France the police are after Charles because he issued cheques without funds ... They are after you both.

Here in Saigon the BNP bank has informed the Consulate General about you and the consul has informed the Immigration Office to arrest both of you on your arrival and send you back to France for trial. Therefore, it is advisable for you not to enter Vietnam at any cost – if you enter you will be in great trouble.

Police were looking for me in Paris also because I was still with him when he bought the watch and issued the cheque, somehow they knew I am his father. I left the country one day earlier, otherwise they would have put me in jail also. God saved me.

I told you in Paris that this boy is no good. He is intelligent but he is number one CROOK. One day he will throw you in the sea or in jail.

Now this country is no good for foreigners, many Indians are closing their shops and going to India. Americans are leaving, so the others also. Please, for God sake, don't come.

Your loving father,
Hotchand Sobhraj

After three months on the road, crossing ten borders and thousands of kilometres, Charles and Chantal arrived in Bombay. This exuberant port on the Arabian Sea, with its florid Gothic buildings, moth-eaten beaches, and red double-decker buses was the financial centre of India and Charles chose it as his base. The couple moved into a cheap hotel near the docks, fragrant with drying fish.

Nine years before, he had stowed away to escape from Bombay, penniless and unwanted. Now he was back, determined to make a success of his life. His first move was to join the Bombay branch of the Alliance Française. This gave him access to leaders of the foreign business community and their rich Indian friends. Chantal, with her beauty and obvious good breeding, was an asset. Everyone adored her. The director of the Alliance Française invited them both to live in his own spacious apartment. On 15 November, Chantal gave birth to a daughter, Madhu.

As the capital of the country's huge film industry, Bombay throbbed with a vitality and glamour unusual then in India. There were families of enormous wealth whose children had cultivated a taste for flashy consumer goods and possessed the means to acquire them, had it not been for the government's ban on their import. At parties in the posh mansions on Malabar Hill, Charles listened to local playboys roll brand names off their tongues like mystical incantations: Rolex, Cartier, Alfa Romeo. Impossible dreams because of the government and its puritanical laws.

Not at all, Charles maintained. He could supply them. With his own Dupont pen he wrote down the orders in his black leather book and took their deposits, telling them, 'Leave it to me.'

When Chantal and Madhu came out of the hospital, Charles rented an apartment on Nepean Sea Road, Malabar Hill, overlooking the ocean. It was there that Chantal spent most of her time, along with the baby and her nurse. For Chantal the hot days and nights passed as slowly as the air stirred by the ceiling fans. Charles was usually off on one of his business trips, away for weeks at a time. He had found his fantasy world at last, a continent where his confidence in himself seemed to be justified.

Chantal could no longer ignore the fact that a lot of Charles' business activity could be better described as criminal, but now, so many miles from home, she found it easier to leave her questions about his life unasked. When she was forced to face up to his crimes she thought of them as mere 'pranks'. When she found out that he had been having an affair with an Indian girl, now pregnant, it was not Charles with whom she had the showdown, but the girl. Despite her husband's unreliability and extra-marital flirtations, and her loneliness, Chantal remained faithful to Charles and to her upright, bourgeois ideal of the devoted mother and loyal wife. Charles was so unusual, allowances had to be made for him. He was not bound by conventional laws.

Sometimes there was no money. At other times, bank notes lay around the apartment like waste-paper. She tried to live philosophically – day to day. Charles would suddenly turn up, empty his pockets of thousands of dollars in various currencies, and then they would go out to the pictures and to dinner at one of the nightclubs in the Taj Mahal Hotel or the Sheraton, where the cocktail bar looked down on the Arabian Sea.

Looking immaculate and handsome, Charles would talk up their future. 'Soon I'll have enough to buy a house for us, darling, a home, in Ceylon maybe. I can write books,' he would muse, his eyes radiating the warmth of a devoted husband and father. The next day he would be off again, to smuggle diamonds to Bangkok and work a currency deal in Beirut, then lose all his money at the casino in Rhodes and suddenly make it all back again through mysterious underworld contacts in Hong Kong. One of his mottoes became: 'Why waste a trip?'

Charles had understood the black market perfectly since he was a boy of six in Saigon. It was a matter of contacts and mobility, being in the right place at the right time. At duty-free ports he bought radios, watches, cameras and jewellery with stolen traveller's cheques or cheques which would bounce. All he needed to run his business was a constant supply of passports and a battery of disguises. Sometimes he would alter the description of the bearer on the passport, and sometimes it was easier to change himself to fit the description. Although his face was strong and unusual, it lent itself easily to disguise. With his Vietnamese and Indian heritage he could make himself look less or more Asian as he liked. He could pass for Filipino, Puerto Rican, French, Italian. A criminal friend taught him the art of disguise in Hong Kong, and it was there that he bought a wig, beard and moustache which he always carried in his attaché case. It was with these theatricalities that he outwitted India's stringent attempts at preventing black marketeering.

India's ban on importing luxury consumer goods required that tourists record any items they were carrying at entry inside their passports. If on leaving India the visitor could not produce the belongings listed, they were compelled to pay their full value in customs tax. So, each time Charles left India on one of his forays, he needed a new passport.

He found the solution to this problem in a crowded hole-in-the-wall called Dipti's House of Pure Drinks on Ormiston Road in the Colaba area. Dipti's stood across the wide palm-shaded road from Bombay's two famous hippie hotels, the Stiffles and the Rex. The yellow paint was peeling from the fretwork shutters of the adjoining Victorian mansions, and on their dirty marble steps sat the ragged travellers with their backpacks and habit of adopting the national dress of whatever country they were passing through. Dipti's was their meeting place, the one spot in Bombay where they could count on meeting others with the same problems: where to buy a student card, where to sell a pair of hiking boots, how to get through Burma, whom to bribe for a six-month visa for Indonesia.

These were the long-haired, pot-smoking types Charles had first noticed on the streets of Paris in 1968. They were young people who were travelling through life in a direction opposite to that of Charles Sobhraj. For such young, middle-class travellers from the West, Asia was the last frontier. Most of them had worked for a few years after school or college, saving money for a leisurely journey across the non-Western string of countries that lay between Europe and Australia. They travelled light and cheap.

Despite his abhorrence of them, Charles came to see these Western nomads as a vast, untapped resource. The irony amused him. He could use these anti-materialists to help satisfy the voracious appetites of his Indian clients. He despised the young wanderers' interest in marijuana and hash and the pleasure they took in discussing how high they were and how many drugs they had consumed. He hated the way they dressed, deliberately separating themselves from society. Yet when he sat down among them, his charisma captivated the travellers. Charles soon learned that these overlanders were often innocent and gullible. He could lift their passports in seconds. Also, having discarded the morality of their parents and society back home, he discovered some of them had a philosophical vacuum he could fill with his own ideas.

After all, what was a crime? To steal from a fat, over-insured tourist, or to shower Vietnam with bombs? Wasn't capitalism simply corporate theft? And in view of this, wasn't it justified for the poor to steal from the rich? If you sold your passport for $50, who was hurt? No one but an overpaid consular official who had to fill in a few forms. There were many ways of making money in Asia, and never any danger involved. Even if you were caught all you had to do was distribute a few dollars among the local officials and the matter would be forgotten. Charles could make anything sound reasonable. And all his schemes – gem smuggling, car smuggling, and stealing from the bourgeois tourists in their luxury hotels – had an element of revolutionary glamour.

Whenever Charles needed an accomplice for one of his growing number of rackets, he could find them at Dipti's or its equivalent in other cities. The advantage of using amateurs was that they accepted a smaller cut of the take. To travellers who paid a dollar a night for a room, a few hundred dollars was a windfall. Dipti's House of Pure Drinks became his employment agency and passport bank. It was a game he enjoyed, picking out a likely accomplice, sitting nearby at one of the grubby tables, striking up a conversation, and analysing their potential using René Le Senne's system of characterology.

Charles' popularity amongst the affluent of Bombay was confirmed when he demonstrated his ability to produce shiny and apparently new Alfa Romeos, BMWs, Maseratis and Mercedes. In the whole of India there was only one car factory, an obsolete British plant which had been dismantled and shipped to Bombay, where it produced fifty models a day of the dull and sturdy Ambassador. Indian playboys dreamed of driving the best Europe could build, but the restrictions made it impossible until Charles arrived on the scene and promised to deliver them at a third of the official cost. He would collect deposits from several customers and fly to Geneva or Frankfurt, where he stole and bought second-hand the requisite number. 'Do you want to earn $200?' he would ask backpackers heading East, and with Charles leading the way the convoy of flashy European cars would speed eastward through Turkey, Iran, Afghanistan and Pakistan.

After showing a car to its future owner, Charles would take a further instalment and promise to present it to them with papers legitimising the ownership. He then booked a room at a five-star hotel, using whatever name or disguise was convenient. The car was taken to a garage he had rented for the purpose and stripped of all its extras. In the back streets of Bombay a crash was staged, involving the shell of the car. From his hotel Charles called the police to report the wreck's whereabouts while one of his accomplices removed its engine and gearbox. The police would report back that thieves had plundered the car. Charles was then entitled to sell it to the State Trading Corporation, which in turn put the vehicle up for auction. One of his accomplices would then buy the shell of the car and along with it the documents entitling him to its possession free of excise taxes. The car would be returned to the garage, repaired and refitted, and presented to its purchaser complete with the correct and necessary paperwork. Who could ever unravel such a complicated chain of minor illegalities?

His new friends found him dynamic, endearingly eccentric, and 'always five jumps ahead'. He had studied law in Paris, he said, and engineering in Japan, but his hobby was psychology. Reading their palms and analysing their handwriting, he talked about self-mastery and hinted mysteriously at his own karate skills. He seemed to have found a hundred shortcuts to the good life, and to be ready to share these secrets with his new friends. There were no limits to his generosity. 'Don't buy anything,' he'd say. 'Just tell me what you need, I'll pick it up in Hong Kong.' He was always the centre of attention. His mere presence made life more exciting. As for the scores of passports lying around his and Chantal's apartment in the Meherina Building, they accepted his explanation that he needed them for his business and learned not to ask questions.

With Chantal he lived simply – their apartment was modest. His wife had been reared to be careful with money. She was amused by the Indians who, having purchased a freezer, would keep it on display in the living room. 'These Indians,' Charles would tell her with a laugh, 'I could sell them the wind.'

After six months in Bombay he counted among his personal friends top-ranking businessmen, stars and directors in the Indian film world, and the upper echelons of the French community living in Bombay. Dinesh Shah, the son of the president of Shah Construction, bought an Alfa Romeo from Charles and became his intimate friend. The two young men formed a business partnership.

Charles had been impressed by the success of 'Le Drugstore' in Paris – a glamorous mosaic of retail outlets aimed at the youthful glitterati. Now he and Dinesh formulated a plan for a Bombay

'Drugstore' and began renovating a building. A pharmacy, a restaurant, a discotheque ... In a city where, ten years ago, he had sat hopelessly on the stone steps of Victoria Gate, penniless and unwanted, Charles now entertained millionaires in the bars of the Taj Mahal, the grand hotel that had once symbolized everything he dreamed of. Now he felt that all the faith Alain Benard had placed in him had been justified, and he knew he was capable of doing anything he wanted. Charles was on his way. Hotchand would be proud of him. In the First National City Bank of Hong Kong he had saved $14,000.

In April 1971, Charles turned twenty-seven. He sent five-month-old Madhu and her nurse to the house of a friend and took Chantal off to Hong Kong and the adjacent Portuguese island of Macao for a holiday. He was rich. He had made it. It was time to celebrate. As soon as he arrived Charles wrote to Alain Benard in Paris:

My dear Alain,

I am now in China. I have truly come a long way, right? I will stay in Hong Kong and Macao on business for twenty days and then return to India. Chantal is here with me, happy, for she has been dreaming for a long time to know this part of Asia.

Yesterday I offered myself a little caprice, a joy, and bought for myself a beautiful golden Rolex watch, extra flat, with a bracelet made of gold. I'm as happy as a kid for I have been dreaming of it a long time, and, as you know, spending half a million francs for a caprice was not always within my means.

At last, Alain, my dear Alain, I do not forget that in my success I owe everything to you. Whether you agree or not, I am your work. Without you and everything you did for me, where would I be? God only knows.

To give you an idea of the money I make in my business, when I return to Bombay at the end of April, my profit will be 530,000 rupees. And, Alain, beginning at the end of June, it doesn't matter how much you need, you will have it. You can have as much as you can as long as you and I will be alive.

About my Drugstore, at last my partner and I decided to buy the place instead of renting it. Isn't that fantastic?

And you, Alain, what are you doing? Life is sad when one's one and only friend stays silent. My little daughter Madhu awaits with impatience the visit of her godfather.

I kiss you affectionately.
Charles

'A Portuguese city in China, you'll love it, a real honeymoon!' Charles had promised. When Chantal and her husband arrived in Macao, Charles booked into the Lisboa Hotel and went straight to the casino. She couldn't believe it. From a few hundred dollars he had won thousands, then hundreds of thousands, while the crowds gathered round. He was betting 20,000 Hong Kong dollars a throw. His pockets were bulging with money and by the time he had won 250,000 dollars Chantal was so nervous she went to bed.

By morning he had lost it all. Worse, he had cleaned out his own savings and was in debt to a Chinese moneylender. She had to remain alone on the island as 'security', while Charles rushed back to Bombay to borrow 60,000 rupees from Dinesh. Yes, it had been a honeymoon to remember. Back in Hong Kong he cashed phoney cheques; money was needed to get home to Bombay and to little Madhu. But Charles could never face his business partner again. The Drugstore project was officially finished.

Four months later, Chantal was home alone with the baby as usual. Charles had disappeared to Delhi, promising to return home with $10,000 from a gem deal. A sure thing, he said.

It was the eve of their daughter's first birthday. Charles had said he would be home to light the candle on the birthday cake, but Chantal had heard nothing from him.

She picked up the morning newspaper, the *Times of India*, and looked through it for the latest news on the deteriorating relations between India and Pakistan. People said there might be a war and she tried to concentrate but every time she heard a car pull up at the curb on Nepean Sea Road, she looked out of the window, hoping it was Charles.

What an impossible husband! After two years of marriage she loved him more than ever. He was strong, charismatic, sexual – anyone could see that, and even those who claimed Charles had cheated them still liked him. Inside, he was something more. Exasperated by his unreliability, Chantal had once threatened to leave him and he broke down and cried like a little boy.

Some of her friends joked that she loved him because she hardly ever saw him – he was always travelling. Business trips, he claimed, but it was clearly a compulsion. She knew now that his business was usually illegal, although he tried to deny it and hide the details from her. She was afraid he would be caught one day, but Charles boasted that he was invincible. 'How could they hold me?' he would ask with a laugh.

Taking a seat at the table by the window to catch the breeze and browse the newspaper, Chantal couldn't keep Charles' latest gambling disaster from her mind.

Half-heartedly, she turned the pages. Her eye was caught by a headline: 'Two Frenchmen Held in City: Delhi Robbery'. With growing horror her eyes raced down the page: 'In a surprise swoop, Bombay police arrested two French nationals allegedly involved in the sensational robbery from a jewellery shop in Delhi's Ashoka Hotel.' Chantal skimmed the rest of the story. It was like something out of a gangster film. The Ashoka robbery, which took place while Henry Kissinger was an official guest at the hotel, was one of the most dramatic and theatrical ever performed in Delhi. A blonde flamenco dancer had been held in her room for three days while Charles tried to drill a hole through the floor to the jewellery shop below. The drill broke, so he had forced the terrified dancer to entice the shop manager up to the room with his best jewels. Then Charles tied him up in the bathroom.

The beautiful flamenco dancer had fallen under the power of Charles' personality, claimed the story. He was a gentleman jewel thief, part of an international organization, he told her. He even left her money to compensate for the trouble he had caused, and ordered her to take a hot bath to calm her nerves. 'You were born to dance,' he had told her, 'just as I was born to be a gangster.' He fled from the hotel with diamonds worth $10,000.

At the airport he eluded police – 'disappeared,' they reported – and flew to Tehran, where he completed some profitable deals selling second-hand gaming equipment to a casino. Now he had been caught.

When Chantal put down the newspaper she knew what she must do. Her husband might be unreliable, incorrigible and untruthful, but she loved him. He was like no other, both superman and superchild.

She found Charles in the Willingdon Hospital in Delhi recovering from an appendicitis operation. He had faked the symptoms to get himself out of jail, where he was being held, and now he was under guard in a small hospital room.

Charles was lying on the bed, playing with Madhu. As his daughter crawled around him, Charles kept kissing her, lifting her up high in his arms, teasing her with nursery rhymes, looking into the small, smiling face. He smiled over Madhu's head to Chantal.

'Darling, play cards with them tonight, or keep them talking. You know what I mean.'

Chantal nodded. She was sitting on the chair next to his bed. One of the guards in the adjoining room, a tall Sikh in military uniform and green turban, called out to Charles to stop speaking French.

'Can't I even say goodnight to my wife?' Charles replied light-heartedly in English.

The guards smiled. They liked Charles. He was always joking with them, handing out American cigarettes, and very polite. He had taught them how to play gin-rummy.

The sounds of the hot Indian night came in through the bars on the open window – crickets, frogs croaking from the open drains, the high-pitched siren of mosquitoes. Chantal sat serenely with her hands folded in her lap. The skirt of her floral cotton sundress came well below her knees, but still the male guards were staring at the curve of her calves and her slim ankles. Their own women kept their legs well hidden beneath their saris, so the sight of this beautiful Western woman was a treat. They could not make Chantal out. Was she a hippie or a respectable memsahib? If she was a hippie, there was a good chance that for a few rupees she might make love. Fully aware of the subject that obsessed them, Chantal kept her smiles friendly but reserved as she watched her Charlie and Madhu laughing together.

'This is the first night the doctor hasn't given me a sedative,' Charles was saying to the guard whom he had called to his bedside. 'He asked me to try to do without it tonight. Do you mind turning off the light for a few minutes to help me sleep?'

The guard was suspicious. Charles had already given his colleagues the slip at Delhi Airport on the night of the robbery.

'All right, Mr Charles, just for a few minutes, but I must chain you to the bed.' He signalled to his assistant. The two guards took a large, heavy pair of shackles, attaching one cuff to the iron mattress frame. The other they locked tightly around the prisoner's left ankle.

Charles turned over and adjusted his pillow, watching the guards move into the adjoining room. Chantal assessed the situation, opened the door to the corridor and joined the guards. The three of them began playing cards while Madhu stayed sleeping by her father on the bed. Charles wriggled his right hand. He had shoved it down the leg of his hospital pyjamas when he was being shackled, now he removed it. It was an easy matter to slip his leg loose. In the next room the guards vied with each other to answer Chantal's battery of questions. It was twenty minutes before they turned on the light and saw that Charles had disappeared.

The city was blacked out and under curfew. A few hours later Charles was caught wandering in his pyjamas around Delhi railway station, and Chantal was charged with aiding his escape.

In jail she discovered that her husband was a criminal celebrity. Among the inmates of Tihar Jail, he was a hero. The notoriety of being the wife of Charles Sobhraj made Chantal as uncomfortable as the jail itself, where she spent her time in a cell with a group of pickpockets.

After arranging for her own bail using an Indian lawyer, the next problem was Madhu. Their money was running low and Chantal wrote desperate letters to Benard for help. But he would not send money. To do so would only encourage her blindness, and Benard thought it was time for Chantal to accept the consequences of marriage to Charles.

India's relations with its neighbouring country worsened. The Pakistani commander of Dacca surrendered to Indian forces and in December the Republic of Bangladesh was established to rule the old eastern part of Pakistan. Rumours were rife that, in retaliation, Delhi would be bombed. Chantal worried about Madhu. She must be evacuated from this beleaguered city. Four days before Christmas she arranged with a woman who was flying to Europe to deliver the little girl to her parents in Paris. Chantal intended to stay in Delhi, an uptight, mean and conspiratorial city, she thought, not as easy-going as Bombay, but her first duty was to her husband.

In January 1972, Charles was granted bail by the Indian courts. Soon afterwards he and Chantal fled the country.

6

Hurtling Towards a Flame

How had they ended up in Kabul? Chantal had no idea, and she wasn't sure if Charles did either. Afghanistan had never been part of the plan, and now things were moving so fast, she didn't know if she could keep up. She had abandoned herself to the challenge of surviving life with Charles. Since fleeing India she had lost track of all borders and distances.

Downstairs at the front desk of the Intercontinental Hotel, the manager was beginning to hint it was time for them to pay their bill and move on. Charles told her they would leave Kabul at dawn the next day to drive the 2,400 kilometres to Tehran, capital of neighbouring Iran. After six months on the run, it was to be their new home, he said.

All day they sped across seemingly endless deserts in a rented car, stopping only for dry biscuits and Coca-Cola in the village oases of a few mud houses clustered under date palms. After Kandahar, where they spent the night, they continued across the Dasht-i-Margo, the Desert of Death, dotted occasionally with the strange black tents of the Kochi tribes, until at sunset they drove into Herat, the last Afghan city before the Iranian border.

The dusty road was lined with casuarina trees and meagre, man-made streams from which women enveloped in ghostly chadors were drawing water to wash their clothes. Men squatted in groups in their baggy white trousers and grey vests. The road was crowded with horses and buggies, beautifully plumed with red and pink pom-poms and ribbons. There was the smell of smoke from cooking fires and manure and dust. They would spend the night here and cross into Iran as soon as the border opened at dawn.

They parked outside the bank and went in to exchange their money, but two policemen stopped them. The car they had rented in Kabul should not have been driven out of the city limits, the police explained. Charles apologized pleasantly and promised to return it the following day.

'We will go with you,' said the police.

'Fine,' said Charles. 'What time should we leave? Where will I find you?'

'We will find you,' the police said, and left them.

If they went back to Kabul they could be arrested for not paying their hotel bill and perhaps for trying to steal the car. It would mean jail. They ate a dinner of rice and meat in a chai shop. They must leave at midnight, Charles said, and drive into the desert as close to the border as possible, then cross into Iran on foot.

In little over an hour they reached Islam Qala, the Afghan border town, and the couple abandoned the car in the street. They walked into the desert. Charles said it would be easy to navigate their way across the border. It lay to the west, somewhere between where they were now and Taybad, the Iranian border town. Perhaps those were the lights in the distance. It was bitterly cold. All night they wandered under the glaring stars towards the lights of Taybad. When dawn broke there was nothing to guide them. They kept walking. It was hot now, over 100 degrees. Chantal was wilting.

'Come on, darling. Soon we'll be in the swimming pool of the Tehran Hilton,' Charles said, trying to encourage her. After an hour or so she sat down. She couldn't go on. Charles pointed to a cloud of dust in the distance, and slowly a truck came into view. He rushed over and asked the driver for water. Of course, the driver nodded, smiling and clearing his throat to spit. It was the police, the ones from Herat. 'You said you would find us,' Charles said with a friendly shrug.

On 3 July, Charles and Chantal were jailed in Kabul on charges of failing to pay their hotel bill, stealing a rented car, and attempting to cross the border illegally.

Once again, Charles wriggled out of jail and into a hospital. He estimated that it increased his chances of escape by about 75 per cent. But the Afghans were more thorough with their shackles than the Indians, Charles discovered as he lay on the straw pallet, both ankles chained to the iron bedstead. All that stood between him and freedom were the bored guards, one on each side of the bed, nodding off with .303 rifles between their knees.

He had got himself admitted into the hospital by duplicating the symptoms of a peptic ulcer. He had learned the trick of removing blood from his body with a syringe and vomiting it up – a relatively easy way to fake it, and superior to appendicitis symptoms because you weren't rushed off and cut open. He would certainly have escaped that time in Delhi if he hadn't still been weak from the operation.

Seeing the night-boy, he called out and asked him to bring some tea. Earlier the previous day, claiming to be in terrible pain, he had asked for sleeping pills. Now he had four of them, probably Largactil. One thing for which he could thank Western hippies was teaching him all about pharmaceutical drugs in Asia, where they were available over the counter without a prescription. Quaaludes, Mogadon, speed, Librium, Largactil, uppers, downers ... and some overlanders actually enjoyed making themselves unconscious. Surely it was the sickness of a generation. Charles tried different kinds, different mixtures, and tested them on unwitting subjects in coffee, whisky and milk. A few downers dropped in a drink had made his getaways easier. Pharmacology had become part of his arsenal.

Now, while he waited for the boy to come back with the tea, he ground the Largactil to a powder in his hands. When the boy arrived with a battered silver tray and three glasses, Charles dropped the powder into the teapot, which he stirred and then roused the guards. 'Hey, chai?' Both men woke up with a start, grinned, and accepted the proffered glasses. They were not supposed to be dozing. They were big men, more than six feet, like most Afghans.

In twenty minutes they were snoring again. Charles stretched out, crawled along the floor on his hands, and just managed to reach the key ring attached to a belt. Within a few seconds he had unlocked his shackles and disappeared into the back streets of Kabul.

Still wearing the dirty prison pyjamas into which he had somehow managed to sew $300, he ran across the bridge where the carpets were hung out to dry. He stole down the steep, narrow streets of the bazaar, lined with rickety vegetable stalls and stands selling pots and pans and stuffed satin quilts, until he came to a clothing store. He pointed to the clothes worn by the proprietor.

'How much?' he asked in Parsee.

The man shook his head and spat fiercely on the floor. He sold only new clothes.

'No, I don't want new clothes. I'll give you five American dollars for what's on your back.'

A few minutes later, wearing a tattered striped coat, baggy grey trousers and an old turban wound around his head, he was transformed into an Afghan. He took a trishaw into the Shahr-e Naw, where the diplomatic quarters and the classier hippie hotels operated behind high-walled gardens.

He left the trishaw and walked down a footpath covered with the antique rugs and jewellery of the street vendors until he saw what he wanted, two stoned-out French boys lounging against the hood of a gleaming white Citroën DS.

'May I speak to you?' he said in French, his voice low and urgent.

They were surprised to hear this stocky, hawk-eyed Afghan speak their language. Charles told the two travellers a tale about how he had been stopped by the police for hash and then jumped from the police station. He offered them $200 to drive him east to the Pakistan border. They agreed.

Near the border Charles waited in the car by the side of the road until he saw a van, which he flagged down. It was full of young Westerners on their way for a holiday in India. Charles told them his colourful story about drugs and persecution. He asked them to hide him. A few minutes later Charles crossed into Pakistan's Khyber Pass on top of the van, rolled up in a Persian carpet.

Sixteen days later, on 19 July, Charles was back in Paris. It was 8 a.m. and warm already. Bees buzzed around the boxwood hedges, and the brass doorknobs shone in the morning sun. The blinds were up in all the windows of the quiet street and one by one the cars pulled out of the driveways as residents left for work. Charles sat in the rented Mercedes opposite the house, watching the front door, waiting for Chantal's father to leave. He knew if the old man spotted him, he would call the police.

It was dangerous for Charles to be in France now. He had been sentenced to one year's jail in absentia for defrauding the bank. But he longed to see his baby daughter. He had a desperate plan to steal Madhu back and return with her to Asia, to reunite the little girl with her mother and rebuild his family.

Charles had also begun to form a plan to break Chantal out of jail. He would park a Volkswagen van with a trapdoor opposite her cell and tunnel under the ground into the jail. Madhu would be waiting in the van. All they needed were three false identities and they could start a new life. Madhu needed stability now; the travelling was harmful and the air-conditioning in hotels gave her colds. Charles did not want her to suffer the same insecurities he had as a child.

The door of the house opened and he saw Chantal's father walk to the car with his briefcase and drive away. A few minutes later, Charles was ringing the doorbell.

'Forgive me for disturbing you so early in the morning, Mrs Lemaître,' he said, smiling reassuringly.

The woman's mouth dropped open. Her son-in-law looked pale and gaunt.

'Chantal is sick and they let me bring her back to France. She's asking for you now and she wants to see Madhu. We're at the Hilton.'

Mrs Lemaître asked Charles into the house. As she got herself ready, Charles embraced his daughter. She had grown so much in six months, and now she was walking. She looked well and happy.

'What's wrong with Chantal? How serious is it?' Mrs Lemaître kept asking.

'She'll have to go to the hospital for tests, but I don't think it's too serious. Come quickly, let's go.' He didn't want to give her time to think.

Twenty minutes later Charles, carrying Madhu, led Mrs Lemaître into the lobby of the Hilton Hotel and up to his empty room. He was registered in the name of a student whose passport he had stolen in Pakistan. Charles picked up the phone. 'Hello, reception? Can you tell me if Mrs Sobhraj is with the doctor now? Yes? Thank you.' He turned to his mother-in-law. 'The hotel doctor is seeing her. She'll be back in half an hour.'

Charles suggested he order breakfast from room service while they both waited for her. Mrs Lemaître accepted the invitation and Charles played happily with his daughter. He hadn't seen her since the night he escaped from Willingdon Hospital in Delhi. Room service arrived with the breakfast tray and Charles added sugar and cream to the coffee and took a cup over to his mother-in-law. She drank it and soon collapsed on the floor.

Charles cradled his daughter against his waist and collected his small attaché case. Outside the door he hung the notice, 'Do Not Disturb'. At the reception desk, where he had already paid two nights in advance, he told them not to wake his elderly relative who needed a long rest before taking an international flight. With the baby beside him, he drove along the Champs-Élysées and headed for the Swiss border.

It had taken Charles three weeks of evasion and adventure to return from Paris to Asia, and now he was on his way to free Chantal. From the front seat of a rented Chevrolet he watched the Pakistani landscape roll past, dusty and drab, while mangy dogs roamed on the side of the road, and in the back his daughter lay curled up on the lap of the English girl he'd hired as her nurse. He could do anything. What was an Afghan jail against Charles?

His life was charmed, he knew, something special. Back in France, he had survived a five-car pile-up in the mists of the Swiss Alps and the police had escorted him to hospital with Madhu for a check-up. Both of them were fine.

At the Yugoslav border there was another narrow escape. Madhu had urinated on his stolen American passport and the photo of himself came unstuck, which aroused the suspicions of the border guards. They had searched the car and found a dozen false passports and a set of radio microphones, which he had planned to smuggle to Chantal. They looked like fountain pens and could tune to any FM radio frequency.

The Yugoslavs had placed him under house arrest at a nearby hotel, but with little Madhu in his arms he wandered into the kitchen – searching, he said, for a special food for his child – then slipped out of the staff door. From there it had been a taxi back to Belgrade and some fast talking with friendly tourists to persuade them to smuggle him and his daughter into Trieste. Freedom again!

In Rome he bought a batch of passports on the black market and flew to Rawalpindi, where he booked into the Intercontinental Hotel. This morning he had hired an air-conditioned Chevrolet from Akbar Tours and told the driver – who, by law, came with the car – that he wanted to explore Pakistan's tribal frontier. Now he was on the road to Peshawar, 160 kilometres to the north-west, a lawless town near the Afghan border.

As Marilyn, Madhu's nurse, struggled with the baby's nappies and bottles, Charles refined his jailbreak plan. He wondered whether Marilyn might, for a price, agree to get herself busted in Kabul, where she would be sent to the same jail as Chantal. He would teach her to draw up a precise set of plans of the layout. With another girl, someone to visit Marilyn and smuggle the plans out, it would be easy to tunnel inside and free his wife. All he needed was money to pay for a fast getaway car. The two Frenchmen who had helped him escape from Afghanistan would be waiting for him now in Peshawar with their Citroën. He had already offered them the job.

Charles looked at the plump Pakistani driver behind the wheel. This one would be no problem. When they stopped for lunch at a small town, Charles took the teapot from the serving tray and passed a glass to the driver.

Leaving Madhu at a cheap hotel with Marilyn, Charles walked down the narrow alleys of Qissa Khawani, the 'bazaar of storytellers', where the frontier tribes – the Pathans, Afridis, Tajeks, Uzbeks

– and a smattering of Western junkies came to buy supplies. Under the relentless sun everyone shoved and pushed fiercely, shouting and spitting. With guns and knives dangling from their belts, their dark hooded eyes under dirty turbans, the men who strutted by ignored Charles. He felt at ease in this town, where the code of the Pathans demanded that all fugitives be granted the right of asylum. At a chemist's he bought disposable syringes, a bottle of Largactil, and packets of Mogadon and Mandrax. The Chevrolet's driver was already sleeping in the boot of the car, but Charles wanted to give him a shot of Largactil before dumping him on the way to their next destination, Darra, known as 'the village of the gunsmiths'.

Charles walked back to the Park Hotel. It was so hot in the green windowless rooms that no one closed their doors. As Charles strolled through the courtyard, his glance fell appraisingly on the array of stoned overlanders stretched out on their beds. He saw a blonde girl wearing jeans. She was travelling alone and accepted his offer of a free, air-conditioned ride to Tehran. Her name was Diana and she was Dutch. Delighted with her luck, she climbed into the back seat with Madhu and Marilyn.

Charles drove south into the hard, rocky hills towards Darra, a town that had been duplicating Western armaments for over a hundred years. It was dusk. The trucks rumbled past them, painted like carousels, strung with lights and rattling with loose chrome. A caravan of camels trod in ungainly shambles on the side of the road. He drove until he came to a long, straight stretch of desert with no further signs of people, and stopped the car beside a crumbling mud hut. He could drop the driver here. By the time the man woke up they would all be lounging by the pool at the Royal Tehran Hilton. He opened the boot and immediately the stench filled his nostrils. The fat man lay in a pool of his own filth.

Charles began to lift him up, but when he saw his face, with its eyes staring unseeingly and the mouth hanging open like a door off its hinges, he realized that he was dead. The boot wasn't airtight, so how could he have suffocated? Unless the Largactil was contaminated or, maybe, the man had a weak heart. Or the heat. It must have been hot in there.

It was irritation he felt more than anything else. Charles already had enough problems. Flies had discovered the corpse and started to buzz around his handiwork as he stood there lost in thought. Then he heard a gasp. The Dutch girl was standing behind him. 'Diana, I told you not to get out of the car,' Charles said.

They got back into the Chevrolet and Charles studied the map. Madhu had fallen asleep. In the now tense atmosphere of the car, Charles wondered whether Diana would tell the police. Luckily she knew nothing about him, not even his name. Still, he would have to make her feel involved, implicated, to buy her silence with fear.

They drove through the night, the country changing from desert to fields and from fields to forest. Somewhere, they crossed a bridge. Charles turned the car down a dirt track between the trees and got out. Moonlight shone across the rushing waters in a silver path. He assumed it must be the Indus river, swollen by the monsoon. Madhu and Marilyn were sprawled asleep on the back seat. He had to get rid of the body – intelligently, coolly.

'Diana,' he said softly, 'lend me a hand. You've seen the beginning; now you must see the end.'

Charles unlocked the boot, averting his face from the smell. He dragged the body through the pine needles to the bank of the river. 'Quick, help me undress him,' he commanded. They stripped the body. Then Charles rolled it into the swirling waters, where it bobbed like a shining white seal before disappearing. Startled by a gasping sound, Charles turned to see Diana doubled up against a tree, vomiting.

'It's all over now,' he said in a soothing voice, curling his arm around her shoulder. 'Accidents happen. Don't worry, no one will ever know.'

The Chevrolet continued its journey westward to Iran.

Charles walked into the lobby of the lavishly appointed Royal Tehran Hilton, owned by the Shah of Iran's family, carrying Madhu in his arms. Marilyn trailed behind holding the baby's gear. It was a relief to check in here after the punishing fifty-hour drive across dirt roads from Pakistan. Madhu had been restless and whining; Marilyn, increasingly unable to cope; and Diana sullen and uncooperative after the unfortunate incident with the Chevrolet driver.

Charles stopped at the desk, where he sensed something change in the clerk's manner; a flicker of awkwardness. Charles guided Marilyn to the lift. Until yesterday everything had gone so well. The contraband passports he had picked up in Rome had been sold, and the two French travellers with the Citroën who had followed him across the border into Tehran were now standing by, ready to take him to Kabul. In order to implicate Diana in the crime, he had persuaded her to drop some Mogadons into the drink of a tourist at the bar of Tehran's Intercontinental Hotel. Then, taking Marilyn with him, he had robbed the room. But yesterday Diana had taken fright and run away. Charles had spent most of his time since searching for her.

Up in his room Charles wondered if the police planned to arrest him. Probably some tourist had complained. Should he run? No, it would not be so serious. With cash, it was easy to smooth things out in Asia, and, anyway, Madhu made flight cumbersome. Watching Marilyn undress his sleepy child and put her in the crib, he said nothing about his apprehensions. As usual, he slept soundly.

In the morning, mist was still hanging over the Elburz Mountains. Charles could see them through the window as he was shaving, and they seemed to surround the hotel like a huge wall. Marilyn was dressing Madhu when he heard the knock at the door. He had not ordered breakfast so he knew it must be the police. Charles stood near the bathroom, naked from the waist up, watching as Marilyn put Madhu on the bed and opened the door.

A man wearing a grey suit and dark glasses came into the room. Charles saw the barrel of a machine gun pointing at him. He knew he was trapped. He would stay cool, smile, cooperate.

'Good morning,' he said affably. 'You want something?'

'Police,' the man said.

Suddenly the room was filled with seven other men in suits and dark glasses, all carrying guns.

'Who is this?' asked the first man. Marilyn, in a T-shirt and panties, sat down on the bed and took the baby on her lap.

'My daughter and her nurse. Do you mind if I finish shaving?' Half his face was covered with foam.

'It will have to wait.'

Smiling politely, Charles dabbed the foam off his face with the towel he was holding. Five men had stationed themselves along the plate-glass window as though they expected him to try to jump from the balcony. The one who appeared to be the boss picked up a black attaché case from the bed.

'Open this, please,' he ordered, gesturing at the combination lock.

'I'm afraid it's jammed,' Charles said.

'OK, we'll blast it open,' said the policeman, starting to take his gun from his holster.

Charles smiled again and shrugged. He flicked the combination and, opening the case, placed it on the bed. Inside were passports and valuables stolen from tourists. Several of the passports had his own photograph inside them.

'Which one of these is yours?'

'That is difficult to say.' He smiled apologetically. He wasn't worried. He had good contacts in Tehran.

'Come with us.'

'Certainly. Just give us a second to finish dressing.'

As Marilyn pulled on her jeans he smiled at her reassuringly. Followed by Marilyn and Madhu, Charles was escorted downstairs and out of the back entrance of the Hilton. Four black Mercedes were parked in the driveway. A few of the hotel staff members who saw what was happening shrank away as they walked by. Charles realized he was in a much worse situation than he had first thought. He was in the hands of the SAVAK, the Shah's secret police.

One of the men blindfolded him, and the car drove off. The police had the rest of his luggage in the car. When they searched it, they would find some hashish, ammunition and equipment for altering passports. Such minor infringements of the law did not interest the SAVAK. It would only be during his interrogation at their headquarters that Charles would learn why he had been picked up by the secret police.

After running away from him, Diana had spent the night with an Iranian. She happened to tell him about a Frenchman she knew only as 'Charles' who had smuggled a load of passports into Iran. Her lover turned out to be an agent for the SAVAK. Aware that the passports could be destined for the anti-Shah underground, he arrested Diana. After she was questioned, the raid was launched on Charles' hotel room. It would take him more than a few hundred rials to get out of this. He was certain they would torture him first and then blast a hole in his head. Forced to sit tight and make a deal, Charles gave them the names of two Iranian anti-Shah activists. In return, SAVAK handed him over to a civilian court.

Back in Afghanistan, in her cramped, cold stone cell, the months were passing slowly for Chantal. There was still no word from Charles. She tried to be brave, to be worthy of him, but the uncertainty of her future was almost unbearable. She had no one she could talk to who would understand. She had written to Alain Benard frequently, without receiving a response.

On 30 October the *Pakistani Times* reported the arrest of a 'gang of international swindlers in Tehran led by a Frenchman named Charles'. At about the same time Chantal learned that her husband had been arrested in Tehran and that Madhu, through the auspices of the French embassy, had been sent back to her grandparents in Paris.

Meanwhile the Dutch girl, Diana, had made a statement to Interpol about the death of the Chevrolet driver and the disposal of the body in the river. Charles was now sought by the Pakistani police for this alleged abduction and killing. The Chevrolet's driver had been Mohammad Habib, thirty-five years old, the father of three children. His body was never found.

A few weeks later Chantal received a cutting from the 22 October issue of the *Journal de Téhéran* which reported the charges against

Charles. It was the usual list of passport forgeries and tourist mug-gings. Charles was also being sought by Interpol, and would be returned to France to face other criminal charges. Chantal was shocked by the news and wrote to Benard. 'What we have always feared for Charles has happened – his extradition!' She wished she could do something. Could Benard help? 'If you saw the face of our Charles in the picture,' she wrote. 'He looks exhausted. I'm afraid he has lost his will to hold on to life. I am afraid he might commit suicide.'

On 18 December, Chantal received a letter from Charles. He was sure he was going to be sent to trial 'for another case', this time in Pakistan. Chantal wrote to Benard: 'I have the impression that this time Charles has reached the summit of all the idiotic things he could do. Since Delhi, he has been behaving like a moth hurtling itself towards a flame it knows will burn it after having, in despera-tion, torn a wing. In search of what? I have no idea. It is inexplicable. It must be some need for destruction.'

On 12 January 1973, Chantal was finally freed on bail. She would not be allowed to leave Afghanistan until she had paid a fine of 50,000 afghanis, about $1,000. It would take her family three months to bypass the stringent French regulations on the export of currency. In the intervening period, as she waited for her case to be cleared up, Chantal met a young American traveller in Kabul buying carpets and silk. They became good friends.

At the end of April, Chantal was at last allowed to go home. She had often written to Benard of how she would like to help Charles prepare his legal defence. Now she wrote: 'My love for Charles has ripened. At present I am clear, Alain, totally clear, because I have suffered. I can't wait to hold Charles and my child in my arms again.'

Six months later, in October 1973, a black Mercedes drove through the gates of Qasr Prison, Tehran. Minutes later it drove back out with Charles in the back. He had just finished a year's sentence. The car swayed along mountain roads past truck wrecks and women hidden beneath their chadors carrying pitchers on their heads. Goats and hens scattered from the wheels. Charles wondered if the hawk-nosed men in the car in their suits and dark glasses would stick to the deal.

The year inside had gone smoothly and he had heard often enough from Chantal. By now she must be back in Paris with Madhu, waiting for him. But he was still afraid. These men knew he was wanted by the police in eight countries. Two of them, Afghanistan and Pakistan, shared a border with Iran.

As night fell, they reached a neat, scrubbed town lined with flags and pictures of the Shah. Charles was given chai and a kebab and put in a roadside lock-up. The next day the Mercedes sped through the desert and then past icy cabbage fields and sooty mud-hut villages. Finally, Charles noticed a long line of parked cars snaking up the mountain. He knew where he was. He had come this way many times. The Mercedes roared past the waiting line and the wayside truck-drivers cooking dinners by campfires. At the top of the hill stood a compound of tin sheds. The Mercedes pulled up and the man sitting beside him opened the door and gestured to him to get out. The man in the front heaved himself out of the passenger door. He took a piece of paper from his pocket and handed it to Charles.

'*Laissez-passer,*' he said and pointed towards the customs shed. '*Alvida.*'

'Goodbye,' Charles said. '*Merci.*'

'*Bon voyage,*' the other man said and shook his hand. The Mercedes made a U-turn, and the two men got inside. Charles picked up his attaché case, now empty of stolen passports, and walked towards Turkey, and freedom.

7

Brothers in Arms

The Istanbul Hilton stood on the steep banks of the Golden Horn, its balconies positioned to catch the view of the blue sweep of the Bosphorus and the minarets silhouetted against the sky on the opposite bank of the legendary waterway.

'*Allahu Akbar . . . Allahu Akbar . . .*' The cry of the muezzin calling the faithful to prayer rose above the screech of traffic and the hooting of ferries.

Charles sat cross-legged on a low stone table. From this vantage point at the edge of Europe, he looked across the crowded waterways towards the ancient fortresses on the darkening shore of Asia. He was free. It was amazing. But there was not that heady rush of euphoria which usually followed a lucky escape. On the river, rush-hour ferries plied between the two continents, making him remember his own first crossing with Chantal, both sitting exhausted on the hood of the battered Triumph.

'Now it's your turn to cross a culture,' he had said to her. As the wind had rustled her long brown hair, she had smiled with the sweet, gentle expression that he loved.

It was a miracle he was still alive. But now he had discovered Chantal was leaving him, and he hardly cared any more. She had taken Madhu and gone to live in America with another man. He was the antiques dealer from New York whom she had met in Kabul after her release from prison. Now she was suing Charles for divorce.

It was dark and the minarets were silhouetted against the sky like rockets. In his meditation position, with his back straight, he stared at the patterns of twinkling lights, letting them blur as tears filled his eyes. His emotions, which he had kept locked in the dark Everglades of his unconscious, had broken free. Everything was hopeless. He was nothing, a nobody, a pariah. The self he had constructed by years of effort had crumbled now that Chantal had left him.

I can't go on like this for ever, he thought. If I do, I'll be destroyed. He had always avoided thinking of his past, but the shock of this betrayal had reopened the wounds of his childhood, when love and security had so often turned into abandonment and rejection. Now it had happened again. This time his own child had been wrenched from him. The cycle of suffering went on.

Charles closed his eyes. He thought back to the hunger strikes in Poissy Jail before he met Alain Benard. He remembered the inner core of hardness, and he slid his mind into a deep, searching meditation. The pain could be stopped. It was his choice. He imagined his mind as an enormous ocean and then he turned this sea into ice. Charles sat straight and breathed slowly. He pushed this mighty Arctic down through his body and brain until it quenched the cauldron of his memories, crushing the pain. Strength, survival, victory – easy.

On 15 November 1973, Charles was waiting at Istanbul's Yesilkoy Airport to meet his younger half-brother Guy Roussel, who was flying in from Paris to join him. They took a cab to the centre of the city. Guy had not seen Charles since he was sixteen, when the older brother he had always idolized came out of Poissy Jail and Charles had brought Chantal down to Villa La Roche to meet their mother.

Only a few days before, Charles had phoned Guy out of the blue at his job at a wallpaper warehouse in Paris and invited him to Turkey. Guy's fantasy of being reunited with his big brother was finally coming true. He left France without a second thought.

At the park surrounding the Blue Mosque and Hagia Sophia, the taxi turned left into a maze of side-streets lined with cheap hotels in cramped terraced buildings with tiled roofs and pots of geraniums. Guy had not been out of France since he was eight, when the family lived briefly in Senegal. All he remembered was his older brother leading the games and stealing toys for him. Charles booked him into the Eiffel Hotel and took him on a tour of the city.

'I work scientifically now, Guy,' he told his brother. 'No stick-ups or knockouts. My main weapon is psychology.'

Little boys trailed them, selling postcards and Turkish delight, as the brothers rounded the corner where a huge glazed dome glittered in the sunlight. Tourists milled around. Guy was filled with the wonder of being twenty-one and on an adventure in a foreign city.

'You look a bit like a chicken coming out of an egg,' Charles said to Guy, who was wearing a brown leather jacket and tight bell-bottom jeans. His brown hair was lightly slicked back with oil. Guy had the same high cheekbones and sculptured features as Charles, but was slightly slimmer and taller.

He smiled at Charles and said, 'I've never been on a plane until today.'

'With me you'll be using them like taxis.'

'I haven't even been in many taxis.'

'Guy, I'll show you a different kind of life,' Charles promised. 'Growing up with our mother and Jacques on his miserable soldier's pay, it makes you think you're lucky when you get a new pair of shoes.'

The two men came to a park surrounded by the dust-caked vans of overland travellers. 'So, tell me, how are Noi and Jacques?'

Charles and his mother had not been in contact for three years. Noi had kept up with his movements through Alain Benard.

'Poor old Jacques is still in the hospital,' Guy said. 'He gets worse all the time. You know, one night he escaped and turned up at the front door in his pyjamas. Noi called the police to take him back.'

Charles showed no surprise. 'If only Jacques had met a nice little French girl instead of our mother, he would have been fine. With Madhu, at least I tried to be a good father.'

'She's beautiful, I saw her,' Guy said.

'When?'

'In Rouen. Chantal came and introduced us to Madhu.'

'Did she say anything about me?'

'She said she left you because she thought you were going to be shot.'

'Who told her that?'

'The French consul in Iran, I think. She stopped there on her way home from Kabul. She was looking for you after she got out of jail. I think she asked to see you, and they said it was impossible, that it was the end for you.'

'That French consul is a bastard,' Charles said. 'I'll get him one day. What else did she say?'

'Oh, that whatever she did in the future would be for the sake of Madhu ...' Guy's manner suddenly became coy.

'Yes?'

'That she still loves you.'

'Yes, she had to do it,' Charles said matter-of-factly. 'I always told her that if anything serious happened to me, she should find someone to take care of her and Madhu.'

At the end of the park Charles led the way across a road to a hippie restaurant, the Pudding Shop. Charles and Guy sat at a table near the door, looking across a chaotic vista of jeans and folkloric costumes with splashes of jade and ivory and a tangle of shoulder-length hair. There were noisy discussions in several languages, and it seemed the only Turks in the restaurant were the waiters and cooks. Signs hung on the walls warning of the dangers of getting caught with hash. Guy grinned broadly at his older brother. For him, this was a bizarre environment.

'So, this is your trip – hippies.'

'No, not really. I work mainly in the big hotels,' Charles explained, 'but anywhere people have a lot of cash and no routine is good. Like where I am now, at the Hilton. Every day travellers deal with new faces, and so it's natural for them to make friends with strangers. Once they decide you're their friend, their guard drops.'

A beefy traveller covered in grime and hauling a huge rucksack came in the door and stood staring at the counter, his eyes fixed on the custard tarts. 'Man, I've been dreaming of this since Isfahan,' he said aloud to no one in particular.

'It's one thing to befriend these kids,' Guy said, lowering his voice a little. 'It's hard not to, but what about the straights who are loaded?'

Charles ordered two Cokes from the waiter.

'Everyone has one weakness, Guy,' he continued in a tone of controlled patience. 'Gambling, women, boys, diamonds, drugs. As soon as you know, you let it drop that you have access to this wonderful girl, or gem-dealer, or drugs, or maybe an amazing investment.'

A woman wearing an Afghan Kochi dress and a gold ring in her nose, her eyes ringed with kohl, smiled at Charles as she went out the door.

'Do you like the fancy dress?' Charles gestured after her. 'For this kind there is one performance, a kind of hippie theatre —'

'But why do you bother?' Guy interrupted. 'What's in it for you?'

'In this business you bother with everyone,' Charles shot back. 'Never turn down a chance to meet anyone. A contact is a resource; if not now, then later. And with the hippies it's quick. It takes, oh, about ten minutes to take a wallet and a passport.'

'But what's inside a hippie's wallet, Charles?' the younger brother asked, gazing around at the Pudding Shop's clientele.

'You'd be surprised. A lot of these kids are carrying a thousand dollars in traveller's cheques; the drug dealers, more. Don't judge by appearances, Guy. Not all entrepreneurs wear suits. I'll teach you better ways to sum up a person's assets than by their clothes.'

'But all these . . . ?' Guy looked around him. 'They must be junkies. So many of them are so thin and sick-looking.'

'That's what I used to think. Actually, most of them are just spoilt students having their last fling before they settle down. Their resistance is lowered from smoking hash. Then they get sick and go down with dysentery. After a few months on the road diarrhoea is just about their only topic of conversation.

'Now, the businessman is just as easy as a hippie. He always has a plan. You find out what it is, subtly, by indirect means, and then drop part of it in your conversation as though it was in your own itinerary.

"'Oh, I'm doing the same thing,'" he'll say, and you smile in surprise. Always let them be the first to invite you to join them.'

Charles and Guy left the Pudding Shop and walked down Unkapani-Eminonu to the Galata Bridge, which rocked on its pontoons. The noise, crowds and traffic closed in on them. Men bent double with huge loads on their backs struggled to pass. Shoeshine boys grabbed at their hands. Pungent cooking smells wafted from cafés, and Guy stopped to buy simit, the Turkish sesame bread. They crossed the crowded bridge, and he followed his brother up the steep cobbled street to Beyoglu and the Hilton Hotel.

Sitting in a quiet corner of the Karagoz Bar, Guy observed the smartly dressed diners flowing into the Terrace Restaurant. He felt high just sitting there nursing a cognac and looking like a regular hotel guest. It was his second day in Istanbul, and he had never felt better. In Paris he had a propensity for gloom. Despite his good looks, he didn't go out with many girls. Most nights he spent at home in a rented room learning English and listening to the Rolling Stones. He began to feel a new confidence in himself and a graceful ease in moneyed society. It was all thanks to his brother.

Charles returned with a portly middle-aged man and a tall flamboyantly dressed woman whose heavy jewellery was obviously genuine. The couple were laughing. Charles ordered a Scotch on the rocks for the man, a crème de menthe for the woman, and a Coke for himself. When she finished her drink, Guy heard her say, 'I'm going off to pack and relax. You two boys have a night on the town.' The man ordered another Scotch and Guy saw his brother's hand move imperceptibly over the glass as he passed it to his jocular companion. A few minutes later the man left the bar.

Charles signalled Guy to join him.

'I spiked his drink,' he whispered. 'He's got the shits. Now he's under my control.'

Charles had discovered from his contact at the casino that the couple, wealthy American boutique-owners, must be carrying $30,000 and the same amount in jewellery.

'We're going to clean them out and be at the airport in three hours,' he smiled.

'But all my luggage is at the hotel,' said Guy.

'Forget it. You can buy new clothes in Athens,' said Charles quickly as the American returned to the bar.

'Hey Richard. Feeling better?'

'Bloody awful,' said Richard, perspiring in his navy blazer and grey flannels. 'What do these wogs put in Scotch?'

'I've got some vitamins. They'll fix you up. We can't let it spoil our last night in Istanbul.'

As the man gulped down two tablets, Charles introduced him to Guy. Throughout the evening, the brothers dragged the groggy American to several nightclubs, and then to the cinema. When the house-lights came up, their new friend was wheezing and snoring. The two young Frenchmen, in a mood of exuberant bravado, walked him back to the Hilton.

'One too many,' Charles said a few times to curious onlookers as, supporting the man at each arm, they helped him up to his room. His wife opened the door. Her make-up had been replaced by a layer of face cream. Guy barely recognized her.

'Your husband's got a bit of stomach trouble,' Charles explained with a look of concern. 'It happens all the time in Asia. What bad luck on his last night.'

'Bring him in, boys. He's such a bore,' she sighed, following them into the middle of the suite. 'In Tangier he tried smoking *kif* and threw up at the dinner table. Put him in the bedroom.'

Holding each arm, Charles and Guy helped the semi-conscious man onto the bed.

'Go and talk to the woman,' Charles whispered. 'I'll search the room.'

Guy wandered casually into the sitting room. His English was still basic. When he tried to relax and begin a conversation, his mouth went dry and he couldn't think of anything to say. He lit a Benson & Hedges.

'Can I pour you a drink?' the woman asked from where she sat on a sofa littered with fashion magazines.

He felt he needed one badly, but before he could answer, the man's blurry voice drifted from the bedroom.

'Hey! Stop it! What do you think you're doing?'

There was the sound of a slap, a thump, and then vomiting.

'You filthy pigs,' the woman screamed, suddenly alert to her predicament. 'I'll call the police!'

Guy froze as she picked up the phone. Charles dashed from the bedroom, turned up the built-in radio, and from behind, grabbed the woman around her mouth.

'Get the kit, Guy,' he said calmly. Guy took the pouch from his shoulder-bag and handed Charles a syringe and a small screw-top jar.

'You do it,' Charles said with a patient smile. 'Can't you see my hands are full?'

Guy filled the syringe as the woman struggled. In the bedroom her husband could be heard stumbling and vomiting. Guy stood uselessly, brandishing the syringe. This was horrible.

'All right, you hold her. I'll do it,' said Charles. When Charles loosened his grip, Guy had trouble subduing her. Luckily Charles had managed to stuff a scarf in her mouth. Next, he lifted her bathrobe and jabbed her in the buttock. A few seconds later – it seemed like ages to Guy – she passed out.

Charles knelt down and twisted a huge diamond ring off the woman's finger.

'OK, Guy, get one of their bags. Fill it with everything, cameras and jewellery. She's got a mink coat somewhere. I've seen her wearing it. Don't leave them with a thing.'

Charles put the man to sleep with an injection and helped Guy stuff the bag. As they left the room, Charles put a 'Do Not Disturb' sign on the door.

'That was really disgusting,' Guy said as they sauntered to the lift.

'Yes? Why do you say that?'

'I can't stand the smell of vomit. It makes me sick.'

At the hotel desk Charles checked out from his own room and showed them the key he had just stolen.

'Would you mind opening my safe, please?' Guy tried to keep calm as Charles was led off to the hotel's vault. Ten minutes later the two of them were in a taxi on their way to Yesilkoy Airport. From the thick wad of stolen notes and traveller's cheques Charles peeled off $1,000 and gave them to Guy.

'Take the next plane to Athens. Book into the Alfa Hotel. I'll be there in a few days.'

'What about you? What are you doing?' Guy asked, shaken by the speed of the enterprise.

'I have business in Copenhagen. Then I must stop off in Spain and Rome,' Charles said. 'I won't be long, three days at the most.'

He handed Guy the pouch containing the syringe and the sleeping draught. 'Get rid of this,' he said, and disappeared into the crowd with the bag of stolen goods.

Guy left the pouch in the gents' and in the early hours of 18 November he boarded a plane for the second time in his life, bound for Athens.

One week later Guy was still hanging around the Alfa Hotel in Athens waiting for Charles to arrive. He had bought two new suits and some casual clothes. Athens wasn't much fun. To quell the demonstrations demanding his resignation, President Papadopoulos had imposed martial law. There was a curfew. Students at the National Polytechnic were protesting against the military junta and the president had sent in soldiers with tanks.

And it was cold, there were no tourists, no girls. He was bored and lonely. His money was running low.

Finally, Charles turned up. In the lobby, he pointed out of the window to where a woman appeared to be waiting in a Fiat.

'Chantal?' Guy exclaimed.

'Looks like her, doesn't she?' Charles said. 'She's American, though. We met in Copenhagen. I can't introduce you. I don't want her to have anything to do with my criminal life.'

In Guy's room the two men sat facing each other from the edges of adjacent beds.

'I feel good today, Guy. Business went well. You know, I've made love twice already this morning.'

Guy was annoyed. His brother hadn't apologized about being late and leaving him short of his share of the money. Now here he was boasting about his sex life. They argued. Instead of giving his brother more money, Charles told him it was time for him to try a job on his own. That suited Guy. Anything was better than hanging around this hotel.

Four hours later he phoned Charles at the Athens Hilton.

'I've done it.' He was exhilarated.

'Already?' Charles asked, doubtfully. 'How?'

'Just like you taught me, Charles,' he said, pleased at his brother's note of surprise, 'with sleeping pills and smiles.'

He grinned at the memory of the friendly Lebanese businessman.

'Two Mogadon in his Greek coffee. He didn't have his passport on him, but I got a lot of cash. I'm still counting it.'

Guy was euphoric again. Here he was, only twenty-one, and making his own way in the world. As he had sauntered back to his hotel with the stranger's wallet in his pocket, the view of the Acropolis in the cold afternoon sun struck him, for the first time, with its beauty.

An hour later Charles came to Guy's room. Their fight was forgotten. 'Tomorrow I want you to do a big job,' he said, opening an attaché case filled with passports of many nationalities. 'These are going to Lebanon for the PLO. You can leave in the morning.'

'I'd rather this afternoon if there's a plane,' Guy said. He was sick of Athens and eager to follow up on his success.

'Sure, if you feel like it.'

Charles packed a set of walkie-talkies into another bag. He wrote down the name of a hotel in Beirut and gave Guy $1,000.

'And this time, don't leave me alone while you chase girls,' Guy called out as his brother slammed the door of the taxi taking him to Ellinikon Airport.

After a routine security check, Guy sat down in the departure lounge to sip a cognac. He felt high and glad that his life in the warehouse was behind him. This was what he had often imagined: fun, travel, adventure, jet-setting the world with his older brother, living in luxury hotels, and making fools of the police. Soon he would be checking into the Beirut Hilton and going on a shopping spree. Then Charles had promised to take him on a big job in India, a sure-fire jewellery heist. At 4 p.m. Guy's flight was called, and he boarded the bus taking passengers to the waiting plane.

A swarthy man in a suit rushed up to where Guy sat with a suitcase on his knee and knelt on the floor beside him, rolling his eyes.

'Allah be praised! Allah be praised!' he shouted. The man bowed his head to the floor as everyone stared. 'Thanks be to Allah. He sent me the thief!'

The man pointed at Guy. 'You! You take my money.' He began screaming, 'You! You!' and jumping up and down, waving his arms.

By two-way radio the bus driver called the police, who rushed aboard and ordered everyone to lie on the floor. It was Guy's bad luck that his Lebanese victim had recovered quickly and was on his way home on the same flight. Guy shook his head at the policeman, showing his French passport and denying that he had ever met the man. The bus returned to the terminal, and the young Frenchman and his accuser were taken to the police station. Guy's luggage was searched. He was arrested and taken in handcuffs to a police station in Athens. The walkie-talkie in his bag was even more sophisticated than those used by the Greek military. Who was this French boy with a bag of passports? He was surely too young to be acting alone. Police questioned Guy most of the night.

The next morning Guy was still sticking to his story when the police led him to a basement. He was acting on his own initiative, he said. An army officer with a silver-tipped cane opened a cabinet and pointed out an array of ancient-looking torture implements. Guy was stripped and tied face-down to a bench. The officer spat on a rag and put it in his mouth. A black hood was put over his face. Other men came into the room and began beating his body with knotted ropes.

At first it was like the times Noi had beaten him. Guy began to pray. Men jumped up and down on top of him. Others began whipping the soles of his feet. They felt as big as balloons, as though they were dipped in molten lead.

'I'm alone,' he wept to himself. 'Charles will never get me out.' He lost consciousness. When the officer revived him with a bottle of smelling salts under his nose and asked again who had sent him to Beirut, Guy sobbed, 'My brother, Charles Sobhraj. He's at the Hilton.'

About an hour later Guy was lying on a filthy bunk in a cell, moaning over his feet, when the door opened and two policemen hurled Charles inside. Unruffled, he said, 'If only you could have held out for another hour, Guy, I would have been out of the country.'

'Oh God, man, I thought I was going to die!' Guy's shame at his brother's arrival made him even more pathetic.

'Remember how I suggested you leave the next day?' Charles said as he walked towards where Guy was lying. He was contemptuous of his brother's bad luck. 'You picked the flight yourself.'

'My feet! I can't bear it!' Guy was fighting back the tears.

'You'll be OK. But you've got to walk. Keep the blood flowing or they'll swell up.' Charles helped his brother to his feet and supported him as they moved slowly back and forth across the cell.

'It will be much easier if you and I swap identities, Guy,' said Charles soothingly. 'Interpol knows me and knows my escape record. It's better they think I'm a first offender. I can skip much easier. Then I can come back and break you out.'

Guy agreed. The two looked similar, and the interrogating Greek officers somehow failed to notice that the young first offender, Guy Roussel, had assumed the identity of the notorious Charles Sobhraj.

It was a heavy yoke for Guy to bear. He was unaware that his brother had been arrested by the Greek police in June 1971, on one of his periodic gambling sprees to the island of Rhodes. Charles had tried to recoup his losses by robbing tourists and had escaped by jumping out of the window of a police station. The court had since sentenced him to thirteen months in jail in absentia. Apart from that, even Charles had lost track of the number of countries which were after him.

After their interrogation, Charles walked his brother back to the bunk. While Guy lay on his side rubbing his feet, Sobhraj sat on the edge of the mattress staring at the floor. He was furious. When the police had arrested him at the Hilton that morning, they had also arrested his new American girlfriend. Now she knew he was a professional criminal and not an affluent European businessman. They'd even pulled the diamond ring from her finger, the one he had given her from the job in Istanbul.

'As soon as I skip this place,' Charles said to his brother, 'I'm going to print myself a document which says I'm a secret agent, maybe for Iran or China. I'll show it to her. It'll convince her I'm not just a gangster.'

Three policemen walked into the cell, chained the brothers together and led them away.

Although Charles attempted to break out of his chains twice on his way to court, both times he was overpowered by the guards. Now, each posing as the other, the brothers were moved to Korydallos Jail in Athens.

For Charles, his year-long stint in Korydallos was the beginning of a dazzling career as an escape artist. His first attempt involved a dozen young foreigners of various nationalities whom he enlisted to dig a sixty-foot tunnel that would bring the prisoners out onto the nearby road. The plan, though foiled just before completion, showed the electrifying power that Charles had over people. Certainly, the Greek authorities weren't taking any more risks with the two troublesome 'Guys'. In February 1975, he was sent to a high-security prison on the island of Aegina. It was a place reserved for incorrigibles and those facing the death penalty. From Aegina, no one ever escaped.

It took Charles a mere two months to do the impossible. First he used his old trick of faking the symptoms of a peptic ulcer to get himself transferred to hospital in Athens. On the morning of 26 April 1975 he was being transferred from the Athens hospital back to the port of Piraeus and then the island of Aegina and its jail. The prison van was crowded. Taking a bottle of cologne which a friend had smuggled into the hospital, he poured it onto rags and lit a fire. He had gambled that the police would open the doors in time. At the last minute, as smoke billowed, the doors opened. Everyone was re-arrested except Charles. With this escape the legend of Charles Sobhraj and his death-defying feats spread through the criminal underworld.

Because of the two brothers' identity switch, Greek authorities believed it was Guy who had escaped. The remaining brother was being taken to court for passport thefts in the name of Charles Sobhraj. From Paris, Benard wrote to the Greek authorities suggesting that there was an identity confusion. Guy tried in vain to prove who he really was. In the end he was recognized by the officer with the silver cane who had tortured him when he was arrested. In his own name, Guy was sentenced to two years and ten months in jail. By the time he got out, Charles would be transformed into the persona destiny had assigned him – an international celebrity criminal.

For now, after escaping from the prison van, which he left smoking behind him, Charles simply needed an unwary student's passport. As he veered off through the side-streets and crowded docks, he knew that the world was his once more. Where would he flee to next? His father was now dead. Rajni, his half-sister, had written to him through Alain Benard while he was still in jail explaining that Hotchand had died of a stroke. His ashes had been scattered over the Saigon River. When the news reached him, Charles had told his jail-mates that he would be rich, but it wasn't true. Hotchand's Vietnamese wife, Chu, had been afraid that all the money would go to Geeta, the Indian wife in Bombay, and had squandered his wealth. As Hotchand lay dying, she sold the furniture around him, spending his life's savings on diamonds and gold. Charles would get nothing.

Now he was a man without a father, without a fortune, without a home. He could never go back to Vietnam. The news had just been announced: the Americans had fled. Saigon had surrendered to the Vietcong, and his birthplace had been renamed Ho Chi Minh City.

If anywhere, it was India that he could best call home now.

8

Following the Heart

On 5 May 1975, as his flight to Srinagar, the capital of Kashmir, was about to take off, Charles was so engrossed in conversation with a French couple that he was unaware of the covert glances of a young woman in jeans and a T-shirt who sat several seats in front of him. She was a serious-looking girl with a sharp, intense face, deep blue eyes, and dark shoulder-length hair. When she overheard Charles speaking French, her own language, she was pleased.

This was the fifth day of Marie-Andrée Leclerc's three-week holiday in India and the first time she had travelled overseas from her small town in Quebec. As her companion, a young, balding accountant from Montreal, fastened his seatbelt, Marie-Andrée looked back at the Eurasian man. She was determined to meet him.

Below, the landscape changed abruptly as the Air India DC9 crossed the barren Pir Panjal Range and dropped into the Vale of Kashmir. The terraced hillsides were patched with neat squares of gold and green, and streams ran down from the Himalayas into a network of connecting lakes which glinted up at the passengers like mirrors as the plane descended.

The famous houseboats on the lakes were rented from their proprietors at the Government Tourist Centre in the capital, four miles from the airport. It was there amid the crowd of gesticulating Kashmiri landlords and earnestly bargaining tourists that Marie-Andrée caught sight of Charles again. He was arguing in English with a Kashmiri man in an embroidered skull cap and waistcoat, with the patient smile of an old hand. Although she couldn't understand what was being said, it was obvious that the man with the compelling Eurasian face was controlling the situation. The Kashmiri almost jumped up and down as he spoke: 'My dear sir, there are three double bedrooms, each one with a flushing toilet, meals included, also morning and afternoon tea. Fifty rupees a night, worth double.'

'We need only two of the bedrooms,' Charles said, 'so why should we pay for more?' He turned to his new French friends. 'This man is unreasonable. There are plenty of other houseboats.' He knew it was a good deal but the locals despised bad bargainers.

'It has all the luxuries, sir,' the Kashmiri pressed on. 'Fully carpeted, with antiques, sterling silver. You will find it greatly to your liking. A very lovely view of a Moghul fort, sir, very high standard, worth the money.'

'No, we won't pay for a room we don't want.'

'May I suggest, sir, that you save money by sharing with other tourist people? It is often done.' He gestured at an uncertain-looking couple standing nearby, and Charles' glance lighted upon Marie-Andrée and her friend, Jules Dupont. He introduced himself and explained the problem. Yes, they would be happy to rent the third bedroom, said Jules. Grinning like a cat in a TV commercial, the landlord hurried them all into his rickety sedan for the drive to Dal Lake.

Intersecting streams gushed beside the road; ducks paddled, dogs barked, women sat on the ground selling apricots. They drove down a track through an apple orchard and pulled up beside the lake. The giant cedars and willows shaded the banks and the huge, fanciful houseboats, each one outdoing the next in its display of woodcarving and paintwork, bobbed gently in the still water that reflected the peaks of the Himalayas.

The landlord led the group to a boat built of yellow walnut carved with Islamic curlicues and with pink gauze curtains fluttering at its windows. The five travellers filed across the gangway to a front porch lined with pots of geraniums and chintz cushions. A miniature flight of steps at the stern led down to the water, where a skiff was tied.

The landlord proudly showed them the rooms and introduced the cook, a stooped old man with a white beard and turban who ran out to show them his book of testimonials dating back to well-fed generals of the British Raj. That afternoon everyone stretched out in deck-chairs on the roof of the houseboat while the bearer served afternoon tea, a British tradition continued on most of the craft on the lake. The white peaks of the mountains turned pink in the setting sun. A man in a long skiff piled with roses and lotus blossoms paddled from boat to boat, calling out: 'Flowers, groovy flowers for your sweetheart.'

As Charles watched, Marie-Andrée stood at the railing looking out across the beauty of the scenery. She reminded him of Chantal.

Marie-Andrée had the same proud way of throwing back her head, and the same apparent stubbornness which, Charles knew, he could overcome, and transform into eternal devotion. Chantal, he believed, still loved him. The divorce had become final while he was in jail. It had been granted on the grounds of his incorrigible criminality. One day, though, they would meet again and he would hold her and Madhu in his arms. In the meantime, Marie-Andrée was obviously very attracted to him, and he liked her. He decided to play a little game. The outcome mattered little; he was not about to become involved again with a woman. Once was more than enough.

In the days that followed, Marie-Andrée, Jules Dupont and the French couple toured the sights of Kashmir. The boatman picked them up at dawn in a shikara, a long skiff cushioned and curtained like a sultan's bedroom, and the two couples floated off to the bazaars and carpet factories, the lakeside palaces and the terraced Moghul Gardens.

Marie-Andrée had loved Jules. At home in Quebec she had spent all her weekends and spare nights with him. They had even built a small cottage in the country together. She'd been happy, except for the times when his mother came to the house and his manner would change and he became nervous and cruel. Was it to show his mother he preferred her to Marie-Andrée? Still, they had loved each other and when he proposed one Christmas she accepted.

Excited, she designed her own wedding dress. Her family was happy for her and she dreamed of children. But as it came close to the wedding, it became clear that Jules Dupont had not yet told his mother about his plans. When she did hear the news from the next-door neighbours, she insisted that the young couple must come and live with her. Marie-Andrée said no. She would not marry Jules Dupont. The wedding was cancelled but they remained friends.

In Kashmir, Charles always refused any invitations to join the two couples' touristy outings. Once he took them all to dinner at an expensive restaurant in the town, but usually he went off on his own or stayed on the boat. Marie-Andrée realized the holiday would soon be over, they would go their separate ways, and life would resume its provincial regularity for the girl from Quebec.

Charles seemed aloof to her, as though he had more important matters on his mind than just enjoying himself. He gave her the impression of being very profound and clever. He spent his time reading and from the fragments of his conversation he always seemed to be speaking from vast experience of the world, a well-spring of learning mixed with street argot and a suggestion of bright lights in faraway cities. He was wealthy, successful, charming, myste-rious, and his physical presence electrified her. Sometimes, passing down the narrow corridor to their bedrooms, their bodies would touch in a way that disturbed her.

There seemed no situation in which he was not in control. At first, the floating merchants had besieged the boat, trying to sell tailored suits of Harris tweed and music boxes carved in walnut. 'Alain', as he was known to her, shooed them away with such offhand authority that they never came back. Sometimes he would gaze across the Himalayas and let drop a cryptic remark about China.

'They talk honeyed words, but they sharpen their stings,' he commented.

Although he looked Eurasian, he seemed very French to her. He was muscled and lithe. She watched him as he stretched out on a deck-chair in the sun. Close to him she felt excited, adventurous. His face, sometimes so scholarly and distant, lit up when he spoke to her. His tone of voice was an instrument of courtship. His business seemed vague, something international which caused him to travel a lot.

One night as the holiday drew to a close and the two couples had retired, Charles remained in the Edwardian-styled living room, stretched out on the crimson velvet sofa, reading. He was always reading. The door opened and Marie-Andrée, wearing pyjamas, walked softly into the room. He looked up over the top of his glasses as she came through the doorway and asked, 'So, you're not asleep yet?'

'No, not yet,' she said, drawing the footstool close to the sofa and sitting down. In the soft pink glow of the lamps she seemed very pretty and vulnerable. Looking into his eyes, as though she had been rehearsing her resolve to make this move, she said, 'May I kiss you?'

Charles returned her gaze without emotion as the boat rocked gently in the silence of the lapping water. In his head he counted the seconds and then said aloud, 'Why not?'

He put his arms around her. For several minutes they kissed until Charles heard footsteps coming from the hallway and pushed her away. Dupont was standing in the doorway in his robe.

'Come to bed, Marie-Andrée,' he said sharply, ignoring the other man.

In the morning, when Charles and Marie-Andrée were alone on the roof of the boat, he asked her what Dupont had said.

'Oh, he was angry,' she said, 'and asked if we kissed. I said no.'

'We'd better stop this here,' Charles said. 'I don't want to come between you.'

'Oh, he's nothing to me, Alain,' she insisted. 'It's over and we're travelling together on the understanding that we are both free to do what we like. I'm under no obligation to him.'

'Maybe,' said Charles, 'but you sleep in the same bed.'

'Yes, but we don't make love,' she told him.

'Well, why aren't you honest with him about me?'

'He might get angry and spoil our holiday.'

The merchants, their skiffs loaded with embroideries and carpets, were already skimming across the lake shouting their wares, and tourists from the other houseboats were heading out towards the bathing barge.

'When we get to Delhi today I'll be leaving you, so it doesn't matter,' said Charles.

'Don't say that. I think I love you,' she blurted out. 'Don't you feel anything?'

'I don't know,' he said. He knew that Western women were useful in Asia, especially pretty ones without criminal convictions. 'I don't like your cat-and-mouse game. Let me speak to Dupont.'

'No,' she said.

'As you like,' he replied, but he had already decided.

After breakfast the two men walked along the edge of the lake. Washing flapped on the lines hung between the willow trees, bright splashes of colour along the lush green of the shore. Charles asked Dupont if he was planning to marry Marie-Andrée.

'If you are, I'll just disappear the moment we return to Delhi.'

'No, I haven't got a chance,' Dupont told him. 'Do what you like.'

After four days on the boat, Charles and the two couples flew back to Delhi. On the plane he sat next to Marie-Andrée.

'I talked to Dupont,' he told her. 'He loves you a lot. Why don't you marry him?'

'I already told you, it's over,' she said impatiently. 'But why did you tell him I made the first move?'

'I didn't want to take the blame for breaking up your relationship,' he said. 'My life is very complicated at the moment. It's not easy and to be frank, I live outside the law.'

Charles claimed later that he knew she wouldn't give a damn what he did, and his candour would only impress her.

'I like you very much,' he said, 'but what's the point? You live and work in Canada. I could never go there.'

'Well maybe ... I could come back.'

'You mean you would come to Asia and live with me?'

'Of course I'd have to think about it,' she said.

'And I'd have to think about it too,' he agreed. 'You know, this is the only time in my life that a woman has ever been the first one to ask for a kiss.'

His bewilderment was genuine. Charles had spent so long in jails that feminism had passed him by.

'I did it because I guessed you would do nothing, and time is short,' she explained.

When they arrived in Delhi, Charles and the two couples took three separate rooms in the Nirula, a small hotel off Connaught Circus. The next day they all took the morning express to Agra to see the Taj Mahal. In the evening they returned to the hotel. Charles asked Marie-Andrée whether she would like him to find a way for them to be alone together and she agreed.

He had not been with a woman since he was arrested in Athens, seventeen months ago. That same evening, the French couple left the hotel and continued their journey to Bali, unaware that his courtship of Marie-Andrée had distracted Charles from drugging and robbing them.

In the morning Charles was the first of the three to go to the dining room. 'Come down to breakfast,' he called through the door of the Canadian couple's room as he passed. At a table in the faded dining room he ordered coffee for three, and Dupont and Marie-Andrée entered as Charles was filling their cups. After breakfast the three of them strolled around the dilapidated circular colonnades of Connaught Circus. Charles kept looking at his watch, waiting for the effect of the five Mogadons he had slipped into Dupont's coffee. After twenty minutes the accountant began to stagger.

'What's the matter?' Charles said. 'Are you sick?'

'I don't know. I feel dizzy.'

'It must be sunstroke from our visit to the Taj Mahal,' said Charles, holding him by one arm in case he fell. 'I told you to wear a hat.'

Marie-Andrée held the other arm and Dupont was helped back to the hotel. Charles brought him a glass of water.

'The best thing for you is vitamins,' he said, handing him another sleeping pill. When the accountant was lying snoring on the bed, Marie-Andrée followed Charles into his room.

The next morning as Marie-Andrée lay beside him in bed, she asked Charles when he expected Dupont would wake up.

'Don't worry. He'll sleep until ten at least,' he said. But according to his calculations Dupont was awake already and he hid this from Marie-Andrée because he wanted the other man to catch them together. It would force them both to face the facts. At seven-thirty there was a knock on the door and they heard the accountant shout, 'Marie-Andrée, I know you're inside. I've been listening at the door for the last half-hour.'

'She will come to see you in your room in twenty minutes,' Charles called through the door.

They took a shower together and he asked Marie-Andrée if she loved him. Oh yes, yes she did. Would she leave her job in Canada and come to live with him? Of course she would.

And so she agreed to be frank with her former fiancé. After she had been with Dupont a few minutes, Charles entered the room and told him to stop shouting at her.

'Listen, I asked you in Kashmir if you wanted me to leave. You said then that you didn't mind and that you weren't jealous. Now you have to face the reality.'

The two men talked it over and the accountant agreed he would have to step aside.

'All right, man, no hard feelings,' Charles said, giving him his hand.

Later that day Charles invited them both on a trip to Kathmandu and Bangkok, offering to pay both airfares and all their expenses. From then on Marie-Andrée and 'Alain' travelled together.

Their three days in Kathmandu were happy ones for Marie-Andrée. Charles was attentive, romantic, generous, perhaps a little in love with her. Still paying the expenses, he swept the Canadians off for eight days in Bangkok. Then, on 25 May, the three of them returned to Bombay, where Marie-Andrée and Dupont were due to catch their flight back to Quebec. It was a month since Charles had escaped from Aegina. At the airport he took Marie-Andrée aside, leaving Dupont to supervise the luggage.

'Alain is not really my name,' he told her and explained that for reasons of business he must travel constantly and keep changing his identity. It sounded romantic, important – he was an adventurer, a buccaneer, a man of a thousand faces. 'In case we lose contact,' he said, writing down Noi's address at Villa La Roche, 'I'll give you my mother's address in Marseilles. What's your address and phone number?'

'Well, Monsieur Dupont,' he said, turning to slap the other man on the shoulder, 'I hope you enjoyed Asia.'

'Yes, a wonderful holiday,' the accountant assured him, picking up the bags as Charles embraced Marie-Andrée.

'You will come back to me and be my little queen,' Charles murmured, his voice low, urgent, compelling, and as he looked into her deep-blue eyes: 'You will share my house ... my life. It's strange, but you remind me so much of my first wife.'

A few days after saying goodbye to Marie-Andrée Leclerc, Charles was walking along Ormiston Road in Bombay to his old recruiting ground, Dipti's House of Pure Drinks. The afternoon sun shone on the mustard-coloured shutters of the cheap hotels opposite as Charles strolled through the door and sat down at one of the grimy wooden tables. The place hadn't changed in the last few years. A few Western travellers stared dolefully into their glasses of beetroot juice with that air of having forgotten their own names. Charles smiled at the girl next to him; she was beautiful, and he began talking to her.

The next day, 5 June, after a French nuclear scientist failed to turn up at Bombay's Atomic Research Centre to deliver a lecture, he was discovered unconscious in his room at the Taj Mahal Hotel with an empty bottle of Chivas Regal by his bed. His valuables were gone, and he had been injected with Quaalude. The last thing he remembered, he said later, was having coffee with a Swedish girl who introduced him to an Asian-looking, French-speaking man.

Two weeks later, when the lobby of the Taj Mahal Hotel was buzzing with the news that Indira Gandhi, the Indian Prime Minister, had been told by the High Court that she had won her parliamentary seat illegally and must give it up, an alert security guard saw Charles walk through the door.

As the man watched him move across the vast white marble foyer towards the Shamiana coffee shop, he remembered the description given by the nuclear scientist of his assailant's peculiar panther-like gait.

But even as Bob Thomas, the security chief, went to arrest him, Charles, with his uncanny sixth sense, slipped away. Thomas checked his files. Yes, the culprit was almost certainly Charles Sobhraj, who was still wanted in India for robbing the Ashoka Hotel four years before.

The Bombay police were alerted and later, as Charles was checking out of the Ritz Hotel with a Chinese man and the Swedish girl, he was arrested and locked in the back of a police van. By the time the van arrived at the lock-up the only prisoner left inside was the girl, Laura. She said later that she was moved to pity by the story Charles had told her of his early life and she wanted to stand by him. Laura was jailed.

On 26 June, after hundreds of political leaders had been arrested, a state of emergency was declared in India and all constitutional rights were suspended. Charles was making his own contribution to the country's chaos as he zigzagged across the continent, leaving a trail of dazed and penniless victims behind him.

Charles next surfaced in Hong Kong in July. Later he would claim that he had come to the colony for more calculated reasons than further petty thefts. From Delhi, he later said, he had let certain people know that he was free to offer his services and had accepted an engagement from a criminal organization based in Hong Kong – a group of Chinese businessmen involved in the smuggling of heroin from Thailand to Europe. This organization, which invested huge sums of money in the heroin trade, had declared war on amateurs – the small-time operators and their young travellers who, for a few thousand dollars, would carry consignments of heroin from the source to the marketplace. They were disrupting the business. Amateur drug rings made a small investment, took high risks, and often got caught. The large organizations based in Hong Kong invested millions of dollars and took minimal risks. Their merchandise was rarely intercepted. But now the carelessness of the small-timers and the constant arrest of their couriers was attracting unwanted publicity and forcing world police and customs officials to tighten borders.

Charles had form with the criminal cartels, and was rumoured to have led drug caravans through the dangerous Khyber Pass. And so this Hong Kong organization decided to discourage the amateurs by recruiting him, or so he would claim. A large fee was to be paid into a bank account. He would be given some names, and discretion to follow up leads. It was suggested that he establish a suitable front in Bangkok, where an assistant would be sent to him. From this point on, he would be carrying out orders.

Charles had met a young French geologist, Denis Gautier, while in Hong Kong, and had stolen his passport. Charles retained the first name from his previous identity ('Alain Gittienne'), and took on the surname of Gautier, which he was soon to make infamous throughout Europe and Asia.

In Singapore on 28 July, he stopped off at the Hyatt Hotel to visit a Cartier representative he had befriended in Hong Kong. Over breakfast he borrowed the key to the young man's room and took fifty silk shirts, just delivered from the tailor, two new suits, a silk robe, two calculators, a camera and a crocodile-skin attaché case. Downstairs he asked for the key to the safe deposit box and cleaned it out. 'A hotel safe is never safe,' he said afterwards.

After buying five diamond rings with the man's credit cards he then flew on to Bangkok. It was from here, three days later, that he made the phone call to the girl from Quebec. The call would change Marie-Andrée Leclerc's life.

Meanwhile, on the other side of the world, it was a hot July afternoon in San Pedro, California. Emma Knowlton said goodbye to her three assistants at Irene's Beauty Salon and walked outside. In her early sixties, tall and rangy, Emma was in high spirits as she crossed Weymouth Road. Her granddaughter, Teresa, was coming to visit her. Teresa had been in California for the past three weeks attending a course on Tibetan Buddhist meditation at Lake Arrowhead.

Emma had not heard from Teresa during the course, where they all took vows of silence. But the minute it was over, Teresa had phoned. She would be coming to stay for a couple of weeks before going home to Seattle and back to college. Teresa was smart, and now that she had settled down to studying seriously she was doing well. Her report card showed A's and B's in everything. Emma now hurried up the driveway of her Spanish-style stucco bungalow. She eased off her shoes, sat on a chair near the window, and lit a cigarette.

It was about three years since Teresa had first told her grandmother that she was into Tibetan Buddhism, after coming home from a trip to the East with her boyfriend. Another fad, Emma had thought, and like the others, this one would soon pass. Teresa had already been a Rosicrucian and a Theosophist.

Theirs had started as a difficult relationship. When Teresa was twelve her parents had divorced and she had come to live with Emma and her husband George. Handling a teenager in the late 1960s had been hell. Teresa got into drugs at San Pedro High School and went boy crazy. In 1970, when Teresa was seventeen, she went off to try living with her mother in Seattle. It didn't work. Teresa grew wilder and took more and more drugs. She left her mother and had herself fostered-out to a part-time security guard at her high school who had lots of other foster children. Emma remembered her granddaughter visiting her with bare feet and dirty jeans.

When she was nineteen, after her trip overseas with a boyfriend, Teresa started talking about a Buddhist monastery in Kathmandu called Kopan. The monks there were from Tibet, she said, and it seemed to Emma they had given Teresa something that replaced the drugs and wildness. The change was a miracle. With its emphasis on death, Emma wasn't sure she liked Tibetan Buddhism. But after what it had done for Teresa, she could hardly complain. They had always loved each other, even during bad times, but now, because she was so open to new ideas, Emma was unusually close to Teresa.

Emma heard the loud toot of the car horn, and she hurried onto the patio. Teresa's red Volkswagen was parked in the drive, and her granddaughter was bounding up the steps with that lovely, big, vivacious smile. But Teresa had changed.

'Teresa! What have you gone and done?' she cried out in shock. As a child, Teresa's mother had thought nothing of spending $70 on having Teresa's hair done with a blonde rinse because she had such beautiful hair. Now it was gone, cut into a rough bob around her ears.

'Aren't you glad to see me?' Teresa laughed as she threw her arms around Emma.

'Of course I am, darling,' said Emma, blinking as she led her into the living room. Teresa was wearing a long Indian skirt and a white cotton blouse which she had embroidered herself with flowers. She was petite, less than five feet, with her grandma's wide smile and firm jaw.

Emma ruffled at her granddaughter's hair. 'Why the heck have you gone and done a thing like that?' she asked.

Giggling, Teresa bounced onto the beige vinyl sofa, slipped off her sandals and sat cross-legged, wiggling her toes. She had cut her hair off at the Buddhist retreat, she said, as part of her spiritual practice.

'The day your mother brought you home from the hospital to this very room, Grandpa and I admired your lovely hair,' recalled Emma sadly.

'Don't take it so seriously, Grandma,' Teresa said.

Emma asked her about the meditation retreat.

'Oh, it was wonderful! We did samsara visualizations. That's when you sit with your eyes closed and the lama reads out the steps that you go through when you die. We use the awareness of death to remind ourselves not to waste a single moment of our lives.'

'It sounds morbid to me,' Emma said.

'It's just the opposite,' Teresa assured her. 'Do I look morbid?'
Emma smiled. Teresa never looked morbid.

'It's just so that when the time comes you'll know what to expect.
It means you can find your way around, and you won't get
frightened.'

Teresa's spiritual teacher was Lama Yeshe, whom she had met on
her first trip to Kopan. A small man with a maroon robe and shaved
head, he had come to America for the first time to teach the course
at Lake Arrowhead.

'Some of the students took Lama Yeshe to Disneyland,' Teresa
told her grandmother. 'He really wanted to go. He went on the ghost
train, and all the kids were worried for him, Grandma. They thought
he'd be scared. After all, he'd only been out of Kathmandu a week.
When he got off the train, he said, "Oh, that was nothing. I've seen
it all before in my visualizations."'

What a joy to see her, thought Emma. So alive and happy, no
longer wild and rebellious and harming herself.

'Grandma, I made a big decision while I was on retreat. It's
another reason why I cut my hair.' Teresa looked so serious, so
intense, Emma thought to herself. What is she going to do next?

'I'm going to go back to Kathmandu in October, to Kopan. I'll do
the meditation course and stay on when it's over to help the lamas.'

Emma was disturbed but she tried not to show it.

'I can teach the children maths, and just being close to Lama Yeshe
is very good for my karma.'

'That's nice, darling, if it's what you want. Are you going with a
group?'

'No, Grandma, I'm going by myself. It's time for me to start doing
things alone. Anyway, at the monastery everyone is a friend.'

As she lit a cigarette, Emma asked how long she would be gone.

'About a year,' Teresa said. She wanted to have time to work things
out and to force herself to be more serious. 'Doing the course is one
thing, but then you get back on a plane, fly home to America, watch
television, and eat junk food again.'

Emma reminded Teresa that she had been doing so well at the Community College in Seattle. 'Why do you want to give all that up?' she asked her.

Teresa had planned it out. She would apply for a year's study leave and continue learning Tibetan for credit. She would also do a paper on the role of women in Buddhist society.

Emma tried not to oppose her granddaughter's independence. Once Teresa had given her a little paper scroll with a saying by Kahlil Gibran, 'Your children are not your children. They are the sons and daughters of life's longing for itself.' She told herself that as long as Teresa was happy, that was all that mattered.

'I'm so excited, Grandma, just to be seeing Asia again. On the way I'll stop off at Hong Kong and Bangkok. It doesn't cost any extra, and I've never been to those cities.'

Emma didn't warm to this news.

'Those places are rough, Teresa. Kathmandu is one thing, you have friends there, you know the place. But Hong Kong and Bangkok are no places for a young girl on her own. Why don't you go straight to Nepal?'

'Oh, Grandma, Hong Kong is on the way and I want to see Thailand. That's a Buddhist society too.'

'I just don't want you to go to those places, Teresa, especially not to Bangkok.' Emma found she was crying. What was wrong? Why did she feel this sense of foreboding?

Teresa came and comforted her, putting her arms around her grandmother's shoulders. 'Silly,' she said. 'I'm a Buddhist, remember? It's like going home for me. No one will hurt me there.'

Teresa stayed with her grandparents until mid-August while she taught a course in meditation to a neighbourhood Buddhist group. She ate raw vegetables from her grandfather's garden, sometimes cooking Emma and George meals with soy beans and buckwheat which they couldn't get down, but Teresa didn't mind. At last they had all learned to respect each other's beliefs.

With a friend Teresa put statues of Buddha in the four corners of the backyard. While her grandfather pottered around in his vegetable garden, the two girls sat in the sun in the lotus position, reciting Buddhist sutras.

In August, as Teresa packed her belongings into the Volkswagen, Emma gave her a small, gold Bulova watch engraved on the back with 'Emma 12/25/37', a Christmas present from George thirty-eight years before. Teresa hugged her grandmother and promised to write from each stop on the way to Kathmandu the moment she arrived. As she watched the Volkswagen roll down the driveway on the start of her granddaughter's journey home to Seattle, Emma Knowlton cried.

Top left: Charles in France in 1956.

Top right: Charles Sobhraj, 'a perfect specimen of the human male'.

Bottom left: The fifteen-year-old Charles at one of his first jobs as a kitchen hand at La Coupole restaurant, Paris.

Bottom right: A young Charles with his mother.

Top left: 'Roong', one of Charles's Thai girlfriends. She is holding Franky, the dog Charles forgot to give an alias.

Top right: Interpol photograph of Ajay Chowdury, the Indian who became Charles's accomplice in at least eight murders. He was last heard of in Frankfurt, Germany, in 1977 and is wanted by Interpol.

Bottom: Marie-Andrée Leclerc, a Canadian from Quebec who flew to Bangkok to live with Charles Sobhraj. 'I swore to myself to try all means to make him love me,' she wrote later, after changing her name to Monique, 'but little by little I became his slave.'

Top: Sobhraj's flat in Kanit House in Bangkok. 'It seemed a nice kind of life, with a lot of young people sitting around with plates on their knees ...'

Bottom left: Dominique Rennelleau. After two months at Kanit House, the sick traveller realized that his hosts were drugging him.

Bottom right: Charles Sobhraj and Marie-Andrée, 'waiting for the opportunity to befriend tourists.'

Top left: Teresa Knowlton in Seattle before she left for the Tibetan monastery in Kathmandu. On the way she stopped in Bangkok, where she met Ajay Chowdury at the Hotel Malaysia and was taken to Kanit House, and, later, to a sex club.

Top right: Stephanie Parry, the French girl who dropped out of a career in advertising to live on Formentera and design dresses. Hired as a courier by Hakim's contact in Spain, she flew to Bangkok to collect a false-bottomed suitcase and take it to Europe.

Bottom left and right: Cornelia Hemker and Henricus Bintanja – 'Cocky and Henk' – the young couple from Amsterdam who had saved for five years for their 'trip of a lifetime'.

Top left: Vitali Hakim, the Turk from Ibiza. 'I wanted his murder to be a message,' Charles told the authors, 'a message to others in the business.'

Top right: Israeli crane driver Alan Aaron Jacobs was found robbed, drugged and strangled in a hotel room in Varanasi he had shared with Ajay Chowdury. 'He was the only one I felt sorry for,' Charles said later. 'He was such a hard worker.'

Bottom: Connie Jo Bronzich (left) from Santa Cruz, California, and Laurent Carriere (right), from Manitoba, Canada, were roommates at a small hotel in Freak Street, Kathmandu. Their burnt bodies were later found in the foothills of the Himalayas.

Top: This snapshot of Charles (centre) with two unsuspecting victims was taken by the third member of a group of young Frenchmen who were exploring Southern India in a van. Charles gave his victims cocktails spiked with sleeping pills, injected them with Largactil and robbed them of their valuables.

Bottom: Then he carried them back to their van, which he crashed against a tree, probably intending to kill them.

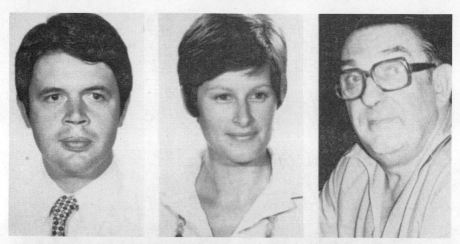

Top: Herman Knippenberg, a Dutch diplomat on his first foreign posting; Angela Knippenberg, whose skill in languages helped unscramble the clues in abandoned documents; Paul Siemons of the Belgian Embassy.

Bottom: Nadine and Remy Gires. It was not until they met Paul Siemons and the Knippenbergs that anyone listened to their story. (From left) Herman Knippenberg, Nadine Gires, Remy Gires.

Top left: Charles Sobhraj, alias 'Alain Gautier' when he was arrested in Delhi in 1976.

Top right: Charles Sobhraj in Delhi, October 1977, with co-author Richard Neville. 'I consider myself a businessman, not a criminal,' he told Neville after recounting his life story, 'and I know I never killed good people.'

Bottom: Heavily guarded, Sobhraj, with Marie-Andrée Leclerc and Jean Dhuisme, is led from the prison bus to the courtroom.

PART III

The Web of Death

August 1975 – February 1976

9

Apartment 504

Marie-Andrée was bewildered when she met Charles at Bangkok's Don Muang Airport on 2 August. He did not hug her or express any affection and behaved like a stranger. 'There's a limousine waiting,' he said briskly.

After her bags were packed in the boot, the couple sat in the back of the Mercedes as it sped along the expressway, passing rice paddies and shoddy wooden houses beside the canals. Charles took four jewellery cases from the pockets of his denim jacket. 'For you,' he said, putting them in her lap. She opened the boxes, holding up in turn a jade pendant, a matching jade ring, a diamond ring and a sapphire ring surrounded with diamonds.

'They're beautiful!' she said, mollified.

'I'm glad you like them.'

'But I cannot accept,' she said, handing them back.

'Not accept? What do you mean? You've come to live with me.'

The countryside was flat and drab. Through the haze of exhaust fumes ahead, the gilded spires of the city looked trashy and make-believe against the gleaming towers of the modern hotels.

'Perhaps later, darling,' she promised, finding it hard to call him 'darling'. He was sitting next to her, but his body was barely touching hers. 'Why don't we see how it works out first? I might disappoint you.'

This flash of independence showed Charles a trait he didn't like in a woman.

'You know that I do some small illegal business here, Marie-Andrée,' he said, looking at her absently over the top of his glasses. 'It's not at all dangerous, and you won't be involved, but maybe it's better for you if sometimes I introduce you as my secretary. And for your protection, we won't use your real name, OK?'

Marie-Andrée breathed the cold air-conditioning and hid her shock behind a haughty tilt of the chin. To pose as his secretary? Use a false name? She didn't have to accept this, she thought, as the car nudged its way into the dense log-jam of Sukhumvit Road. Panoramic advertising hoardings stood at intersections, depicting gory scenes from local horror films. Children pushed garlands of jasmine and frangipani against the car windows.

The car pulled up at the Rajah Hotel, a concrete box rushed up in Bangkok during the building boom of the 1960s. Heat shimmered up from the asphalt. American soldiers lounged in the lobby as bar-girls with vacant smiles circled aimlessly in hot pants and platform shoes. Asia did not seem quite so romantic this time, thought Marie-Andrée as she unpacked her clothes. Why was he so distant? Why had he changed so much?

Before Marie-Andrée's arrival, Charles had been juggling an assortment of girlfriends, one of them a Thai girl, Ann, who managed a jewellery shop. It was always handy to have a local woman attached by bonds of love, he thought. If there was trouble, she was security. If he had something hot to drop, she could keep it. She could be his spy, his translator, and arrange useful business contacts.

The day after her arrival when he took Marie-Andrée to meet Ann, he explained all this to her. 'At first, if I introduce you as my secretary,' he told her, 'she will have time to get used to the idea that you are more to me than that. In a month she will accept you as my wife.'

Charles had chosen a new name for Marie-Andrée. Like the Thai girl, she was being forced to submit. She would now become 'Monique' Leclerc, sometimes wife, sometimes secretary of 'Alain Gautier'.

In the following days she spent much of her time alone in the hotel room. He did not like her roaming around the city on her own. She read paperbacks and wrote letters home to her family, hiding her unhappiness to save them from worrying, but hinting that she might be home sooner than expected. During their first nights together all his coldness melted, leaving her feeling physically and spiritually close to him. But he quickly stopped making love to her, even though they still slept in the same bed. 'I'm tired,' he would say, or, 'I have too much on my mind.' Marie-Andrée felt that her lovemaking did not please him and that Alain no longer desired her. She became frustrated and felt deceived.

Actually, Charles did feel affection for her but, as he insisted to himself, that 'Quebecois pig-headedness had to be eliminated'. It was a psychological game – he would break her. He rose early, and often she was still asleep when he went out. Charles dressed like a businessman and carried his newly acquired crocodile-skin attaché case, which was full of papers. But what he did exactly, he kept a mystery.

A week after she arrived she passed Charles on his way out.

'Darling, can you lend me five hundred dollars?' he asked. 'It's a Thai holiday and my bank's closed.' As Marie-Andrée signed the traveller's cheques back in their room, he asked her whether she had decided to stay with him. 'You always say you are waiting to see whether it will work out,' he said. 'What do you think?'

'I still don't know. You have other girls here,' she told him. 'You don't seem to care for me. Maybe it would be better if I went back to Canada.'

Her indecisiveness suddenly infuriated him.

'It's as you like, little girl, but make up your mind. I haven't time for this uncertainty. In my business I can't afford a girl who's unsure of her loyalty.' Suddenly he shouted at her: 'Learn to be either black or white, not always different shades of grey – do you understand?' Taking her traveller's cheques, he left her sitting on the bed and slammed the door.

Marie-Andrée was aware that she had hurt his masculine pride. Of course she was undecided. His coldness was not an inducement to stay. She felt she was a woman who had suffered in love so much already. And now here was Charles, a man full of secrets, with Thai girlfriends, false names and a murky background. Could she really dream of setting up a home with him? One full of sunshine and children? Maybe she would try. At least he seemed like a man who was master of his own destiny.

After fifteen days in Bangkok, when her landing visa expired, Charles arranged for its extension. He borrowed another $500 from her, the last of her money. 'I'm too busy to go to the bank,' he told her. 'Soon I'll return it with interest.' He was so offhand, as if he had access to unlimited funds. And when her visa came up for renewal again at the end of August, he promised to take care of it. Instead, he let it lapse. Now she was an illegal alien without cash or a return ticket.

She realized she was his prisoner.

On Thursday 4 September, an Australian couple lay on the sand of a Thai resort, their stomachs raw and rumbling in the aftermath of a bout of diarrhoea and vomiting. Next to them the French-Vietnamese psychiatrist and his wife ate crabs the fisherman had caught that morning. A jumble of giant rocks marked the southern edge of the beach, giving a name to the oldest resort in Thailand, Hua Hin, 'Head of Stone'. It was an apt description of how the two Australians felt; it was difficult to keep their eyes open.

'We heard you being sick last night,' said the psychiatrist. 'It sounded quite violent. Did you ever get to sleep?'

'No. We were up all night,' moaned Russell Lapthorne, a university professor travelling overland through Asia with his wife, Vera. They had first met 'Jean Belmont' and 'Monique' a few days before at Pattaya, a beach resort on the opposite shore of the Gulf. Over a few beers the psychiatrist suggested that they team up and travel south to Singapore by train, stopping at beaches on the way.

Monique played in the sand with her fluffy white puppy, Franky. 'Jean Belmont', her handsome husband, swam a few minutes in the water, showing off his taut, muscular body as he ran back up the sand and picked up his towel.

'I'm going to the shop,' he said, hardly out of breath. 'I'll buy some tinned milk to soothe your stomachs, and by tomorrow you'll feel much better.'

The night before they had eaten together at a local shellfish restaurant. Later the Australian couple had rushed back to their room at the Railway Hotel, pale, shaking, and wracked with stomach cramps.

'Seafood is always risky,' said the psychiatrist, smiling down at them as he patted himself dry. 'I remember my wife once, after a bouillabaisse in Marseilles, I thought she would die.'

At 3 p.m. Russell and Vera, weak from their illness, stretched out on deck-chairs on the shady veranda, where the potted palms rustled in the afternoon heat. Jean Belmont emerged from his adjoining room carrying a tray of glasses filled with chocolate-flavoured milk. He put a bowl on the floor for the puppy and passed a glass to each of his Australian friends.

'Thanks, Jean,' said Vera, gratefully sipping the milk. 'I still feel a bit dizzy. I think I'll go to bed.'

Monique threw a rubber ball along the veranda for Franky to chase, and Russell curled up in his chair with his book, *Oil Politics*. It was the rainy season. The air was sticky, and clouds were gathering for the afternoon thunderstorm over the South China Sea.

When Vera Lapthorne woke up, she got out of bed and fell over. The surroundings were strange. She tried to rouse her husband and then passed out again. It was Saturday 6 September, thirty-six hours after they had drunk the glasses of chocolate milk. When the hotel maids found them sprawled on the floor, both of them were taken to the local health clinic. While they were unconscious, their stomachs were pumped.

Vera was the first to make it back to the Railway Hotel, where their passports, marriage certificate, driving licences and all other identification were missing, as well as $900 in currency. Gone too was a cine-camera and Vera's jewellery – a diamond ring and a gold chain. Vera knocked on the door of the adjoining room and was answered by an unfamiliar voice.

Jean Belmont and his wife Monique had vanished. All they had left behind was a used battery from a cassette recorder and Franky's rubber ball. Vera stood on the veranda of the Railway Hotel, stunned by the meticulous treachery of the charming French couple.

Back in Bangkok, Charles and Marie-Andrée were already signing a lease for an apartment. Kanit House was a five-storey, U-shaped cement structure built in the 1950s, now run down, but convenient and respectable. A kidney-shaped swimming pool in the central courtyard added a token touch of glamour.

Their apartment, number 504, was on the top floor at the end of one of the wings. Through the bedroom windows they could see the gleaming white tower of the Dusit Thani Hotel among the rows of red-roofed bungalows and shops, like a symbol of the affluence and success Charles so desperately wanted.

There were two bedrooms, a balcony, and a living room with a kitchenette partitioned by a padded vinyl bar. On the liver-coloured rubber tiles stood a cane sofa and two chairs.

Charles saw the apartment as his business headquarters as well as his home. He had picked it mainly for its location, close to the tourist section of Bangkok and near the bars of Patpong, as well as most of the big hotels and shopping arcades. Charles had no belongings to add warmth to the barely furnished rooms except for his black leather punching bag which he hung near the door. It was for his guests. They would come to do business and end up fooling around with the bag. That would put him in a position of strength. Another distraction for the people he planned to entertain was Coco, a tiny gibbon monkey bought at a stall in the Sunday market. Coco was kept in a cage on the cement balcony that overlooked the swimming pool in the courtyard.

'We have an apartment, and that gives me hope,' Marie-Andrée wrote in her journal. 'At last we spend the night, just the two of us, in our home. This makes me really happy.'

For her complicity in the drugging of the Lapthornes, Charles finally rewarded her with a night of lovemaking.

Meanwhile, dizzy and destitute in Hua Hin, Russell and Vera sold their Kodak Instamatic to pay for their hotel room and took their story to the local police. An interpreter recorded a statement, and the police, bemused, shook their heads smiling. Nothing could be done. A sympathetic businessman lent them the train fare back to Bangkok, and they went to their embassy for help. A few days later Russell collapsed with a high fever and abdominal pains and was rushed to the hospital, where he remained for two weeks.

Marie-Andrée was not to have Charles to herself for long. A fortnight later they drove 800 kilometres north-east from Bangkok to Chiang Mai, taking with them a plump, middle-aged Frenchman called André Breugnot.

Chiang Mai held many attractions for a visitor. Elevated about 300 metres above sea level, the climate was temperate, and the ancient capital had a reputation for its roses and beautiful women. The streets were lined with the traditional wooden Thai houses on stilts standing in gardens shaded by flame trees. A towering backdrop to the city were the mountains of the Golden Triangle that border Laos and Cambodia. These were the home of the hill tribes who divided their time between embroidering costumes and cultivating opium on steep, inaccessible fields that supplied 70 per cent of the raw material for the world's illicit heroin market.

According to Charles, his passenger Breugnot had been sent to Thailand by a European heroin ring to pay off local suppliers. The Frenchman, allegedly, was one of the first names on the list supplied by his Hong Kong employers, or 'investors' as Charles preferred to call them.

Charles had been told that Breugnot, posing as an antiques dealer, would be flying from Paris to Bangkok via Hong Kong in early September and checking into the Royal Hotel. Charles later claimed to have hung around the Royal Hotel until he caught sight of a solitary Frenchman sitting at the bar. Charles took a seat nearby with one of his Thai girlfriends and began to drop phrases in French. As so often happened with the French in Asia, Breugnot was delighted to hear his own language spoken and quickly struck up a conversation with the charming Eurasian. The rest was easy.

According to Charles, who knew Chiang Mai was Breugnot's destination, he mentioned casually that he was planning a trip there with his wife, 'Monique'. Later, when they met for another drink, Breugnot volunteered that he too was going, and Charles offered to drive him there.

And so, on 20 September, they arrived in the old city together. After a sightseeing tour and a few drinks, Charles said goodbye to Breugnot, whom he had mildly dosed with laxatives, and drove back to Bangkok.

For this trip another passenger had joined them in the car – Dominique Rennelleau, a bearded young bank clerk Charles had picked up at an overlanders' restaurant. For most of the journey the young Frenchman was unconscious.

When he next opened his eyes, Dominique was in a shadowy room cut with slats of sunlight. For a few minutes, as he realized how much his head was throbbing, he watched the specks of dust moving aimlessly around in the sunbeams. Where was he? Another hotel room? Yesterday – or was it the day before? – he was in Chiang Mai. Alain and Monique were charming, a nice straight young couple, and really, he thought, the man's conversation was fascinating. They lived in Bangkok, they had told him, where Alain had a gem business.

It was after the dinner they had shared that Dominique's memory faded out. He remembered rushing back to his dilapidated guesthouse in a trishaw, only just making it to the grim cement squat lavatory before his bowels exploded. Sweating, shaking and vomiting, it continued all night. The next morning he had woken up on the floor of his room. Alain, with his strange sallow face and bottomless black eyes, was looking down at him.

'Well, you've got the bug, haven't you?' he said, looking concerned. 'I know all about it. You'd better come home with us. We'll look after you.' They had helped him into their car and given him something that 'would set his inside like concrete'.

And now? There was a tap on the door, and his host entered the bedroom. He was smiling and carrying a glass of white medicine.

Dominique drank it. Then his limbs and head felt light and yet heavy at the same time, and consciousness washed away from him again.

Charles would say later that one reason he had taken Dominique Rennelleau back to Kanit House was to create an alibi for the job he had planned. After tucking his house-guest into bed with another sleeping draught, Charles caught the afternoon flight back to Chiang Mai, where a Thai friend met him at the airport and drove him to the Chiang Inn, the most luxurious hotel in the city. There, resting in his room, was André Breugnot.

It amused Charles for years to recall the way Breugnot greeted him when he walked into Room 207. 'Who are you?' said the Frenchman, realizing immediately that he was in danger. 'I thought you were my friend.'

Charles had heard this before. It was his style to use friendship as a weapon to break and enter into his victim's life. Intimacy and pills. Laxatives first, to induce illness so he could diagnose their complaints and offer helpful advice. Later, when their trust had been won and defences disarmed, he would move in with heavier weapons: Largactil, Quaaludes, Mogadon and other assorted soporifics.

Once he had dosed a man with Mogadon for a few days, Charles discovered he could make him do anything. What happened that afternoon between him and Breugnot would later be recounted in his own words:

Breugnot was surprised when I suddenly appeared at the door and told him that we had business to discuss. I asked him, 'What did you come to Chiang Mai for? As a tourist or on business?' At first he denied everything and I continued to question him. Later I gave him a Japanese slap on the side of the head, and he fell to the floor. When you're hit like that you don't see anything for a few minutes, and you get confused. 'What is your trip, tourist or business?' I kept asking. He didn't answer so I kicked him and lifted him up by the shirt. He was a fat fellow. 'You're from the Thai police?' he asked me, and I laughed. 'No, I'm French,' I told him.

'What do you want from me?' he cringed.

'Your contacts in Bangkok,' I said.

He told me he knew nothing and that he only came to Chiang Mai once a year.

'You're not a small boy,' I told him. 'You're over forty – you must know a lot.'

Later, I made him take a Mogadon and waited for it to take effect. I didn't want to leave any marks. I showed him a gun.

'Either you speak up, André, or I work on you,' I said, all this time speaking softly. 'No one will ever know what you tell me.'

'If I speak to you they will kill me,' said Breugnot.

'No one knows you're in this room, André. In a few minutes you can be free.'

This was a classic Sobhraj deployment of psychology. Now he set about moulding Breugnot into a conspirator. He knew how insecure Europeans often felt in Asia, and how susceptible they were to a sympathetic listener.

'I picked up a paper napkin from the breakfast tray and tore it in half,' Charles continued. '"This one is your life," I told him, laying down one sheet in front him, "and this one is your death. Which one do you choose?"

'Then he asked me, "Are you sure no one outside this room will ever know?"

'"No one will ever know," I assured him.'

According to Charles, Breugnot then revealed details of his heroin business and gave him the names of some couriers who would be coming to Thailand.

'Afterwards, I made him take some more capsules,' Charles recalled. '"It's just to secure our getaway," I said. "When you wake up everything will be fine."'

When Breugnot passed out I undressed him, and I put all his clothes neatly on the bed. I carried him to the bathroom – he was fat and heavy – and put him in the tub and turned on the

tap. I laid his pipe near him on a stool by the bath and propped
a newspaper, half in the water and half on the outside of the
tub. I left some sleeping tablets on the sink. I didn't touch his
passport or wallet. I held André Breugnot's head underwater
until he was dead. Then I dusted my fingerprints, locked the
door behind me, and put up a 'Do Not Disturb' sign. I had
worked fast and reached the airport in time to catch the afternoon flight to Bangkok.

Records at the French embassy in Bangkok showed that an André
Breugnot, aged fifty-six, was found dead in a hotel room in Chiang
Mai on 21 September. The maid found the body in the bathtub,
blood dripping from the nose, and local police concluded that there
was no trace of foul play. Charles later described this operation as 'a
cleaning' and boasted about it. It was the perfect murder, one still
officially listed as an accident.

Among the contacts Breugnot had given to Charles was Vitali
Hakim, a Turk from Ibiza known to his friends as 'Ved'. He would
be coming to Bangkok in October to buy heroin, which would be
packed in false-bottomed suitcases for the couriers to take to
Europe.

For some time, agents of the US Drug Enforcement Agency based
in Thailand had been putting pressure on the authorities to increase
surveillance of all travellers flying from Bangkok bound for Europe
and the States. The new smugglers' route now went via Kathmandu
where, Charles knew, 'You could take a cow out through the airport.'
The second name that Breugnot allegedly gave him was that of a girl
who would come from the United States to take a consignment of
heroin from Bangkok to Kathmandu. From there it would be smuggled to Europe. Charles would claim later she was Teresa Knowlton,
the girl from Seattle who was now packing her bags for her trip to
Kopan Monastery in Kathmandu.

When Dominique woke up again in Kanit House a few days after
the killing of Breugnot, he felt better. My God, how lucky I've been,

he thought. If Alain hadn't found me in Chiang Mai ... I could be dead by now.

His train of thought came to a stop. How did he find me? I never told him where I was staying. Now here he was ensconced in the guest bedroom. It was simply furnished with a bed and a chest of drawers. He pulled up the venetian blinds and looked down into a courtyard with a swimming pool, a rock garden and sugar palms. He felt strong enough to get up and that night his host invited him out for a tour of the city.

In green neon script, the sign above the window in Nana Nua Road spelled out the name of the Grace Hotel, and beneath it hung a banner that read 'Willkommen Liebe Gäste'. Noodle stalls cluttered the pavement outside. These were for the customers who needed to sober up before they went to bed with one of the bar-girls from inside, Charles explained to a bemused Dominique.

'That's where the girls go,' he added, pointing to the small, short-stay hotels that lined the street. 'Three dollars for two hours, five dollars the whole night.' Cab drivers lounged near their cars, and two Thai bouncers watched the *farangs* – foreigners – filing in and out under the red canopy.

Inside, it took a few minutes for Dominique's eyes to adjust to the smoky darkness. The room was large with a full-length bar, and waitresses circulated with wet trays of beer as two juke-boxes boomed out American rock. He followed Charles to a table. Everywhere he looked were girls, all so garishly dressed and brightly made-up that it was hard to tell the young from the middle-aged or the women from the ladyboys. There was dancing, chatter, loud rock music – this was a perpetual party where the female 'guests' were for sale.

Dominique would never have come to a place like this alone, but Charles was completely at ease, his hawk's eyes taking in everything that was happening. Some of the girls smiled and waved at Charles.

'Do you like these Thais?' Dominique asked his host nervously, not wanting to say the wrong thing.

'Not in the way you think. I've never had a prostitute in my life. I only come here to meet the tourists for my business,' said Charles.

He was just starting out, he explained, but soon he would build the biggest cut-rate gem business in Bangkok. This was a city where few failed to succumb to gem fever. The most sacred Thai statues were coated with gold and encrusted with precious stones. Society women spent hours in beauty parlours, their perfect manicures showcasing expensive rings which glittered with sapphires, rubies and diamonds. Hundreds of jewellery shop windows, like Aladdin's caves, lined the main streets, while the alleys of Chinatown, with their red shopfronts, presented a rainbow of jade, gold of high purity, and gems.

'I can buy direct from the mines, cut out the Chinese middlemen, make a thousand per cent profit and still give my customers a bargain,' Charles revealed. 'Maybe I'll take you to the gem mines at Chanthaburi,' he suggested above the noise of the juke-box. 'You can take some stones to Paris and make a profit.'

Dominique reached into the back pocket of his jeans to pay for a round of drinks and realized that his wallet was gone. Nor had he been able to find his passport and traveller's cheques when he had dressed that evening. His $1,100 had been hard-earned on the tobacco fields of Australia, where he had worked for months to pay for a leisurely overland trek back to France. Nonplussed, he turned to his new friend.

'Oh, I meant to tell you,' said Charles, 'I've put all your valuables in my safe at the bank. You're still so sick and I'm out all day. While you're my guest I feel responsible for you. Let me know when you need them.'

Charles had other plans for Dominique's passport, and for the young man himself.

After a week at Kanit House with the French couple, Dominique was ready to move on. He wanted to see more of Asia and be home by Christmas, and asked Charles for his passport and money to be returned.

The next day he was sick again. He couldn't seem to shake off the stomach bug. Alain and Monique are being so wonderfully patient, he thought to himself as Marie-Andrée put his glass of milky-white medicine on the cocktail bar. On top of the diarrhoea, he felt weak and sleepy. When he woke in the morning he didn't know where he was. But Charles stuck his head in the bedroom doorway on his way out, asking, 'So, how are you today, Dominique? We'll soon have you cured.'

Why did they put up with him? he wondered.

Early in October, Dominique started to feel better, and Charles said he could stop taking the medicine Marie-Andrée had been dispensing for the past ten days and accompany them both on a trip to Pattaya and the gem mines at Chanthaburi.

For six hours Charles wandered up and down the shabby streets of Chanthaburi, 480 kilometres south of Bangkok. With a bored Dominique and Marie-Andrée in tow he sifted his hands through the sapphires and rubies piled on the pavement trestle tables.

'See, most people would think this is valuable,' he said, picking a large blue sapphire and holding it up to the light. 'But it's not. The sparkle is caused by tiny flecks of green.'

The old Chinese dealer behind the table nodded at Dominique and Marie-Andrée. 'Your friend is an expert.'

Back in Bangkok, at Kanit House, Charles installed metal filing cabinets in the living room and filled the drawers with small white envelopes of stones from Chanthaburi. He acquired scales, tweezers, magnifying glasses and other paraphernalia. And just as Dominique was planning to leave he was struck again by the mysterious illness.

One morning while he was still ill, a handsome young Indian boy arrived at the door, smiling. Dominique noticed his fine white teeth. Charles welcomed him in and put his small cardboard suitcase down near the punching bag, which he sparred with jokingly. The boy was slight, and wore dark trousers, a white shirt and a thin moustache, which added to the impression of personal neatness – in contrast, Dominique realized uncomfortably, with his own unshaven face and crumpled clothes. The young Indian – Ajay Chowdury – professed himself to be 'hip' and addressed Dominique as 'man', speaking English with an Indian accent. Dominique could barely understand him.

Over breakfast Charles made a surprising announcement.

'By the way, Dominique, I'm afraid I have to ask you to move out of the spare room. Ajay is going to need it; he'll be working for me. You can sleep on the couch.'

Dominique had often heard Charles make jokes about Indians as if he despised the whole race. But he concealed his irritation at losing the room to the newcomer. After all, he would be leaving in a few days.

'I met Ajay in the park,' Charles explained. 'He was lost.'

'Yes, I still get lost around here,' the Indian nodded, sitting almost upright on the sofa.

'Where have you been staying?' Dominique asked politely.

'At the Hotel Malaysia. It's a good place. I like it.'

Why does everyone stay there? Dominique wondered.

'Ajay is going to find me customers at the Malaysia. I think he'll be very good at it,' Charles said as he ate the sandwiches Marie-Andrée had prepared.

Dominique tuned out of the conversation. English required too much concentration. Ajay didn't speak French, and Dominique was feeling queasy again.

From then on, Apartment 504 became crowded with a passing parade of visitors, all potential customers, and the coffee table was usually littered with white paper packages of gems, ash trays and coffee cups. Young travellers from the cheap hotels were drawn in droves to the apartment by the stories they had heard from Ajay about 'Alain Gautier' and his cut-rate sapphires and rubies. Sometimes Dominique was asked to come into the room and pretend he was a good customer, one who made many profitable trips to Paris, selling the stones he had bought at Kanit House. Dominique didn't know how to refuse. He felt so guilty about always being sick, and Marie-Andrée kindly nursing him. Charles was paying for his upkeep. The least he could do, he thought, was to help the family business.

Quickly the apartment turned into something like a youth hostel. There were French, Americans, English and Germans, and Charles spoke to them all in their own languages. But it was only when Charles was out on his mysterious rounds that the atmosphere really relaxed, for everyone knew that the hard-nosed businessman was not sympathetic to the wondrous lifestyle of wandering the world in a haze of marijuana smoke.

'Drugs are the sickness of your generation,' he would often say, rolling up his shirt-sleeves to show he had no syringe marks. 'So many people have tried to convince me to smoke hash; so far, no-body has succeeded.'

Dominique had travelled the same roads as the visitors who flocked to Kanit House, but always with a map and a guidebook. So many of them, he realized now as he talked with them, drifted across Asia not knowing where they were going or why. Wide-eyed, they spoke of the restaurants in Bali that served omelettes prepared with hallucinogenic mushrooms; their illegal border-crossing into the territory of the hill tribes of the Golden Triangle; their foolhardy excitement at crossing the Khyber Pass while on LSD. Many travellers pined secretly for the comforts of home, and at Kanit House there was a kitchen where they could drink Nescafé and cook a steak. It was a luxury to lie around reading *Newsweek*, and to play badminton in the courtyard. It was a break from the chain of dollar-a-night hotels that had plastic jugs of water instead of toilet paper, and menus written in Urdu. You could walk out of number 504 with a pocket full of sapphires or a ruby ring, they believed, and when you got home you could sell the stones for such a profit that you wouldn't have to work for another year. Then you could take off again, maybe to South America.

Marie-Andrée had been briefly happy when she and Charles had first moved into Kanit House. But now their apartment was always crowded with strangers and, unlike Charles, she was not adept at hiding her feelings as she served endless trays of pineapple and papaya and poured cups of coffee. Sometimes Charles would catch her scowling at the guests, and he would hurry her into the bedroom and shut the door.

'Come on, darling, smile, be polite,' he would say. 'Don't scare away my customers.' She tried. She had sworn to herself to do anything to please him. Her love eclipsed anything she had felt before for a man. She knew she was becoming his slave. She was the one who had always to be available, smiling, on call twenty-four hours a day – if only to please him. But her devotion was not paying off. Charles was always elsewhere, busy promoting his gem business, seeing his Thai girls. How little she meant to Charles, she fretted. 'I'm just an employee satisfying his whims.' Yet strangest of all, her love for Charles kept growing.

It was on one of those afternoons when the living room was filled with visitors that Ajay turned up with an American girl. As soon as she walked in the door with a wide smile and sat down on the cane sofa, it was as though she had brought a party into the room with her.

'Hi,' she said, 'my name's Teresa.'

Wanting to be hospitable, Dominique offered to go out and get some beer while Teresa was telling everyone about the monastery in Kathmandu where she was going to become a Buddhist nun. She flashed a smile at Dominique as he went out.

When Teresa had arrived in Hong Kong from Seattle she had stayed at the Boston Guest House in the cavernous Chungking Mansions in Kowloon. A week later, on 12 October, Teresa Knowlton took Air Siam Flight 909 to Bangkok. Arriving early the next day she checked into the Hotel Malaysia on 13 October.

Built in the 1960s to attract American GIs on rest and recreation from Vietnam, the hotel sat behind a high wall in the narrow Soi Ngamduplee, and resembled any one of thousands of modern motels across America. It had achieved a word-of-mouth reputation on the drifters' trail by being one of the few budget hotels with a swimming pool, air-conditioning and Western plumbing. When overlanders first set out to cross the continent, dollar-a-night hotels with rope pallets or lice-infested mattresses were a novelty, but by the time they reached Bangkok, a mid-point, they were willing to spend $3.50 on newly appreciated luxury.

The Hotel Malaysia was the place where most overlanders stayed. Day and night the foyer and adjoining coffee shop were crowded with footsore travellers. There were clean-cut students on their maiden voyages, idealistic and innocent, eager to talk politics with the locals, as well as bedraggled, taciturn veterans with only a bed roll and a string of Nepalese prayer beads; junkies, executive drop-outs and buoyantly healthy backpackers.

Downstairs, next to the lift, was a notice board of the road which guests used to swap Afghan lapis lazuli for jungle boots or to hawk forged student cards or perhaps find someone to cross a desert with. Around the swimming pool of the Malaysia, bright blue, heavily chlorinated and lined with coconut palms, it was possible to draw one of the only generalizations that could be made about the over-land travellers. By the time they reached Bangkok few of them were fat. A sign said that bar-girls were prohibited from entering the pool. Guests lay on deck-chairs and smoked joints or drank beer. Frequently the Malaysia was raided by the Thai drug squad, but guests were usually tipped off in advance.

Among the other foreign travellers at the Malaysia when Teresa arrived were a young couple from Amsterdam who had been on the road for seven months. Cornelia Hemker, nicknamed 'Cocky', was a tall, quiet twenty-four-year-old woman with blue eyes and flowing fair hair who had worked as a secretary while saving for her 'trip of a lifetime'. Her boyfriend of five years was Henk Bintanja, who had inherited swarthy skin and dark hair from his Indonesian father and bright blue eyes from his Dutch mother. By travel standards they were withdrawn, usually keeping to them-selves as they conscientiously visited every sight recommended by the guidebooks. They took photographs and sent them back to their families, all the time recording their daily experiences neatly in exercise books.

When Cocky and Henk had packed up their small flat in Oosterparkstraat eight months earlier, Amsterdam had been blan-keted with snow, and the canals were frozen hard. They put their bicycles in storage. Henk was close to completing his PhD in chemistry at the University of Amsterdam when he decided to take this year off and see the world before settling down. His laboratory work on the purification of water was finished, and while on the road he was completing some of his paperwork, corresponding with his course supervisor and even correcting proofs for his technical articles and posting them back to the university. Cocky's sister Marijke and her husband, John Zant, a psychologist in an Amsterdam clinic, had joined them on this trip for three months in Bali. It was there that Zant noticed Cocky and Henk had become less excited by the novelty of travelling and often preferred to spend time alone in their hotel room reading and writing in their journals. After Marijke and John returned to the Netherlands, Cocky and Henk flew to the Malay Peninsula, then travelled north towards Thailand by train. On 29 September they took the twenty-four-hour trip from Butterworth in Penang to Bangkok and booked into the Hotel Malaysia. In one of their journals they wrote:

October 2nd – 15th: We arrived early. Knew the Malaysia was one of the cheapest hotels. There were many tourists whom we saw on the train, and we had to wait for our room until 10 a.m. It was 13 guilders. When we got inside, better than expected. Reception desk leaves something to be desired; if you ask for assistance, the girls yawn into your face and look annoyed, perhaps because they spend the nights on their backs with the tourists. Later, shopping in Silom Road. To tourist office for info. Going by bus we are glued together. Unbeliev-ably humid especially when the bus stops, because of exhaust fumes. At the tourist office it becomes clear that for tourist visa, extension is difficult. Easier to go to Vientiane in Laos to get new visa.

Unimpressed by Dusit Zoo.

Went to Wat Phra Keo, 2nd visit but didn't regret it. It was again thirsty weather; we sat somewhere and ordered milk but got soybean milk. At Oriental Hotel saw Thai dances; tickets 50 baht, the cheapest. We took a small beer, 44 baht, highly inflated price. Looked awfully five star. After show wanted to get food. Lunch was 90 baht ($4.50) so we declined. Walked down New Rd. but couldn't find anything.

They had seemed like ordinary tourists, but Charles would say later that his men in Hong Kong had put their names on his list.

By the time Dominique returned to number 504, eager to see Teresa again and with two dozen bottles of Singha beer, the group of young travellers was in fits of laughter. He had never seen the living room so lively. Even Marie-Andrée had discarded her familiar gloominess, and her thin body was shaking with incredulous giggles. Two visiting Americans, a Thai girl, Ajay and Marie-Andrée were all absorbed in Teresa's account of her sex life in Seattle.

Dominique opened the beers, put them on the coffee table in front of the guests and then sat on the sofa next to Teresa. His English was basic and he wondered if he misunderstood what Teresa was talking about. Her brown eyes were sparkling as she picked up her beer.

'And so when he asked me to sleep with his friends,' she said, shrugging, 'I thought, well why not?' In an undertone Marie-Andrée began questioning Dominique in French to make sure she understood the gist of the stories Teresa was telling.

It was a hot night and everyone kept drinking beer as Teresa chattered on. As she talked, she began stroking Dominique's thigh. Startled, he went to the refrigerator for more beer. Was she getting drunk?

At 11 p.m. the door opened and Charles came into the room, looking trim and business-like in a light-blue open-necked shirt and dark trousers, and carrying an attaché case.

'Oh, darling,' Marie-Andrée called out, 'come and meet Teresa, she's fantastic!' She went up to Charles and kissed him and led him into the room.

Charles glanced around at the chaos of empty bottles and cigarette butts, then focused his attention on the new guest.

'Hello, Teresa,' he said, smiling and walking towards her. She looked up at him and flashed a sultry smile. It seemed to the others that an electric current passed between them. 'I hope you will allow my wife and I to take you swimming one weekend to Pattaya. It's a beach resort. We have a bungalow there.'

The invitation was so direct and unprompted, as though Charles had planned to ask her before he had even opened the door, that Dominique would always remember it. Charles' claim that when he walked into the room that night he had already been instructed to kill Teresa has been impossible to prove, but it must be considered as motive.

Charles made his rounds among the guests and then sat down next to Teresa. She was wearing a long maroon skirt and halter-neck top. Her skin was smooth and tanned. Around her neck she wore a woven red string, a protective Buddhist charm.

'And so what's all this about your sex life?' Charles asked.

'Oh, all sorts of things,' Teresa giggled. 'Sorry you missed it.'

'My wife tells me that you're off to a monastery in Kathmandu,' he said, focussing on her. 'I was born in a Buddhist country. It's the greatest of all the religions, I think, and I've studied most of them.'

Already their intimacy had eclipsed the other house-guests. Teresa was giggling in erratic bursts and it was easy to see she was drunk. Charles knew the type well, he thought, he had used a hundred like her on his old jobs in Bombay.

'Maybe you think it's weird for me to be drinking and talking about sex before going to a monastery?' Teresa said.

'There are a thousand roads to reach Nirvana,' Charles replied. 'It doesn't matter which one you take.'

Buddhism was a flexible religion, that's why he liked it. Even the Thais kept an open mind. They were not supposed to kill, but Thais liked to eat fish, and fishermen must feed their families, so they solved the dilemma by believing that, having simply taken the fish from the water, they died of their own accord.

'Do you expect to reach enlightenment,' he smiled, 'up there in those hills, where Buddha was born? Do you really have the self-discipline?'

'I don't have a real lot of self-discipline, but I'm working on it,' she replied, suddenly serious. 'How about you?'

'To me, it's the most important quality a man can have. You know, Teresa, when I was a little boy, I was like you. Running around, searching for something ... reading Buddha, the Bible, philosophy, and in the end I realized that here, inside me, I had truth.'

He could see he had touched a chord in her. It was so easy with this type.

Dominique was the first to wake up the next morning. The others had headed out to Patpong on Charles' instructions, and must have had a late night. He folded his sheets carefully and finished cleaning up after last night's party. He couldn't get Teresa out of his mind. She was so outspoken it had shocked him. Still, that was America, Dominique thought. And then she had put her hand on his thigh. At first he thought that she must be attracted to him, but later he had seen her doing the same to Ajay.

He wondered what she must have thought of Patpong, the outrageous sex district only a few blocks from Kanit House. Package tours flew in daily from Frankfurt to the precinct, which was famous the world over for its sex clubs, hustlers, tarts and transvestites. Thai boys thrust cards in tourists' hands promising 'Elephant smokes hash', 'Love with a goldfish', and other unlikely delights. The clubs, supposedly illegal, were Patpong's attraction. The atmosphere was relaxed and cheerful, with men and a few couples served drinks by Thai waitresses while naked women on stage light-heartedly penetrated each other with dildos or inserted goldfish into their vaginas and then flipped them into buckets across the stage. Using the same highly trained kegel muscles, performers could puff cigarettes or pop ping-pong balls across the room.

When Dominique came out of the shower, Marie-Andrée was up frying eggs and making the morning coffee.

'How was last night? Where did you go?' he asked.

'To a sex club,' she said, indicating by the tight set of her mouth that she was in no mood to elaborate. Marie-Andrée was angry with her husband again, he thought. There was psychological warfare going on between those two and he couldn't quite work it out. Sometimes he watched them go off into their bedroom and lock the door, and he heard low, angry voices. She was always sulking while Charles rarely dropped his friendly, warm-hearted sociability.

Marie-Andrée measured his medicine, a half glass of Kaopectate for his diarrhoea, and pushed it across the breakfast bar.

'Here you are, Dominique,' she said with brisk efficiency. He took a sip and decided to save the rest until he had eaten, thinking to himself that despite her cool manner, his hostess had a heart of gold. Without her he never would have remembered the medicine. His own memory often lapsed these days – but she never forgot.

The phone rang and he hurried to answer it, trying to make himself useful. A girl's voice asked in French, 'Is Charles there, please?'

'Charles?' Dominique replied, not connecting the name to his host Alain. 'There's no one named Charles living here.'

Charles' voice called from the bedroom, 'Tell whoever it is to hang on a minute.' A few seconds later he hurried out and took the phone.

'Yes? Oh, it's you. Yes, I'm here. No, I don't like the name Charles, so I have my friends call me "Alain". How are you this morning? What are you doing? Well, why not come up now. My wife is just making some coffee.'

When he put the phone down he told Dominique that he had met a French girl who lived downstairs. She could be useful in his gem business.

In the apartment below, twenty-one-year-old Nadine Gires hung up the receiver and stood in front of the bedroom mirror, tidying her brown hair and hurrying on some pink lipstick. She was tall, with an olive complexion, an attractive face and a straightforward gaze. She had been married for two years to a chef named Remy, and after he had been appointed chef at the Oriental Hotel, had lived in Bangkok for the past eighteen months. Remy worked long hours in the kitchens, and Nadine was lonely in 307a, their tiny Kanit House apartment. She had grown up in a suburb of Paris, the eldest of four daughters of a baker and a lady's maid, and was used to the convivial conflicts of a hardworking but happy family. So, the life of enforced leisure in Bangkok had been getting on her nerves. Sometimes she worked part-time at the Laotian embassy, translating English press cuttings into French. She attended the activities of the Alliance Française, but most of the French people she met there were of another generation and another world. They were snobbish and stylish. She had no patience with the fashion-plate diplomats in their white suits and their wives for whom Asia was a place to collect antiques.

Yesterday, she and Remy had been on their way out when a neighbour had come up and introduced himself as a fellow Frenchman. He was charming and very friendly and told them he was starting a cut-rate gem business. He flattered them by asking their advice as long-term residents of Thailand. Did they know of a printer for his gem catalogues? What did they think of the Thais?

'Don't trust them,' Nadine and Remy had said laughingly.

After he had come down and had coffee with them, he had suggested that since Nadine was at home alone most of the day, he might be able to offer her some work. She had asked him his name and he said it was Charles.

The upstairs apartment was on the opposite side of the building, and to reach it Nadine had to cross an open-air walkway that lined the two wings. She looked down over iron railings at the swimming pool, a small orange spirit house on its pedestal, and the car park. She disliked Kanit House, but it was cheap and close to the Oriental Hotel so Remy could walk to work and avoid the hellish traffic jams. Passing down a dim concrete hallway to the end of the wing, she reached number 504 and knocked on the turquoise door.

Charles opened it with a welcoming smile, dressed as he had been yesterday in dark slacks and an open-neck business shirt. A flat gold Rolex watch glinted on his wrist, hinting at a prosperity that was not echoed inside the apartment. It was much larger than her own, and a door opened onto a cement balcony that ran the length of the living room, shaded by white aluminium awnings. But the room was shadowy and dank and she was surprised to see a black punching bag hanging near the door. It seemed to be the only personal touch apart from a dog-eared stack of gemology magazines and books on the coffee table. In the corner stood a grey metal filing cabinet.

A dark-haired European woman looked up from the kitchenette where she was busy with cups and a jar of Nescafé. Charles introduced his wife, Monique, and his house-guest, Dominique, a thin, apologetic young man with a kind face. Then he disappeared back into the bedroom saying he had to finish getting ready for an appointment.

Marie-Andrée put the mugs on a tray. She did not look very friendly.

'I told you to take your medicine,' she said to the house-guest, adding the glass of milky liquid to the tray, which she set down on the coffee table.

'What's wrong with you?' Nadine asked.

'Oh, I don't know,' the boy smiled self-deprecatingly. 'My latest theory is malaria. I caught it in Chiang Mai three weeks ago, and I've been staying here ever since.'

'Haven't you been to the hospital?' Nadine asked.

'He doesn't need to do that,' Marie-Andrée said quickly. 'My husband is an expert on Asian diseases, and we're already looking after him here. Why should we pay for a hospital as well?'

'I'm quite willing to make a contribution for my upkeep,' Dominique interjected. 'Alain is taking care of my money, and . . .'

'My wife is a little bad-tempered this morning,' Charles said, coming swiftly out of the bedroom, his hair combed and shoes on.

The four of them sat drinking coffee. Ajay's bedroom door was closed. He was either still asleep or out. Sometimes he stayed overnight at the Hotel Malaysia.

Charles questioned Nadine about the French community in Thailand while Marie-Andrée played with the dog. He was curious about the contacts Nadine had made through the Alliance Française and the embassies she had worked for.

'Diplomats make great customers,' he said, holding a ruby up to the light. He was selling quality gems at wholesale prices, he told her. If she brought him customers, he would give her a 10 per cent commission. Apart from the sapphires and rubies he bought at the mines in Chanthaburi and the diamonds he got from Hong Kong, he had his own goldsmith in Bangkok who could design the settings according to his customers' specifications, or to his own.

'Well, think about it, Nadine, and we'll talk again later. It was lucky that we met, don't you think? Not that I believe in luck.'

Kissing Marie-Andrée lightly and picking up his attaché case, Charles excused himself, saying he had a business appointment. Nadine wondered if she should leave, but decided to stay since it was pleasant, sitting around, talking French. She lit another cigarette and walked to the windows overlooking the balcony. In a cage beside the railing she noticed a small monkey with its head in its hands. Marie-Andrée began clearing away the coffee cups.

'You should have been here last night,' said Marie-Andrée, who had started to enjoy Nadine's company. 'There was an American girl, Teresa. She told us such funny things about her sex life.'

'Americans are so outspoken,' Nadine smiled. 'How long have you been married to Alain?'

'Oh, we're not married. He just calls me his wife. He says that in Asia it's better for business. It makes a better impression. I've been living with him for a few years now,' she lied. 'I used to be a nurse in Canada.' That was another lie.

As she helped her clear up, Nadine thought that Marie-Andrée seemed nice, but there was a pained, resentful expression in her blue eyes. If they became friends, perhaps she would confide in her. It would be fun to have a girlfriend in Bangkok, Nadine thought.

After her first visit to number 504, its occupants became a part of Nadine's life and she dropped in every day. She was friendly with people from the airlines and embassies who were always looking for bargains to take back to Paris, so she agreed to work for Charles.

One morning Nadine went up to find that the monkey, Coco, had died. Marie-Andrée was very upset. 'It's your fault,' she said to

Dominique, who, Nadine noticed, seemed to be wasting away from his illness. 'You always leave your medicine around. Coco must have drunk it.'

On 18 October, five days after Teresa had first visited Kanit House, a fisherman dragged his small wooden boat into the gentle waves off Pattaya Beach. The red and yellow prayer flags knotted around the prow floated on top of the transparent green water as he threw his nets out and hauled them in.

It was a rhythm Chid Chamuen had known since he was a boy. He rowed adjacent to the beach, south of the resort area where the long white strip of sand was usually deserted. The sun was rising over the distant mountains as he passed the Sea Gull Bungalows, which were newly built and still secluded. Once Pattaya had been miles of white beach backed by jungle: no speedboats, no tourists. Now seafood restaurants lined the strip of Pattaya Beach. Chid had grown wealthy selling his catch directly to their kitchens. He rowed on, trailing his nets. Then, looking to the left, he saw something floating in the water. He rowed towards it. Sometimes the turtles came in, turtles as big as men. Their shells were valuable. As he came closer, he saw that it was not a turtle, but the body of a girl in a bikini, a drowned *farang*. She was floating face-down in the warm green water.

Blue blotches mottled the body. The short brown hair looked like seaweed as it washed back and forth. Chid believed it was bad luck to touch a corpse. He took the rope that was coiled under the seat and looped it around the body's neck and tied it to the side of the boat. With the red and yellow prayer ribbons floating beside it, the body was brought back to land and laid out on the beach in the sun. The local people gathered around in their sarongs and bamboo hats, looking curiously and hurrying away.

At 8.30 a.m. the local police arrived. There was no sign of injury on the body except a small cut on the neck believed to have been caused by the fisherman's rope. The fingers and toes were already turning blue. The eyes were closed. The right earlobe was pierced, but there was no jewellery on the body, nothing to identify the

tourist who had apparently drowned. The sergeant in charge took a
photograph of the body with his Instamatic.

On 4 November the *Bangkok Post*, an English-language daily, carried the photograph of Teresa lying on her back in a bikini with her
arms outstretched. Unable to identify the body, the police had sent
the picture to the newspaper. 'No traces of any foul play and police
and doctors inspecting the body concluded she must have drowned,'
the newspaper reported. An appeal was made for anyone who recognized the body to contact the police.

How did the body of Teresa Knowlton come to be floating in
the water that morning? Later, in another country, Charles would
offer a confession: knowing Teresa would check into the Hotel
Malaysia, he had sent Ajay to captivate her with his talk of cheap
gems. After she had visited his apartment, Teresa had been
delighted to accept Charles' invitation to join him for a weekend at
Pattaya. With Ajay he had picked Teresa up at the Hotel Malaysia.
He could not remember the exact date. Teresa was surprised that
Monique was not going with them to the beach resort. Charles
said she had stayed behind at Kanit House to look after their sick
house-guest.

With Teresa sitting between the two men, Charles drove the
rented Holden Torana south along Sukhumvit Highway, leaving the
city at 6.30 p.m. The road passed through rice paddies with black
buffaloes plodding through the water. During the journey Teresa put
her hand on his thigh, but he pushed it away, saying, 'No, Teresa, not
now.' He thought she was a nymphomaniac.

Teresa talked cheerfully and Ajay sat quietly, staring out the window, ready for whatever his boss might ask him to do. He was a
smart fellow, Charles thought, and he would claim later that the
Indian had been sent to him as an able assistant by the men in Hong
Kong.

There could be few more romantic bars than the one to which
Charles said he and Ajay took Teresa for her last drink. Under the
roof of thatched palm leaves, the view from the bar swept across the
Gulf of Thailand, through the silhouettes of palm trees that lined

the beach, to the sun setting behind the jagged offshore islands. To the left, the black sweep of the beach continued, unpopulated. Music from nightclubs and discos on the docks hung in the air. It was not the Asia that Teresa loved, the austere beauty of the Himalayas, the temple bells, the silence of the lamas at their ancient meditations. It was tourist Asia at its most seductive. As she looked across the bar, where the fishermen pulled their boats onto the beach, Charles dropped a sedative into her drink.

'I've got business on the strip,' Charles said. 'Let's meet back here at midnight and we'll drive to the bungalow. Maybe we'll have a swim before we sleep.'

He strolled to the Sandbox, a nearby disco where local rock bands blared out Western hits. During a break in the music a sheet of canvas was rolled out on the dance floor, and the crowds returned to their tables or sat close to the improvised boxing ring. Two teenagers with quivering muscles and bright satin shorts came on stage. With a quick balletic gyration each one made the ritual sign of homage and then they began to punch and kick each other. As bets were placed, money flashed among the audience as Charles filled in the hours until it was late enough to finish off his business with Teresa.

It was nearly twelve when he walked back to the car, where the smiling American girl and Ajay were waiting for him. They were leaning against the hood, joking with the strolling bar-girls and the children hustling cut-glass 'diamonds from Burma'.

'OK, let's go,' Charles said.

He drove south again, along Sukhumvit Highway towards Cambodia. Because of the fear of bandits who roamed the surrounding jungle, few people strayed from their homes or the brightly lit tourist areas, and traffic was sparse.

After about ten minutes, Charles turned towards the ocean at an ornate Buddhist temple on the side of the road, its five flashy pagodas standing out against the sky. He drove for 3 kilometres until he reached the edge of the beach, where the road was briefly paved. He drove past two construction sites for new tourist bungalows. He kept going for a short distance until the road reverted to dirt and there was no sign of settlement. It was deserted although less than a mile from the Sea Gull Bungalows. After bumping across a field he turned off the lights and the engine. The field faced a long, grey strip of beach that stretched away endlessly to the horizon and down the coast towards Cambodia.

Charles would later claim that he could remember his last conversation with Teresa quite clearly.

'Do you know the reason I brought you here?' he asked as they got out of the car.

'Yes,' she answered, 'for a weekend at the beach.'

'There is something else, too,' Charles said, moving around the car to her side. 'Who do you work for?'

'What do you mean?' she asked, surprised. 'I'm not working. I'm on my way to Kathmandu. I'm going into retreat at Kopan Monastery, to teach the children.'

'Teresa, I don't think you are telling me the truth,' he said softly, putting his hand on her shoulder as if she were a little girl.

'Yes, I am.'

'You know, this really doesn't interest me. I've been engaged in illegal matters for a long time now, and I know you came here to do a little business.'

'Oh, well, sometimes I have done some business,' she agreed.

'Yes, and many people who have lived in Kathmandu like to take a little powder through,' he said.

'You mean from here to there?' she asked.

'Yes. It's easier to take from Kathmandu to Europe. From here direct is getting difficult.'

'I suppose so.'

'Tell me, Teresa, do you have to take something from here to Kathmandu this time? Do you?'

'No,' she said, and continued to deny that she was involved with heroin. But Charles was not to be convinced.

'Come, Teresa, I think you have to do a little business,' he said, his voice low but resolute. Ajay was staring straight ahead.

'No, Alain, you're crazy,' she insisted, shaking her head at his questions, starting to feel foggy and confused from the capsule he had dropped in her drink.

'I think you do have to carry some powder, Teresa, and you are silly to hide this from me. You see, I already know the one who has to give it to you.'

'You do?'

'Yes, I know.'

They stayed silent for a while. There was just the sound of the waves. When she seemed to relax again, Charles said, 'Teresa, how do you like Kathmandu? How do you like the life there?'

'It's good,' she said. 'I can't wait to get back.'

'Don't you think what you are doing now could harm another human being? You know what it's like at the other end of the heroin market. You say you study meditation, and part of this philosophy is to respect the human being. Don't you think that what you do is contrary to this respect?'

This was a game he loved – ensnaring people in their own contradictions.

'Well, you know, Alain, I only do it for the money.' And then she said, 'Did you put something in my drink? I'm feeling weird.'

'It was only to relax you, Teresa, because I must tell you that I think I have to do something bad to you.'

'What's that?'

'Well, you choose your way of making money. You know the risk of it. Sometimes the risk can be high.'

'What are you going to do to me?'

'It's not my fault. I have the order to do something to you, and I have to carry out my order.'

'Are you going to beat me up?'

'No, Teresa, I am not going to beat you.'

'What are you going to do?'

'Something better.'

Ajay opened a vacuum flask and poured coffee into a cup, then he took three capsules from his pocket. In each of these, according to the story Charles would later tell, was fifty milligrams of Mogadon, five tablets ground to powder and packed inside. Charles dropped these capsules into the coffee.

'Drink it,' he commanded.

'I don't drink coffee,' she said.

'This time you will have to make an exception, Teresa.'

'What will it do?'

'You will just sleep. I want to keep you asleep.'

'What for?'

'We are going to visit some people now to talk business. I don't want you to see the way. Afterwards, we will ask you some questions, and you can go.'

'Really?'

'Yes, Teresa. Just drink up and it will all be over soon.'

Later Charles described how he and Ajay undressed Teresa Knowlton, put her in a bikini and removed her jewellery. She didn't struggle. Then he took a two-way radio from the back of the car and walked through the prickly pear bushes and low scrub to the road. Ajay stripped to his underpants. Charles searched for signs of traffic or people, and then whispered the signal to Ajay, who backed the car onto the road and parked it on the grassy bank by the beach.

'Take her for a swim,' he told Ajay, who put her arm around his shoulder and his hand around her waist. He helped her from the car and down the embankment. Then he dragged her across the sand to the water's edge, picked her up, carried her into the water and swam out with her. Then he let her go.

On 18 October Teresa was found by the fisherman. Charles would claim he killed Teresa on the same night he collected her from the Hotel Malaysia, but records show that she checked out on 14 October – four days earlier. Her whereabouts during those days remain a mystery.

With no responses to the *Bangkok Post* story forthcoming, Teresa's unidentified corpse was wrapped in a plastic bag and buried in the local Sawang Boriboon Cemetery. On the day she was buried, her grandmother, Emma Knowlton, wrote to her at Kopan Monastery:

'I am very worried about you. I haven't heard from you since you left, and I can't understand it. Anyway, we are fine here. Steve and Grandpa are getting on well, and the garden has been lovely, with a big crop of courgettes.'

For seven months the body of Teresa Knowlton rested anonymously in the overgrown field.

10

The 'Hit List'

On a steamy afternoon in late October, Nadine lay in a deck-chair beside the swimming pool dabbing suntan oil on her shoulders. She took off her sunglasses and looked up when she heard Marie-Andrée calling down to her from the balcony of the top-floor apartment.

'You don't go in, Nadine? You're always sunbathing.'

'Come and join me,' Nadine shouted back, waving, 'and then I'll go in.' She was nervous in the water, and usually splashed around in the shallows of the chlorinated pool.

'I'll be down in a few minutes,' Marie-Andrée called.

Over the last few days the two women had come to know each other better. Marie-Andrée was obviously lonely. She was in love with Charles, but Nadine thought this seemed to make her miserable. She could see why Marie-Andrée was so crazy about the gem-dealer. What an unusual man, prosperous in business, charming, intelligent, a real man of the world. She sensed there was something curious about their relationship, something secretive and hidden. It was very different from the intimacy and companionship she had found with Remy. But then, the two men were such opposites.

Nadine had to admit that Charles was charismatic, sexy and domineering in an almost hypnotic way. Even so, at the back of her mind she wondered if he was using tricks he had learned from all the psychology books lying around his flat. Remy wasn't sure about him. Charles made him unaccountably suspicious and he rarely went up to number 504.

Marie-Andrée arrived by the pool. Her hair was pinned up, and in the glaring sunlight the lines of her forehead were etched deeply. She sat down, hunching her arms around her knees. Nadine asked her why she looked so unhappy.

'So many people coming and going and doing business, and I'm the one who has to clean up after them,' she replied.

'But doesn't Dominique help?'

'He tries, but he's so sick.' Marie-Andrée paused and then added bitterly, 'Charles has met another Thai girl. Roong!' She spat out the name like a curse. 'We were having lunch at the Indra coffee shop, and he started talking to the waitress. I could see what was happening. She's eighteen. Now he sees her every day, and he says, "You know that this is only for business. I need Thai girls to help me." He buys her presents, takes her out. And me, I am just his wife, and his wife is just the woman he is cheating on.'

Marie-Andrée was not the first European woman to confide in Nadine about a husband's Thai mistress. In diplomatic circles it was often said that only a strong marriage could survive a posting to Bangkok.

'You know, Monique, you don't have to stand for it. If it makes you so unhappy, you can always leave.'

'I know. Sometimes I think I'll go, then he says he needs me, and I know he does. If it wasn't for me, I'm sure he'd never eat. All he thinks about is his business.'

They lay side by side in the deck-chairs, their eyes hidden from one another by sunglasses.

'Nadine?'

'Yes?'

'My name isn't really Monique. My name is Marie-Andrée, but Alain doesn't like it, so he gave me the name Monique.'

Nadine remembered that Charles had once said: 'I don't like the name Charles, so I ask my friends to call me Alain.'

'I think Marie-Andrée is a nice name,' she said, glad that her neighbour was beginning to confide in her.

On 5 November, the day after the picture of Teresa's body appeared in the *Bangkok Post*, François Dubily sat on the sofa at number 504, mentally reviewing the events that had brought him there.

He didn't like it when his life went out of control, as it had been since he arrived in Bangkok with his old friend Yannick Masy. It was more than irritating, and Charles had not failed to make jokes about the fact that both men were ex-detectives and both had now been robbed on the same day.

Yannick was talking with Charles about the gem business. He seemed happy to be here and not at all bothered that his passport and traveller's cheques were gone. Yannick's pale-blue eyes were alive with adoration for their suave French-Vietnamese host, who had introduced himself as Alain Gautier. Yes, François knew all the signs. Yannick was being swept away again.

A similar passion had led to his friend's resignation from the police force in Paris in May 1968. Yannick had been so inflamed by the rhetoric of the student revolutionaries that he had switched sides. Naturally he was fired, and François, a quiet, solidly built young man with a dark-brown beard and pale skin, had resigned in solidarity. They had worked at other jobs in France to save money to travel, but not enough. Bangkok was a city where many young men stayed longer than they had originally intended. By the time they were ready to leave they were so low on funds that they were ready to listen to the American they had met one night in the Blue Fox, a bar opposite the Hotel Malaysia. He had told them about 'Alain Gautier'. It seemed that the name was on every traveller's lips. The following night 'Alain' himself turned up at the bar and assured them he could help them all find work.

First, he took them to the immigration compound, folding a 100-baht note inside each of their passports. He had arranged an extension for their visas. Then he had given them a ride down to Pattaya, telling them that they would certainly find work in one of the big tourist hotels. Yannick had been a chef before he became a policeman. But none of the hotels that lined the palm-fringed beach strip were interested in employing them.

Now, back on the sofa at Kanit House, François tapped out his pipe and rummaged in his pocket for a tin of tobacco. There was a knock on the door, and Nadine ushered in two new customers whom she introduced to Charles. Then she joined François on the sofa and asked him what had happened when he went to Pattaya with Charles.

'It was very strange,' he began. After breakfast at Sangkew Bungalows, François had suddenly felt sick and went to lie down in the room he shared with Ajay. When he woke up, his passport and remaining traveller's cheques were gone. Charles had told him it must have been one of the staff at the bungalows. Then at dinner that night Yannick had become dizzy. He was helped from the table and they all walked along the strip, but Yannick remembered he had left his shoulder-bag behind. They rushed back. The bag was gone.

'It's probably as well for the French police force that you two have left it,' Charles joked, and then suggested they both come to stay with him at Kanit House. While waiting for their new passports and traveller's cheques, he offered, they could help him sell gems. He would rent the adjoining apartment for them.

'Yes, he's so generous,' Nadine said. 'You were lucky to meet him.'

François nodded in agreement. 'I think my friend Yannick is almost glad that it happened. He thinks Alain is some kind of guru. He isn't even bothering to apply for a new passport. Me? I've been going to the embassy every day. It takes so long. Now Alain says he will employ me to sit around the bars and tell people about his bargain-priced sapphires and rubies.'

The two new customers Nadine had just brought to the flat walked over with Charles and sat down, both looking pleased.

'Your friends want to go snorkelling at Pattaya,' Charles said to Nadine. 'Ajay and I are going to Chanthaburi for more stones tomorrow, and we can drop them on the way.'

Yes, Nadine thought, he really was a helpful neighbour.

The next day, at midnight, Nadine and Remy were in bed when the phone rang.

Remy answered and listened, his face becoming grim. 'OK, you'd better come back here and spend the night. And go to the police in the morning.'

'What's wrong?' Nadine asked, sitting up and lighting a cigarette.

'Looks like your friend Alain Gautier is a thief,' Remy said, putting down the phone. The call had been from their two friends who had gone to Pattaya with Charles and Ajay. They had just returned to the bungalow they shared with them and discovered that everything was gone, their passports and $4,000 of traveller's cheques.

'I told them to stay at the Tropicana and put their money in the hotel safe,' Nadine said to her husband, 'especially after what happened to François and Yannick. Why didn't they listen? Air France employees get fifty per cent off at the Tropicana, and it's much nicer than that creepy bungalow.'

'Your friend Mr Gautier can be very persuasive, my darling,' Remy said as he turned out the light and got back into bed.

In the morning after she had spoken to her two friends, who had thumbed a ride back from Pattaya, Nadine walked slowly upstairs to the apartment on the top floor. Marie-Andrée opened the door. She was wearing flared jeans and a black nylon T-shirt, and obviously hadn't brushed her hair.

'Is Alain back yet?'

'No. Come in, Nadine. Have some coffee. They're still at the gem mines.'

'Monique, forgive me for asking, but how well do you know Ajay?'

'He's a good friend of Alain's. I like him, don't you?'

The two women sat on bar stools while Nadine told Marie-Andrée that her friends said Ajay had left them suddenly during dinner, which was when their money was stolen.

'Oh, Nadine, that's dreadful. How can you imply Ajay is involved? Alain will be upset.'

That night Nadine was home alone while Remy worked late at the Oriental. The phone rang. It was Charles, and he sounded angry.

'It's ridiculous what you're saying about Ajay,' he said to her, 'and very unfair. His father is a big film producer in Bombay. The whole family is rich. He doesn't need to steal.'

By the time she put the phone down, Nadine was reassured. Charles was so certain about Ajay and, after all, he had confronted her head on, not like someone guilty or suspicious of his friend.

Later, Charles spoke to Nadine's two friends. He told them their allegations were slanderous and unfounded, and that Pattaya was renowned for its high crime rate. The two young men were by this time less certain that it was Ajay who had stolen their belongings. It was flimsy and unconvincing evidence, really. 'Circumstantial,' Charles called it. So they apologized.

'While you wait for the return of your money,' Charles told them, 'I will rent you a downstairs apartment and lend you some cash, but before you leave Thailand, you must repay me.'

He drew up a contract to that effect, and they signed it. 'I must tell you,' he said, 'that in Paris I studied law, so if you do leave Bangkok without paying me back, I could sue you in the courts.'

Nadine was now reassured that Ajay had nothing to do with the thefts at Pattaya and that the incident a week earlier with the two French policemen was a coincidence. Remy, however, was not convinced. 'You know, darling, you can keep working for him if you like, but my nose is good, and in my opinion there's something about this clever friend of yours that smells bad.'

Nadine did keep working for Charles. During the International Gem Convention at the Bangkok Indra Hotel, she marvelled at his ease with the managers of the most exclusive jewellery shops in Paris. His business was booming, and he was planning to buy his own jewellery shop. His Thai girlfriend Ann would be the official owner since it was illegal for foreigners to own businesses in Thailand.

One day after a trip to some jewellery shops, Nadine happened to be standing behind Charles when he opened his attaché case to remove customers' business cards and saw a false beard and a moustache in a plastic bag. 'Alain,' she giggled uncomfortably as she reached to pick them up, 'what do you do with these things?'

He grabbed them from her and put them back in the case, snapping it shut as he said coldly, 'In this business, Nadine, you have to be prepared for anything. It's a rough game. But that's not your problem. Your job is to bring me more customers.'

Now he smiled warmly at her. 'You've been doing very well.'

As Charles' fortunes swelled, so too did the ranks of his followers. In the short time Nadine had known him, she saw Charles enlist the two French ex-detectives, Yannick and François, and a young German boy called Reiner Stein, whom she had introduced to Charles and who was helping plan the new gem shop.

Then Nadine met a new visitor at 504, Ved, a handsome Turk who had just arrived in Bangkok. He had seemed stoned. But the next evening, when she arrived at number 504, he looked pale and barely seemed to know where he was.

Ved's real name was Vitali Hakim, a Sephardic Jew whose ancestors had fled to Turkey from the Spanish Inquisition. His family owned a thriving textile business in Istanbul and Ved had been groomed to inherit it. He was well educated and spoke five languages fluently. But despite his gifts, Ved had partied, getting into LSD when he moved to the golden beaches of Ibiza. Smuggling was an island tradition, with several eighteenth-century pirates commemorated on an obelisk in the main square of Ibiza Town. Bringing marijuana to the people was considered a noble profession; the locals had long funnelled whisky and cigarettes to mainland Spain. Ved soon began smuggling marijuana, and then moved on to heroin. A kilo of pure 'No. 4' heroin could be bought for $4,000 in Bangkok. Heavily diluted it would fetch $250,000 on the streets of New York or Europe. The merchandise changed, and so did Ved's style. He became a careless dealer, sloppy and indiscreet. To those who knew him, it was a tragedy to watch his decline. He had become a junkie.

All of this was unknown to the residents of Kanit House. To Nadine, Ved was yet another hippie traveller come to Bangkok to get high and crash out in Charles' apartment. But as Charles was later to claim, Vitali Hakim was the other name that André Breugnot had given him just before Charles had murdered him in Chiang Mai. So Ved was the next on his hit list.

By the summer of 1975, Ved's next trip to Bangkok had been organized. It would be financed by a fellow Turk who was living with a Danish woman on the island of Formentera, another Balearic paradise off the coast of Spain. Their operation was known locally as 'the Danish–Turkish connection'. The couple would arrange couriers to collect consignments of heroin from Ved and bring them into Europe. Having spent time himself on Formentera, Ved had met a twenty-four-year-old Parisian girl called Stephanie Parry. She had come to the island three years before, in 1972, to see her older sister and had decided to stay. She was a beauty, but withdrawn. Spellbound by the island, she moved into an old stone farmhouse and made her living by designing dresses to be sold at boutiques in nearby Ibiza or in Madrid. Still, she missed home. Stephanie had told her family in Paris that she would be back for Christmas. That was her plan. She didn't mention that she would be flying there via Bangkok.

When he had closed his house up earlier that month in Ibiza, Ved personified the extravagance of the 1970s – long, wavy hair, embroidered shirts and platform heels. As he said goodbye to his friends he was carrying enough cash to provide for his own needs and two couriers. Assuming that each of them could smuggle 2–3 kilograms, he must have had $10–20,000 on him when he landed in Bangkok.

On the evening of 27 October, when Nadine entered number 504, she found Hakim slumped in one of the armchairs. Reiner was sitting at the bar going over the lease on a factory space that he and Charles were planning to rent, while Charles was talking quietly with Yannick, whom he had put in charge of his filing system. Tall and fair, the ex-policeman looked self-important as he nodded in agreement with Charles.

'Hi, Ved,' she said, 'how are you?'

'Good to see you, Nadine,' he said wearily, pushing his long hair back from his face and neck with be-ringed fingers. 'I think I'm getting sick. It began, I don't know, after dinner last night.' She touched his forehead. It was hot.

'Alain, Ved's getting a fever,' she called across the room. 'You know, I've been in Thailand eighteen months now, and until I started coming to your apartment, I'd never seen so many people sick,' she laughed.

'At least I'm looking after them, Nadine. Do you expect me to abandon them to Thai medical care?'

Several people in the room laughed.

Later, his friends thought that Vitali Hakim's carelessness in consorting with a complete stranger like Charles reflected his constant need for company. Heroin dealers on business trips normally kept to themselves. Most chose middle-class hotels and behaved discreetly. The flamboyant clothes and platform boots reflected his insecurity. To him the suave Eurasian who held court over a group of nomadic Westerners would have seemed supremely self-assured, even mesmerising. Moreover, Ved was back on heroin after trying to give it up, and weighed only 57 kilograms. Oddly, when Charles later confided about the night of 27 October he recalled Ved as 'a hard man, a strong man, a real Turk'.

At about 11 p.m. the other guests in the apartment were surprised to learn that Ved was going with Charles and Ajay to the gem mines that night. Charles told them that Ved had decided to make such a large order of stones that it was necessary to go to the wholesalers.

Dominique, still an unwitting captive of number 504, later recalled that when Ved left the apartment, loosely supported by Charles and Ajay, he seemed to be staggering.

Charles wanted this to be a different kind of murder. His instructions from Hong Kong, he would later say, suggested it was time to make an example of one of these amateurs. It was for this reason that he had already packed a can of petrol in the boot of his car – a maroon Holden Torana that was parked downstairs.

Vitali Hakim was still very drowsy, lying in the back seat, when the car came to a halt soon after they had set off. Charles and Ajay opened the back doors, rolled him onto the floor and handcuffed him to the bottom of the seat. Stuffing his mouth with a rag and taping it shut, Charles told his guest that soon he would be asking him some questions. Leaving Ajay in the back, he slipped behind the wheel and drove south.

Later that night the car stopped at the fishing village of Si Racha. He needed rest, Charles said, and he wanted to leave the Turk some time to think, a few hours of silent terror that would break down any resistance or loyalty. The Turk had names and addresses that Charles needed. Ajay stayed with the prisoner that night, while Charles slept in a bungalow.

Late the next day they set off in the direction of Chanthaburi.

'Did you give him the sodium pentothal?' Charles asked Ajay, who was checking on the sleeping figure under the blanket. The Indian smiled back – he had Charles to thank for teaching him to use a syringe.

Dozens of dirt roads branched off the highway and Charles turned right on one of them, stopping when he spotted a secluded clearing through the trees. With Ajay's help, Charles ungagged Vitali Hakim and dragged him into a field. His eyes stared up at their moonlit faces.

Charles began the interrogation by asking him the names of his contacts. 'The operation was small,' Ved protested, 'only a family business.' He said the couriers were just hippies living on Ibiza.

Charles wasn't satisfied. He thought the man was sly, revealing a fragment in order to hide the whole story. No one could beat Charles at that game. He had practised the technique in police stations all over the world.

Ajay re-cuffed Ved's hands and squatted on the grass near him, watching. With others Ajay could be lively, but working with Charles he usually looked on silently, a mute gravedigger.

'We're professionals, Hakim,' Charles said. 'If you don't tell us, you will disappear and nobody will care. You're in Asia, so who's going to help you?'

Later he would claim to reveal what happened next:

When I had beaten him enough, I took off the gag. The first person he told us about was Stephanie Parry. We beat him some more, and then he said he had two people in Peshawar. I was writing the names and addresses down on a piece of paper about the size of a chequebook. He said these two men could come anywhere to help him or the courier if there was any trouble. I beat him again, and then he told me about Spain. He had another Turk there, someone with a joint bank account. I wrote it down. This was the man who knew all about the

Danish–Turkish connection to the Copenhagen operation. I
beat him for about another twenty minutes, and he told me
about Hong Kong and the name of a top dealer there. He used
to buy hash in Hong Kong. And he also gave me one of his
contacts in Amsterdam and some small fry, a few couriers he
had used before. I just took all the names. He told me that
Stephanie Parry was coming and would stay at the President
Hotel. I sent Ajay to the car for the scissors. This was in case
the fellow had anything more to tell. He had long hair, and so
to break down his last resistance, I cut it all off.

Charles and Ajay re-gagged Vitali Hakim, put him in the car and
drove back towards Pattaya. Before reaching the resort, they turned
right off the highway, along the road to the Siam Country Club.
After 5 kilometres they turned right onto a dirt path and drove a few
metres. As the path curved, it was hidden from the road by tapioca
plants and palm trees:

Ajay and I dragged the Turk out of the car, and – clack! – I
broke his neck. I took out the petrol and left it next to the body.
I reversed the car back onto the road and faced it in the direction of the highway, about 600 metres from the track. Then I
came back to Ajay, and we threw some rags over his face and
poured petrol on it. It burns better that way. The rags stop the
liquid from evaporating. If you put it straight on the face, most
of the petrol just runs to the ground.

I poured some more under the head and the body, and all
through his clothes, soaking them, otherwise it would have
just burned the grass. You know, this is one job I wanted to be
a message. Not for everyone – just the people who sent him.
That's why I took him back to Pattaya. I wanted it to be in the
same area as Teresa. I wanted it to be a deterrent to the others
in the business.

And so, after the petrol had soaked through everything, I say
to Ajay, 'OK, in one minute you light, and as soon as you do,

run towards the car.' Already I started hurrying to the car because I knew there would be a big flame. I got in the car, turned on the lights, and then I saw it. *Whoooooosh!* A big red flame, the whole sky lit up. Ajay came running, and we drove off.

The small wooden house of Tuan Chanmark, a rice farmer, lay a few kilometres from the sea, down the road to the Siam Country Club. The house was set back half a kilometre from the road, hidden behind a grove of coconut palms. The country that surrounded it, emerald-green rice paddies and the lighter green of the tapioca fields, was still bathed in the monochromes of the cool dawn when, at 4.30 a.m. on 28 October, Tuan arose and went outside to start his day's work. It was then that he saw a fire in the direction of the road, about 500 metres from his house, but he paid no attention to it, assuming that a farmer was burning grass or rice stubble. At 6 a.m. when it was full daylight, he happened to walk up the track and came across a charred body, still smoking. It lay at the edge of a bamboo patch beside a tall coconut palm. The eyes in the blackened face were closed; the nose half burned off. There was something reminiscent of the praying mantis in the way the hands were raised as though in supplication. The legs were splayed out, the head was thrown back.

Tuan Chanmark walked around the body. The last tongues of flame that had consumed the figure's black shirt, with its pattern of yellow stars, had gone out. Later that day the police arrived at the scene. The ground was hard, so they found no tyre marks on the grass that led from the road to the corpse. The clothing that remained, a pair of blue underpants and zippers at the wrists which had burned into the skin, might have furnished clues but they weren't examined. One of the villagers who came to look noticed that there were a few hairs still left on the legs, and that they were light brown, but this wasn't reported to the police until much later.

Lieutenant Suthipong Ramawong, who was in charge of the investigation, assumed the case was a suicide. It was probably one of the many Thai ex-employees of the former American bases flocking to Pattaya in hope of getting work. These people were impossible to trace, and the death of one of them was not of enough importance to warrant an investigation. Without ceremony, the corpse of Vitali Hakim was wrapped in a sheet of plastic and buried in the Sawang Boriboon Cemetery, only a short distance from another unmarked grave, that of Teresa Knowlton.

When Nadine visited number 504 the next day, wondering if the Turk was feeling better, she was told that he had gone off on a trip with Charles and Ajay.

'And so, what happened to him?' Nadine asked Marie-Andrée.

'Oh, Alain says he met some of his druggy friends in Pattaya and decided to stay there.'

'But what about his things?' Nadine asked. She had noticed his silver necklace lying on the coffee table, and his case was still in the bedroom.

'Oh, he'll be coming back to collect them in a few days,' Marie-Andrée said.

A few days later Dominique sat on one of the stools next to the cock-tail bar idly reading the label of a bottle of Kaopectate. This was the medicine Monique had been giving him since he had first arrived, and he had been drinking it dutifully. But strangely, it was only when he did not get around to taking a dose from the bottle that he ever felt better. 'Do not use for more than two days or in the presence of high fever,' said the tiny print. He began to wonder – it was impos-sible – if he might be being poisoned? Surely not. What would be the reason?

He felt better today because he had not taken the medicine recently. But Monique and Alain were angry, saying that he was cost-ing them so much money by being sick that if he wanted to get well, he should take more Kaopectate. Sometimes Monique had to bring his meals to him in bed. How could he suspect them of drugging him? This illness was affecting his mind. But he did suspect. In that case all he had to do to test his theory was to take the medicine one more time and note its effects. Yes, he would have to be sure what was happening.

Despite his illness Dominique had enjoyed the communal lifestyle at Kanit House for the first few weeks because there was always so much happening around Charles. He had a zest for life which the mild young banker had never experienced before. The first few days had been something out of a fantasy; nightclubs, discos, expensive restaurants, gambling, and trips to Pattaya and the gem mines.

It was on one of those very enjoyable weekends that Yannick and François had both been robbed of their passports and money. Later, when Nadine's two friends had lost theirs in similar circumstances, the coincidence disturbed Dominique. Was Alain a passport thief? Well, it's none of my affair, Dominique had decided. But I'd better get out of here as soon as I can.

It wasn't so easy. Each time he asked Charles to return his passport, he just made an excuse, saying, 'Oh, tomorrow, tomorrow, it's still in my safe at the bank.'

He had also noticed that Ajay had started to carry a nine-inch flick-knife, which was not uncommon in Bangkok. The Indian was always asking Dominique to do the laundry or to make coffee. In fact, he and François did most of the daily chores now. Yannick had become more of a personal secretary to Charles. The gem business was booming. All over the apartment, saucers were filled with sapphires and rubies, and customers constantly streamed through the door.

When Nadine's two friends who had lost their valuables at Pattaya returned to Paris, Dominique and François were moved downstairs into 103, the apartment they had vacated. Alain said that he wanted him off the couch because so many customers were coming to buy gems.

Dominique had watched Yannick counting out piles of 100-baht notes. One morning he saw Charles walking down to the car with wads of baht in his hands, almost as if he wanted everyone by the pool to see how much he was making. He was spending a lot, too, with the five people he supported in the apartment and all the people coming through. Sometimes Charles would sell the stones at a huge profit. At others he seemed to sell at a loss, just to meet more people. It didn't make sense.

Dominique now often thought of Les Sables-d'Olonne, his village, with its yachts and fishing boats bobbing peacefully in the port and the string of waterside restaurants with candles, shiny silverware and red-checked tablecloths where he used to eat with his family. His mother was worried, as well as grateful. She had promised Dominique that she would 'send Alain Gautier a wonderful Christmas present' in return for looking after her wandering son. Dominique was determined to be home by Christmas. He had seen enough of the East.

The young Frenchman poured himself a half glass from the Kaopectate bottle. He knew he must be feeling a little better even to do this experiment. For the past eight weeks he had not had enough clarity to make any decisions at all. He had lost 9 kilograms in weight. Sometimes he tried to force a decisive act, but in the end he just sat around, inert, unable to budge. Always there was the sensation of falling, falling. He would soon know. Dominique gulped down the chalky white liquid. He began counting. By the time he reached sixty, he felt dizzy again and began to sway. Then crash! Dominique fell to the floor.

Behind the million neon lights of Kowloon, the mountains of China were black, almost invisible forms against the night sky. But from Nathan Road and the windows of the Chungking Mansions all that could be seen were the lights of Hong Kong, doubled by their reflection in the wet streets and multiplied by the illuminations of Christmas. It was 8 December, only seventeen more shopping days to go in the shopping capital of the world. Cardboard faces of Santa Claus hung between the vertical signs of Chinese characters. All the storefronts glittered with artificial Christmas trees, and the record shops played carols over the din of the traffic.

Cocky and Henk, the two thrifty Dutch travellers, were in their room at the International Guest House of the Chungking Mansions. One dollar a night for a comfortable room with Western plumbing and a television lounge, it was on the same floor as the Boston Guest House where Teresa Knowlton had stayed. It wasn't the first time their paths had almost crossed. The Malaysia in Bangkok was another bargain hotel where they had stayed at the same time as Teresa.

They had left Thailand, the two wrote home, because of the rainy season. Since arriving in Hong Kong three weeks ago they had visited the nearby Portuguese island of Macao, where they stayed ten days before taking the ferry back to the British Crown colony and the guest house. Here they had left most of their luggage. Over the last few days they had been occupied with buying Christmas presents for their family and with getting to know a most unusual man. Cocky still found time to keep up her correspondence. That night she wrote to her sister and brother-in-law in Amsterdam, Marijke and John Zant:

Hong Kong
8th December 1975

Dear Marijke and John,

It is now 1.30 a.m. and we have just come back from a night-club. The reason why I am writing to you so suddenly is the following: I have a white golden ring set with a deep blue sapphire and surrounded by 14 tiny little diamonds. It is so beautiful that I immediately wanted to write to you. But I will tell you first how this all came about.

Henk was sitting watching TV yesterday in the hotel here, but as the film wasn't any good, he started talking to a Frenchman, who seemed to deal in precious stones between Bangkok and Hong Kong. He told Henk that he and his wife liked travelling very much and were even earning their living that way. He knew that we were going to Bangkok and asked if Henk was interested in seeing the mines. This morning we went to his hotel room in the Hyatt Regency Hotel (refrigerator, closet with pushbuttons: when you pushed a button, you got whisky, cognac, Coca-Cola, gin, etc. all in small bottles, colour TV, wall-to-wall carpeting, radio etc.). He wanted to teach Henk how to appraise precious gems and showed us all kinds of stones. He then asked us to have lunch with him, but we declined because the hotel was so expensive, and we didn't want to appear too greedy by accepting it. In the evening he came to our hotel (he has a friend who lives here) to give us his address in Thailand and he asked if we would join him to have a drink in the bar of his hotel. I told him in the bar that I was interested in stones, but only in order to make a ring. After we went back to his room, he got a white gold ring with a light blue sapphire. I looked a long time before deciding on a very pretty one. With a lot of pressing we put the stone in the setting and the ring is really very pretty. We got the setting at factory price, but not the stone, because that was the prettiest in the collection that he had just bought. All in all, the ring was very cheap because here you can buy diamonds very cheaply and in Thailand sapphires and rubies are cheap, as long as you buy them in large quantities.

Later in the evening we had dinner in the Hyatt and sat afterwards in the nightclub. He insisted on paying and it really added up, and he also asked us to stay at his apartment in Bangkok. We were already offered a typically French meal, because a French cook will be staying with him when we are in Bangkok. Something to look forward to.

With all his generosity it could work out that the ring will cost us nothing ... sounds very greedy, but we have offered several times to pay for things and he didn't want to hear about it. Just send me a souvenir from Holland, he said.

When Cocky's brother-in-law read the letter in his Amsterdam apartment, he thought it strange that anyone would be selling such a ring so cheaply. He said to his wife, 'Cocky and Henk have met someone playing Santa Claus.' He did not worry about them. Cocky and Henk were wary people, and he felt sure they would not be easily tricked.

Zant was right. Henk recorded his misgivings about the gem-dealer in his journal:

I was already wondering last night if our French friend was not a swindler who was adeptly cheating us by asking a high price as we don't know anything about precious stones. That's why we looked at the shop windows of the many jewellers who are nearby and there are dozens of shops in the neighbourhood. I find out that we bought the ring for roughly half the price they ask in the shops.

When Charles returned to Kanit House from Hong Kong on 9 December, Dominique informed him that a girl had been phoning all the previous day asking for Ved. 'She sounded worried,' he said.

Dominique was trying to present his normal, everyday front to Charles. Since his Kaopectate experiment he was confused about exactly what had happened to him – and why. He was waiting for the chance to get his passport and go.

'Did the girl leave her name?' Charles asked as he threw his attaché case on the sofa.

'Yes,' said Dominique. 'It was Stephanie, I think.'

Charles went into his bedroom, shut the door and called the President Hotel. He asked for Stephanie Parry. The courier from Formentera had checked into the hotel two days earlier, on 7 December.

'Hello, Stephanie. This is Alain,' he said when she answered the phone. 'I'm a friend of Hakim's.'

'Where is he?' she asked.

'Let's talk about that when we meet. I have a message for you from him. Could you be in the foyer at eleven?' he asked. 'Sit near the reception desk and read a copy of the *Bangkok Post*.'

As Charles would later tell the story, it was ten minutes to eleven when he walked through the revolving door and into the foyer of the President Hotel. Prosperous-looking tourists were milling about or sitting at the small gilt tables writing postcards. Charles sat on a sofa opposite the lifts – he wanted to observe the girl for a few minutes before introducing himself, just in case she was under the protection of another organization. A very pretty girl stepped out of the lift, and, looking at her, Charles did not need the agreed-upon signal of the newspaper to tell who she was. She was wearing a mauve floral dress without a bra. Her eyes were circled with black kohl. With her long brown hair and glowing suntan she stood out from the other tourists.

He watched her as she sat down and a few minutes later he joined her. She said she was worried that Hakim had not returned the phone calls. Charles told her that her friend was on a short trip to the gem mines.

When Stephanie seemed relaxed, Charles said, 'Actually, I'm going to Pattaya this afternoon, which is near the mines. I could take you to meet Hakim.'

No doubt disturbed by Ved's failure to make contact, the young Frenchwoman had nowhere else to turn. Alone in Bangkok on a dangerous mission, and short of cash, Stephanie welcomed this invitation from a sympathetic go-between and checked out of the hotel with Charles.

Much later that night, she found herself sitting in a car on a deserted road south of Pattaya, with Charles and Ajay each side of her. Charles was not interested in questioning her. She was just a courier. The dose of Mogadon he had given her at lunch had begun to take effect. He looked across at Ajay, pointed to a spot and got out of the car.

'OK, Ajay, let's get this done,' Charles said as he dragged the groggy woman out of the front seat of the car and propped her up against a tree on the bank of a tidal creek.

The Indian squatted down beside her, his hands circled her neck, and then he choked Stephanie Parry to death.

11

Everything Falls into Place

On Friday afternoon, 12 December 1975, three days after Stephanie
Parry had checked out of the President Hotel, Nadine walked up
the stairs at Kanit House, curious to meet the new arrivals. The
previous evening, Charles had mentioned that he would be picking
up a Dutch couple at Don Muang Airport and bringing them back
to stay.

She opened the door to the two apartments. Charles now rented
number 503 as well as 504, and had built an extended entrance, which
joined both of them. As Nadine walked towards the bedroom of 503,
she heard voices. Accustomed to the casual atmosphere of the apartment by now, she opened the door. She saw a dark-bearded, heavy-
set man in his twenties sitting on the bed talking with Charles. She
guessed he must be the Dutchman.

'Hello,' she began.

'Oh, Nadine, please go and see Monique,' Charles said quickly.
'We're discussing business here.'

He seemed angry, which surprised Nadine. He was usually courteous, to the point of excess she sometimes thought.

'I'm sorry,' she said. 'Excuse me.' She hurried into the kitchen of
the adjoining apartment.

'Hi, Nadine, coffee?' Marie-Andrée asked as she made herself a
cup of Nescafé.

Nadine sat on a stool at the bar. 'Alain is in a bad mood today. He
just sent me out of the guestroom,' she said as she crossed her long
legs and lit a Gauloise.

'Oh, you know him. He likes to keep his business private.'

Another woman walked into the room. She had blue eyes and long, fair hair. As she picked up an ashtray and walked back through the door, she smiled warmly at Nadine.

'Is she Dutch?' Nadine nodded after the young woman as Marie-Andrée sat down next to her.

'Yes.'

'She's so beautiful.'

'I must tell you, Nadine, I don't like these Dutch. They can't talk proper French.'

'That's hardly enough reason to dislike them so soon.'

Marie-Andrée shrugged. She was very tense.

'I am exhausted physically and morally,' her diaries would later reveal. 'I feel sick, depressed and lonely. The dangers and risks of the business mean that I can never relax any more. At every moment I have to play a role. Our business makes me more and more nervous and scared.'

Downstairs in apartment 103, two more of Charles' house-guests were sitting at the kitchen table discussing how soon they could leave Bangkok. Since his experiment with the Kaopectate, Dominique had only pretended to drink his medicine. He was feeling better and had trimmed his beard. The other man, the stocky, slow-talking François, had just received a refund of $810 on his stolen traveller's cheques, and a new passport was waiting for him at the French embassy.

'Now I've got to get my passport back from him,' Dominique was saying to François. 'I know he's still got it. It's in the new safe he's installed. I've given up all hope of getting back my eleven hundred dollars.'

In the past weeks both of them had painted number 504 blue and done other repairs around the two apartments, as well as taking care of most of the shopping and the laundry. Yesterday Charles had asked them not to enter 504. From now on they were to have their meals in 503.

François was also beginning to suspect that as well as Charles' gem business, which seemed to be flourishing at the moment, he also stole the passports and valuables of tourists. But he did not raise the matter because, in a curious way, he was quite grateful to Charles for having put him up for the past two months, feeding him and giving him cash for odd jobs. Although he did feel sad that he had lost Yannick to Charles, who had just bought Yannick two pairs of new shoes and a suit and employed him as his full-time secretary.

'You should tidy yourself up a bit,' Yannick had told François a few days before.

Yannick wasn't even bothering about the return of his traveller's cheques and passport. In Asia such formalities required constant pressure and form-filling.

Dominique and François wandered upstairs to prepare dinner. Afterwards Dominique sat on the couch next to the Dutchman, who introduced himself as Henk Bintanja. The two of them discussed the usual subjects, travelling and gem stones. Henk told Dominique that he had been on the road for almost a year now. While they still had some money in the bank, he and Cocky were thinking of making an investment. If they made the right purchases now, later, when their funds ran out, they could make a profit. Henk seemed a nice man, and although the two of them spoke in a halting mixture of French and English, Dominique, who was well disposed towards most people he met, recognized a kindred introvert.

The next morning, Saturday 13 December, Dominique came upstairs to 503 and noticed that the bedroom door was shut.

'Shall I make coffee for the Dutch couple?' he asked Marie-Andrée, who was fussing at the stove.

'No, don't. They're sick.'

'Already? This place is becoming like a hospital,' he said, immediately regretting his outspokenness.

'Oh, they take drugs,' Marie-Andrée said. 'Marijuana. That's what makes them sick. And Alain doesn't like it.' Everyone who came to Kanit House knew that Charles would not tolerate drug-taking. Dominique remembered the night Ajay, the Turk and some other travellers had hidden in the guest bedroom, furtively passing round joints.

'Why did he bring the Dutch here, then?' he asked.

'Oh, to sell them stones. They have money, and Alain will sell them more than they want,' Marie-Andrée replied.

Dominique nodded. He had seen Charles in operation. He was uncanny in his talent to make people buy more than they planned. He also had a method for calculating how much money they possessed. By finding out how much they planned to spend on gems and where they were staying, he used a crude index to calculate the total funds at their disposal. Dominique was fascinated by Charles' almost mystical understanding of money.

Nadine came into the room to say goodbye – she and Remy were leaving for a brief holiday. When she heard the Dutch were sick, she couldn't help commenting once again on the seemingly inevitable misfortunes of Charles' guests.

'It's because of their drug habits,' said Marie-Andrée angrily. 'And Alain's generosity with travellers who don't know how to be careful with Asian food.'

'Or he could be drugging them,' Dominique said.

'Oh, really?' Charles said as he walked into the room.

'Well, the medicine you gave me, Alain,' said Dominique, surprised to hear himself speaking up, 'it never cured me. It must have been mixed with something?'

Nadine smiled uncomfortably but Charles burst out laughing.

'What a sense of humour, Dominique! It's good to have you around. That's why I drug you, so I can support you. That's why I work hard, to earn enough to buy your toilet paper.'

Everyone was laughing now, even Marie-Andrée.

It's true – it just doesn't make sense, Dominique thought to himself. Of course it's not him. Maybe Monique doesn't know as much about nursing as she sometimes says she does. Maybe she mixed the medicines up, who knows?

'Well, I'll see you all in a week,' Nadine said, rising from the couch and playfully tousling Dominique's hair. 'I'll think of you all when I'm lying on the sand at Hua Hin.'

'I have to go too,' Charles said, opening the door.

As Charles left the room, Marie-Andrée turned to Dominique and said, 'We have so much important business going on here now, Alain would prefer it if you and François could stay down at 103 for the next few days unless we phone you that it's OK to come up.'

'Sure,' Dominique said, wondering what was going on now.

Nine kilometres south of Pattaya a red dirt road used to run off through the tapioca fields and the scrub of Nipa palms that lie between the highway and the beach. The road was called Haad Sai Thong, Golden Sand Road.

At 6 a.m. on 14 December 1975, a truck driver pulled up on Route 3 beside the small compound of peasants' houses that stood at the junction and began walking down Golden Sand Road, unzipping his trousers, looking for somewhere to relieve himself. Some of the leaves on the trees that shaded the road were curled into brown cylinders that were the homes of ginger ants. The truck driver took this into account as he looked around for the right spot. A ditch ran on either side of road, dank with tea-coloured water. Fifty metres along the track, the truck driver saw something that made him run back along the road, holding up his trousers. The peasants he alerted in the nearby house rushed back with him, an old farmer and his toothless daughter in their muddy sarongs and bamboo hats. They looked over the edge.

The body of the *farang* girl lay with its feet pointing at them. This was very bad luck. It lay half in the water, and the girl's face was submerged, her long brown hair floating, her eyes closed. Her dress was bunched up around her waist revealing a pair of red bikini pants. Ants were crawling all over her.

The next day Reiner, the young German, was packing his bags in the bedroom of 504. He was taking a flight to Frankfurt to be home with his mother for Christmas, although 'Alain' had been urging him to postpone the trip. Reiner was excited about the future of his gem partnership with Charles. Already Charles could hardly satisfy his customers' orders. They had decided to rent office space in the Air Egypt building. He was always planning for the future; looking for furniture, shop space, good gem supplies, machinery, designs, contacts. Reiner had seen how successful Charles had been at the Indra Hotel with the gem cutters from France. He had taken thousands of dollars' worth of orders.

It was not only Charles' business sense that gave him confidence in the partnership. Reiner enjoyed being with him. Just the other day, when they were driving around the city speaking in German, Charles had poured out his ideas on philosophy and psychology. The Dutch couple had just arrived in Bangkok and were sitting in the back. When they got out, Charles had turned to him and asked, 'What do you think of them?'

Typical travellers, he had thought, a bit on the hippie side.

'I'm thinking of getting them to do some travelling for me,' Charles had said.

Gems, Reiner thought. Charles was always asking people to smuggle gems for him – to take emeralds and rubies to Iran or fly diamonds in from Hong Kong to save the 25 per cent duty. He had also talked about giving that Turkish fellow, Ved, a job.

He didn't know much about Charles' other affairs. But lately Reiner had begun to notice that Charles was gulping down little white tablets. 'Speed,' Charles said. 'This business is getting too big.' And Charles was certainly rich. Reiner had watched Yannick counting the money in the safe, bundling up wads of 100-baht notes. It must have been 20,000 baht at least. Reiner closed the lid of his suitcase and checked his airline ticket to Frankfurt.

Suddenly there was a shattering scream. A thud. Another scream. A banging noise and someone swearing. He rushed into the living room where Monique was tidying up as if she hadn't heard a thing.

'What was that?'

'Oh, it's those Dutch drug addicts. I wish Alain would get rid of them, always so sick, and I have to cook for them all the time.'

Reiner stared at her for a moment, uncomprehending, and then walked into the hall and tried to open the door of the adjoining apartment. It was locked.

'Who's that?' Ajay's voice called out from behind the door.

'What's going on?' Reiner demanded.

'Oh, nothing much, man,' Ajay said, coming out of the room and quickly closing the door. 'The Dutch have had some kind of fit. They're sick. Alain's with them now.'

Ajay was grinning and sharply dressed. Partly because the two were among the youngest at Kanit House, Reiner and Ajay had become friends over the past few weeks. Earlier that day they had had lunch together at an open-air restaurant on Silom Road and Reiner had mentioned the Dutch couple.

'It sounds as if they could be dangerously ill,' he had told Ajay. 'Don't you think you should call a doctor?'

'Yeah, Alain probably will. He knows about medicine,' replied the Indian, averting his eyes.

That night Dominique and François sat at the little kitchen table downstairs in 103 discussing their growing realization that Charles was a petty crook.

'I don't know why he bothers,' Dominique was saying. 'He makes so much profit from selling gems.'

'Yes, but he throws the money away as quickly as he makes it.'

'Yes, maybe he enjoys it.' Dominique was becoming obsessed with trying to figure out the mystery of Charles. 'I often have the sense he's playing a game with you and your friend Yannick. He's fascinated because you were both once policemen.'

François made a quick sign to his friend to lower his voice. Both suspected the apartment was bugged. They sensed Charles didn't trust them so much any more. In the last two days Dominique had become more and more insistent about having his passport returned. He was determined to get home by Christmas. Even when they were away from Kanit House, they both sensed they were being watched. Two days ago, Charles had given them some money to go to the bars in Patpong. When they came out into the street after a night of chatter with the bar-girls, they bumped into Ajay, who had obviously been following them.

Now the kitchen door opened and Ajay walked into the room.

'Alain wishes to see you both,' he said with a cold, formal smile.

'Sure, let's go,' Dominique said casually.

'No, not together. One at a time. You first, François.'

François slowly got out of his chair and went upstairs. He walked into 504 and saw Charles sitting at his desk. On it was Ajay's nine-inch flick-knife and a pair of handcuffs. Looking smart in his new suit, his old friend Yannick sat on the couch.

'Sit down,' Charles said.

'I prefer to stand,' said François. Then nervously he changed his mind and sat on the opposite chair.

Ajay stood near the door.

'You say you are taking a trip to Penang,' Charles began. 'Aren't you really going to Paris to complain to the French authorities because you know what kind of jobs we do in Bangkok?' His face and voice were expressionless.

'You have no need to worry. I've suspected that you stole my passport for months now, but I did nothing. I'm going to Penang to have my visa renewed. That's all. It's so much easier there than with the Bangkok Immigration.'

Charles smiled. 'Tell me, François, if a French policeman disappeared in Bangkok, what do you think would happen?'

'There would be a big search,' he said. Was Charles serious? No, it must be a game.

'Not here, François. Who cares about life here?'

'Interpol would take the case. And, of course, they are very thorough about disappearing policemen. Why do you ask?'

'I want to know if you can be trusted,' Charles said.

'Look, Alain, I'm only in your flat because you promised to help me. When I return from Penang, if you have jobs for me, I'll stay. Otherwise I've got my traveller's cheques back.' He shrugged. 'In the end I've lost nothing.'

This answer seemed to appeal to Charles. 'OK, François, I'll see what I can do. You don't seem to be an undesirable.'

'Sure,' François smiled with difficulty. He was told to return to 103. He tried to saunter out of the room with his hands in the pockets of his baggy jeans. He avoided Dominique's questioning

glance as he was led into the apartment for fear it would be inter-
preted as collusion.

Dominique stepped back suddenly when he saw the three men he
had thought of as friends looking at him like a tribunal of
gangsters.

'Yannick tells me that if I let you go back to France, you will say a
lot of malicious things about me and try to have me arrested,'
Charles said as though he was only mildly interested in the proceedings. 'He says you will go to the French Ministry of Justice and tell
them I steal passports.'

'That's not true,' Dominique said angrily. He looked at Yannick,
who did seem embarrassed. He knew that Yannick had said no such
thing and that if this was a test it was as much a test of Yannick as
himself.

'And François just said the same thing as Yannick.'

'No. It's impossible,' Dominique said. 'We never mentioned anything like that.'

Charles repeated the charge, and Dominique kept wracking his
brain for the right words.

'How could I complain about you, when you and Monique have
been so kind? I've been here now for three months.'

'So, you will keep your mouth shut?'

'It's cool. I know you need passports for your work. It's none of
my business. But I wish you would give mine back now.'

'OK then,' Charles laughed. 'Tomorrow morning, you'll get it.'

Later Charles would tell the chilling story of the Dutch couple's last
days. 'I could have easily hidden their bodies in the jungles of
Thailand,' he explained:

> I got a message to go to Hong Kong and pick up the Dutch. I
> didn't make a profit on that sapphire ring. It was just the bait. I
> had been told that they were on their way to Chiang Mai to set
> up a smack deal. After that they would have sent back dates to
> Amsterdam to the couriers. I could have killed them in Hong

Kong, but it's too small. Although many bodies are dumped in the harbour there, I wanted this cleaning to make a big impression. Another warning. Like the Turk.

Instead, he drugged Cocky and Henk at Kanit House the day after he picked them up at the airport:

I told Yannick we had to keep them a few days, not to kill them, just to get some information. Because of the drugs, it was easy. I used psychology. The guy was a bit scared because he sensed after two days that something was wrong. They were so much under the influence of drugs they couldn't think coherently, and the questioning was slow. Sometimes Henk would get dozy, and I'd shake him and say, 'Answer this man, answer this!'

By the time we took them from the house, they were down, although they could just about walk. I'd said to the guy in the morning that they were sick, and I'd take them to the hospital, so in the car they were convinced that's where they were going. Ha!

Late on the night of Monday 15 December, Charles and Ajay helped Cocky and Henk down the corridor and across the walkway. The city was dark – only street lights, the red tail-lights of cars and the white tower of the Dusit Thani Hotel illuminated with flood-lights. Cocky's head lay on Ajay's shoulder.

'Come on – it will soon be over,' Charles said to her gently.

'Where are we going?' she asked, hardly managing to form the words.

'You're both very sick, Cocky,' said Charles. 'We have to take you to hospital.' The gentle, caressing voice seemed to reassure her.

Charles drove fast towards Don Muang Airport and continued through rice fields to the small town of Rangsit. The car crossed a canal and passed a police checkpoint on the lookout for overloaded trucks. Traffic was scarce, and the rhythmic acres of paddy fields were broken occasionally by a well-lit junction or a cluster of shops and restaurants open late for truckers hauling teak from the north.

The shadowy pagoda roofs of Wat Kudi Prasit which doubled as the village school were visible from the highway. Two kilometres past this the Toyota, the latest in Charles' string of rented cars, came to a stop.

Cocky was sleeping deeply with her head on her boyfriend's shoulder. The back doors were opened, and Ajay and Charles dragged the couple out of the car.

'What's this?' Henk asked. 'Where are we?'

As Charles would later recall, 'When the Dutch guy started resisting, I hit him in the stomach, and he fell down. He was stocky, and he started to move, so Ajay kicked him in the stomach and then choked him. But he began to move again. He was strong, even under drugs.'

It had been raining heavily. Charles and Ajay dragged Henk over to a puddle of water and held his head under it.

'The girl never really knew what was going on. Ajay bashed her over the head, I think. On the side of the road we splashed them with petrol.'

As their car sped back to Bangkok, flames leapt up beside the highway.

At dawn on the Tuesday morning a group of village schoolchildren on their way to Wat Kudi Prasit saw smoke rising from the long grass and found Cocky and Henk lying near the road, side by side, on their backs. The bodies were still smouldering, Henk's right arm resting protectively on Cocky's shoulder. His neck was broken in three places. Cocky's knees were bent as though in fitful sleep. Her teeth were clenched. Her denim skirt, pulled above her thighs, was covered with mud.

Later that morning, at 11 a.m., Dominique went upstairs and knocked on the door of 504 to retrieve his passport.

'Oh, Alain's expecting you, but he's still in bed,' Marie-Andrée told him, still in her dressing gown as she answered the door.

Dominique went into the bedroom, where Charles was in bed reading a copy of the *Bangkok Post* in which a story about Stephanie Parry had just been published:

EUROPEAN GIRL MURDERED

The body of a teenage European girl was found lying on a bank of a tidal creek near Pattaya yesterday, and police are treating her death as a case of murder.

Police are working on the theory that a person or persons held her under water until she drowned.

It was only 2 months ago that the body of a second foreign girl was found floating in the sea off Pattaya. The police have still been unable to identify her.

Charles would later claim to have killed Stephanie Parry on 9 December when she checked out of the President Hotel. But her body was found by local villagers on 14 December and she had been dead only a few hours. A similar discrepancy hovered over the timing of Teresa Knowlton's death.

Charles carefully put down the paper and handed Dominique a manila envelope. 'Here is your passport,' he said smoothly, 'but as you will see, I've been using it.'

The young Frenchman opened the envelope and saw what was left of his passport – a loose collection of pages, all falling apart, in different shades of blue, and Charles' photo stuck where his own should have been. Dominique didn't know what to say.

'Don't worry. I'll fix the photo for you in a minute,' Charles said, explaining that he had removed some of the pages with the visas he required to insert them into other passports. 'So now I have taken some pages from other French passports and put them into yours, see?' Charles then cut a piece of one of the mismatching blue pages from the passport. 'I'll take this to Hong Kong where I've got fifty passports and I'll match the colours.'

'But, Alain, I want to leave soon.'

'OK. I'll be back in a week – next Tuesday. Monique and I will go for Christmas to Hong Kong.'

'But the passport picture?'

Dominique was amazed that Alain had come out into the open now.

'I'll fix it up now for you. Have you got a picture of yourself?'

Dominique handed him a passport photo he had picked up a few days before.

'OK, you wait next door while I do it,' he said as he got out of bed.

Dominique knew that Charles kept a lot of seals and stamps and other printing equipment in the refrigerator.

'What about the Dutch?'

'Oh, they're not in there any more. Last night I took them to the hospital.' He shook his head sadly. 'These people come to Asia and take too many drugs.'

Dominique went into the apartment next door where he noticed that Henk and Cocky had left some of their bags in the room. A few minutes later Charles called him back into 504 and handed him the passport, which now had his own photo inside and was stamped with the embossed seal of the government of France.

'It's not such a good job. I'll do a better one when I get back.'

They were by the kitchenette, and Dominique noticed a rubber hose-pipe smelling of petrol on top of the refrigerator.

'Listen, Dominique, could you do me a favour? We leave for Hong Kong tomorrow.' He handed Dominique a pair of his trousers which were wet and covered with mud. 'Get these dry-cleaned, please. Same-day service.'

The mud oozed all over Dominique's hands. Alain was usually so impeccable about his dress. Where on earth had he been?

Two days later, on 18 December, Dominique was downstairs alone in 103 when Yannick burst into the room. 'You've got to go!' he cried out wildly. 'You've got to get out of here! Today!'

Yannick's new clothes were crumpled, and his eyes were blazing. His long fair beard seemed scraggy and wild.

'I am going, Yannick,' Dominique replied a trifle coldly, 'but why are you suddenly so interested in what I do?'

'If you don't go now, you'll never go. Look at this.'

Yannick thrust a copy of the *Bangkok Post* at Dominique.

'I've just come back from driving the three of them to the airport. Alain, Ajay, Monique. I bought a copy of the paper. And I just read this upstairs. Don't you recognize them?'

Dominique opened the newspaper and saw the headline: 'Australian Couple Killed and Burned'.

'Australians? I don't know any Australians.'

'Look closely. Can't you recognize the skirt?'

Dominique went into shock. Yannick was beside himself.

'It's Cocky and Henk! Alain and Ajay took them out late that night. I opened the gate of the compound. They were both drugged. Look, read the story.'

The partly burned bodies of a young Australian couple have been found in a ditch alongside a highway 58 kilometres south of Ayutthaya.

Police tentatively identified the couple as Johnson and Rosanna Watson who had apparently been touring the Central Plains.

A 'Made-in-Holland' T-shirt worn by the young woman indicated they may have arrived here from Europe on their way back to Australia.

Dominique put down the paper. 'It says it's two Australians.'

'I tell you that's a mistake,' Yannick exclaimed, grabbing the paper again and waving it at his friend. 'Look at this, it says the T-shirt the girl was wearing was made in Holland.'

Dominique tried to take the paper calmly. He saw his friend was right.

'We've got to get out of Bangkok before they get back!' Yannick shouted hysterically.

'I've got no money,' Dominique whispered, the awful truth dawning at last. 'Did he leave you any?'

'No, just a thousand baht to feed the stupid dog!' Then Yannick stopped. 'But I have the key to his safe.'

The two men fell silent. Dominique looked again at the picture of the two burned bodies. The caption read: 'They had come halfway across the world for a date with death.'

'Oh, my God! What about François? He was supposed to be going to Penang three days ago. Do you think Ajay really took him to the bus station?'

Three days before Christmas, Nadine and Remy stood on the balcony of a lavish mansion overlooking the Chao Phraya River. Out front on the gravel driveway limousines were lined up, their Thai chauffeurs in crisp white shirts, smoking and talking amongst the shrubbery. Paper lanterns were strung throughout the garden. The lights in the house were blazing and music filled the humid, scented air. Guests laughed and chatted in groups as they took a break from the dancing. Nadine and Remy usually circulated at these parties thrown by French expatriates, but tonight they huddled together, looking out at the lights moving up and down the river.

'It's a nightmare,' shivered Nadine. 'We must tell somebody.'

'Not yet, not until we get the whole story,' Remy replied slowly, smoking his Gauloise. 'It sounds crazy to say, "Excuse me, there's a killer next door."'

That morning when they had returned from their holiday at Hua Hin, they had gone upstairs to ask if anyone in 504 wanted a quick game of badminton before they went to the party.

Yannick was alone in the apartment and looked very strange, his pale-blue eyes unfocussed, his face drained of colour. He told them he couldn't leave the apartment because he was expecting Charles to phone from Hong Kong. If no one answered the phone, Charles might suddenly return.

'So what?' Nadine asked.

'We've all got to get out of here,' he blurted out. 'He's a murderer. He killed the Dutch couple.'

Then he showed them the story in the *Bangkok Post*.

'But come back later and I'll tell you everything.'

Now, as the party inside cranked up, Nadine turned to her husband, desperate for reassurance.

'What if Yannick is dreaming all of this – and he's just a homesick detective?' she asked.

They both jumped when a voice called out from the doorway. It was one of their friends, an ambassador's wife, elegant in a Thai silk dress.

'Merry Christmas, you two! But why so miserable?'

'Oh, nothing,' they said a little stiffly.

'Where's your friend Alain?' the woman demanded playfully. 'I'm mad at him. I ordered a heavy gold chain for my husband's birthday and I've not heard from him.'

'Alain is due back in Bangkok in a few days,' said Remy quietly.

As soon as they could, the couple left the party and rushed back to Kanit House.

When they returned, it was Dominique who opened the door. He too looked haggard and scared.

'Why them, not me?' he kept saying. 'It's all I can think about.'

Number 504 was a shambles, cigarette butts spilling out of ashtrays and saucers, dirty dishes, newspapers scattered on the floor. Franky the dog was whining for food, and the place smelled of dog shit.

Dominique took the piece of hose-pipe off the top of the refrigerator.

'Smell it,' he said, handing it to Remy. 'Petrol. It was there this morning after they took out the Dutch. They were going to the hospital, they said. At two in the morning?' He was shaking. He told them how Charles had handed him the muddy trousers, and how later he noticed that Charles' shoes were covered with mud.

Yannick stood stroking his wispy beard. 'I don't think they were the only ones,' he said.

They decided to search the two apartments.

In 503 Nadine opened the top drawer of a bureau and saw two hypodermic syringes, a walkie-talkie, some radio microphones and a pair of handcuffs. She picked up a silver necklace.

'I remember the Turk wearing this, the one who never came back from the gem mines,' she said turning to Yannick, who pointed to a stack of suitcases in the corner.

'They belonged to Cocky and Henk,' he said.

Nadine moved to a handbag on the table and looked inside. There was a purse of Dutch coins, and a package of contraceptive pills. She held them up to show Yannick. She knew the pills did not belong to Marie-Andrée, who had a coil.

'Why would she leave without taking these?' she asked.

Back in 504, Yannick led them to the safe and took out a manila envelope. He tipped a pile of passports onto the cocktail bar. His own was among them with Gautier's picture inside. So were the passports stolen from Nadine and Remy's friends in Pattaya. Another had belonged to the girl from Formentera, Stephanie Parry.

'I think this one's dead, too,' he said. 'She came back here one day and later –' Yannick drew his finger across his throat '– she was found strangled near Pattaya.'

'But why her and not me?' Dominique asked again. 'I cost them more than they got out of me.'

'Why anyone at all?' Remy said looking through bundles of traveller's cheques, some wallets and fifteen passports.

Yannick put the envelope back in the safe and sat with Dominique and Nadine round the coffee table. Remy sat on a bar stool under the harsh fluorescent lights from the kitchen.

'OK, let's discuss what to do next,' he said, making an effort to remain calm.

'That's just what we've been doing since Thursday,' Dominique blurted out, 'and every time we decide on a course of action, the consequences rule it out.'

It would be useless, even dangerous, they agreed, to go to the Thai police. The only language they understood was money. What about the French embassy? No, Alain had too many friends there too. Maybe that was why he always sold his gems and gold to French diplomats at cost, often less than cost.

'What about Interpol, the international police agency?' Nadine suggested. But they decided that because its headquarters were in France at St-Cloud, operating with a few telex machines, there wouldn't be a representative in Thailand.

'When I get back to France I'll go to Interpol,' said Yannick. 'They can send a man out to arrest him.'

'But Alain and Ajay are coming back tomorrow,' cried Dominique. 'We have to get out of here.'

'Don't worry,' Remy said. 'Tomorrow morning you can come with me to the bank as soon as it opens. We'll lend you the money for your tickets, and you can be out of Bangkok by tomorrow night.'

Nadine was now in shock, compounded by a terrible sense of guilt. Remy had often warned her about Alain, and she had laughed at him. She had presumed he was jealous. With his big moustache Remy looked like a comic-book French chef. It was true that he spoke only French and worked long greasy hours in the kitchens of the Oriental Hotel. And yet now he did not say, 'I told you so.' Instead of voicing recriminations, he had taken control and was calm and rational.

The lights of the city were dimming, and the darkness was brightening into dawn. Dominique made coffee as they sat chain-smoking.

'When I was driving the three of them to the airport,' Yannick revealed, 'Alain told me he was on the way to make the best deal of his life. Then he gave me the keys to the safe and asked me to take care of things here until he got back on Tuesday.

'I knew something must have happened to the Dutch couple, but Charles insisted they were still in the hospital and that after what he had done, they wouldn't remember anything for six months. And he told me, "Don't worry, nothing will happen to me in Thailand. I'm protected."'

'But what about François?' said Dominique. 'He was supposed to be back from Penang yesterday.'

For half a minute everyone was silent. The same thought had hit them all. The stolid ex-detective was last seen climbing into the car with Ajay.

Nadine and Remy got up to leave. The other two would meet them at the bank at 9 a.m. When they got to France they would go straight to the police – and then they would cable the money back.

On their way out they stepped over Charles' files, which were scattered all over the floor. Kicking one open, Nadine saw a large glossy photo. She called the others over. It showed a Vietnamese soldier standing in a charred field. In each hand he held a human head, dripping blood.

The next morning Remy went to the bank to meet Dominique and Yannick. Nadine was looking out of the window smoking when she saw a familiar, sombre figure by the pool. It was François. Relieved to see he was safe, she called him up to her apartment and told him what had happened.

'Everything falls into place,' said François, shaking his head.

'What do you mean?'

'A few days ago, I saw my passport in his room, the passport that was stolen in Pattaya.'

'It's so strange,' said Nadine faintly. 'I suspected something. So did Dominique, you, Yannick. And yet we all kept quiet about it. Why?'

'Alain just has a way of making people not see things they don't want to see,' said François, with a fatalistic shrug.

When Yannick and Dominique got back to Kanit House their bags were already packed and waiting in the hall downstairs. Their flight was not scheduled to depart until midnight, but they would spend the whole day at the airport where they felt safe. There was one catch – Yannick still had no passport. The one in the safe upstairs had Charles' picture inside. So he asked François to go with him to the French embassy so that he could get an emergency *laissez-passer*. Dominique, who had barely slept for days, arranged to meet them at Hua Lamphong railway station. From there they would go straight to the airport.

The three of them said goodbye to Nadine. Dominique kissed her warmly. They had been good friends. He wondered if being close to Nadine had actually saved his life. She would have asked too many questions if he had disappeared.

At the embassy, Yannick was told that his *laissez-passer* would take days, so with his flair for seizing the moment, he created a scene. He was a detective due back in Paris on urgent police business, he said. He would make a scandal at a high political level if they refused to help him! Within an hour he was issued with the document.

The three frightened men arrived at the airport before lunch. Dominique suggested they check the times of all incoming flights from Hong Kong.

'I might as well tell you,' confessed Yannick, twisting a strand of his beard, 'they haven't gone to Hong Kong. That was a decoy. They've gone to Kathmandu.'

The other two were nonplussed. Why was Yannick issuing such potent pieces of information like this in fits and starts, instead of telling all from the start?

'Back in Paris I'll tell you everything I know,' he promised, fumbling in his pocket as he spoke. He took out a key, the one to the safe at Kanit House, and hurled it in the trash can.

'Sapphires and rubies,' he offered when his friends noticed several white envelopes bulging from his pockets. 'Just part of what Charles owes me for my work.'

That night while the three Frenchmen waited to board their plane, Remy was in the Oriental's cavernous kitchens supervising chocolate mousse for the Christmas banquet when he was called to the phone.

'Hi, Remy. This is Alain. I'm just back from Hong Kong. How's everything?'

'Fine,' Remy said, trying to sound relaxed yet busy.

'Where's Nadine?'

'Isn't she at home?' asked Remy, knowing that Nadine had agreed to stay away from Kanit House until he could meet up with her later. 'I guess she must be visiting friends.'

Remy waited.

'The others seem to have disappeared,' said Charles calmly. 'And there's no sign of Yannick. Did they leave any message?'

'*Non* – they told us you phoned them from Hong Kong and asked them to meet you there. Did you miss them?'

There was a pause.

'OK, thank you so much my friend,' said Charles. He sighed. 'I might see you tonight if I'm not too busy.'

At midnight, when Nadine and Remy returned to Kanit House, they saw lights on in the upstairs flat. Remy hauled a huge cupboard across their door. They spent the night huddled tight.

The next morning when they looked through the blinds of their bedroom, they saw Ajay Chowdury walking along with two Thai men in overalls bending under the weight of a two-handled metal tool box.

'They've come to open the safe,' whispered Nadine, clutching her husband's arm. 'Yannick must have had the only key.'

In the early hours of that same morning, Christmas Eve, the three Frenchmen checked in for their flight back to Paris. Dominique had been terrified that the Thai immigration authorities would question Charles' crude alterations in his passport. But all three boarded without a hitch. They clicked shut their seatbelts, and Dominique buried his head in his hands.

'Come on, man,' said François kindly, leaning forward to shield him from the eyes of the other passengers. 'It's all over now. We're safe. We've been lucky.'

'But why not us?' Dominique muttered, his body convulsing involuntarily. 'Why not us? Who's going to stop him?'

'Try not to think about that until we get to Paris,' said François sensibly. 'We can go and see the police and the Minister of Justice. They will have him arrested. And Yannick has promised to pay a personal call on Interpol.'

It was not until he got to Paris, twelve hours later, when he stood outside the railway station saying goodbye to the others, about to begin his journey home alone, that Dominique broke down and wept uncontrollably.

12

Freak Street

'Kathmandu!' a voice rang out from the back of the bus as it rounded a hill and the passengers saw tattered prayer flags flapping from poles; but the cry was premature. It was just another village of terracotta clay on the edge of the Himalayas. The bus pulled up at a scruffy hut and the overland travellers scrambled out for bottles of Fanta and the home-brewed soda sold in old Coca-Cola bottles.

The bus resumed its precarious crawl on the rollercoaster road from Pokhara, a town in the west of Nepal, to its capital city. For hours now, the scenery had been a relentless spectacle of great gorges, roaring rivers, vistas of terraced hillsides. The road was so sinuously death-defying that one false twist of the wheel by the jovial Irish driver would have plunged them into a ravine. The bus had set out from London months ago, and now, 14 December, it was nearing its destination. Among its youthful passengers, most of whom had climbed aboard at Victoria Station, the excitement was reaching a crescendo. There was laughter and cheers at the children squatting on the roadside to pee. Hash smoke wafted along the aisle, someone played a flute, and a hip flask of Gurkha rum travelled from mouth to mouth. Through the window they could see women winnowing wheat, wearing fist-size lumps of coral and turquoise around their necks, babies tied on their backs.

With her long dark hair parted down the centre, a red kurta and jangling collection of Asian jewellery, twenty-eight-year-old Connie Jo Bronzich looked like a Nepalese hill woman herself, although she was Italian-American. She had joined the bus in Delhi, after travelling overland from Athens. She looked scruffy and run-down, as would be expected after so many miles on the overland trail.

On the road, chance acquaintanceships turn into fast friendships overnight. At the last stop, three students had joined the bus, and were now responding to Connie Jo's weary, dislocated conversation with the wry indulgence of the captive listener. Connie was stoned; that was obvious, or she wouldn't have been talking so much.

She had her own house, Connie said, in the redwood mountains of Los Gatos outside Santa Cruz in California. It was so beautiful, but she had to get away. Too many bad vibes. The mountains frightened her. It was a heavy heroin scene around Santa Cruz, and in those mountains most roads weren't even on maps. The police just left it alone. 'Sure,' said one of them. Luke, a journalism student at University of Texas, had teamed up with the two girls sitting next to him. Sally and Katy were law students from Australia. 'Santa Cruz. Murder and drug capital of America.'

Connie, it seemed to him, was freaked out and a bit desperate.

'Yeah, my old man was in the smack business, but after a time it gets you down,' she told them. 'All these scumbags kept coming to the house trying to do deals. Man – it was heavy! In the end it all blew up, and I had to get away.'

She had come to the East to break her heroin habit, she said, which to Luke made as much sense as going to Mexico to give up chilli peppers.

'I'm down to my last hundred dollars,' she confided. 'When my sister comes to Kathmandu for Christmas, I'll probably have some more, but, anyway, this is gonna have to be a business trip.'

The Kathmandu Valley, surrounded by the peaks of the Himalayas, looked as green and ordered as an opera backdrop. Connie stopped talking as suddenly as she had begun and spent the rest of the journey staring out the window.

Finally they reached Kathmandu – which in 1975 was a city leaping headlong into the fourteenth century, and the ultimate summit of the international freak scene. Those in the bus were cheering and singing and two girls unfurled a Union Jack and hung it out the back window.

Shaky wooden two-storey houses and shops leaned into the narrow streets. Lamps and candles lit windows of dark, tiny bare rooms like tableaux from the Middle Ages – blacksmiths hammering, tailors sewing, small children mending shoes. In the gutter a butcher disembowelled a side of buffalo. Beside him, a woman crouched in a long crimson skirt beside her fruit stall, where a half-dozen passion fruit lay in a line.

The bus crawled the cobbled streets into Durbar Square, almost nudging the men in loincloths carrying huge bundles of firewood and straw. Meandering in the ancient square, flanked by palaces and pagodas, were dogs, goats, chickens, holy men and snake charmers. The bicycle rickshaws whizzed past, their drivers hissing to warn the crowds. As soon as the bus pulled up children surrounded it, whispering through the windows the endless litany of the road: 'You want hash? Grass? Thai sticks? Best cocaine from Colombia?'

That night, Connie stayed at the ramshackle Star Hotel with the bus driver, and the next day she moved on to Freak Street, checking into the Oriental Lodge where her other three friends from the bus had taken rooms.

Like most Nepalese buildings, the doors and ceilings of the Oriental were so low that Western visitors had to hunch up while inside. Its stairs were dark and precipitous, and even during the day the only source of light was a candle which burned on the reception desk. Connie's cell-sized room contained only a narrow cot. A tiny window looked down on the grubby stone courtyard. It cost ten rupees a night – about a dollar. The hotel lobby led into Freak Street.

In 1975 genuine Tibetan treasures were still on sale in hole-in-the-wall stalls along this fabled alleyway. As well, there were versions of Tibetan and Nepalese national costumes which were run up by busy tailors for the hordes that arrived ready to swap their precious blue jeans for strings of amber, and their sneakers for red felt boots embroidered with flowers.

If only she had money, Connie said as she browsed with Luke, Sally and Katy. So many beautiful things. She was crazy about jewellery.

It had been fourteen months since hashish had been half-heartedly proclaimed illegal in the Kingdom of Nepal, under international pressure, but on Freak Street its heady aroma billowed out from the upper windows of cheap hotels. In the tea shops, where hash was optional in biscuits and chocolate cakes, loudspeakers blared the music of Bob Dylan and the Doors.

In the twilight of the Don't Pass Me By restaurant, the four new arrivals sat down and giggled over the menu. 'It must be the worst food in the world,' Luke said in a Texan drawl. 'Well, what will it be? Buffalo balls or yak-butter toast, or buffalo balls on yak butter toast?'

As they waited for their order, he told them about the Bangkok newspaper stories he had seen about some young tourists burned by the roadside.

'Yep, burned black – two Aussies – like crispy critters.'

'Don't freak us out, Luke,' Sally said.

Later in the day, Connie persuaded Katy to accompany her on a visit to one of Kathmandu's landmarks, the Pie and Chai Shop. As they walked along the ancient streets, they passed shrines wreathed with marigolds and smeared with a sticky red paste. Candles burned beside statues, and rats scuttled up and down their elaborate silk costumes.

A low doorway led into a room of six tables. It was dirty and bare, and a tiny girl was crouching on the floor, washing dishes in a bucket. The pies were lined up on a shelf behind the fly-screen and there were more on the counter: lemon meringue, apple, banana, custard, pumpkin and chocolate meringue – an anomalous array, and a legend from Bali to Istanbul. Connie went to the back of the shop and spoke to a man. A few minutes later, with the dexterity of a hardened junkie, she shot herself up with morphine.

A portrait of Connie Jo at the age of seven still hung in the comfortable living room of her parents' home in Saratoga. Wearing a light-blue dress and her hair in long brown pigtails, she was beaming at the white puppy she held in her arms. Her bedroom was a confection of pink nylon curtains and fluffy stuffed animals to which she returned to do her homework after piano and ballet lessons. The adored only child of a prosperous business couple, the pretty dark-eyed girl with the eager grin was just one of the gang in high school and enrolled in Stanford College to become a radiology technician.

But before graduation she was asked to leave. She took a job with a local doctor but suddenly left that too without explanation. Some people who knew her at the time say it was because she had begun using hard drugs.

She was twenty-six when she married John Bronzich, a motor-boat salesman who drank and loved motorcycles. It was a garden wedding, California style. Connie wore traditional white, and the bridegroom wore a tailored leather suit. Now she had turned up alone in Nepal, wearing a lot of turquoise and coral, with a thirst for friends and a taste for morphine and smack.

Luke, Sally and Katy didn't see much of Connie Jo Bronzich until three days later, 18 December. In one of the larger rooms of the Oriental Lodge, a group of the young guests was sitting around on the three beds, passing joints and listening to a guitarist and a har-monica player warming up for a jam session. Connie joined them around a hash pipe. They had managed to avoid her company. Her morphine habit depressed them.

'I feel great today,' Connie said. 'I've had my first hot shower in weeks.' Her long dark hair was smooth and shining, and she looked fresher and more alert than she had since her companions had met her. 'It was the first real luxury bathroom I've seen since Istanbul.'

'How did you manage that?' one of her friends asked.

'I met this guy, a gem-dealer, he's really amazing. I had drinks back at his room in the Oberoi, and—'

'Connie! You mean to say—' Sally broke in teasing.

'No, you jerk. His wife was there too. He showed me some stones. They were incredible. He buys them at the mines in Thailand and sells them cheap! I might stay with them if I go to Bangkok. They were both really nice, even bought me drinks. They've got a car, too. He said he'd take me to visit the garnet mines sometime.'

Now another man entered the room, bending low to get through the door, wearing a checked flannel shirt, hiking boots and jeans.

'Hi, Laurent,' Connie said. 'Come and meet my friends.'

The Australian girls were surprised. Connie had not mentioned that she was expecting anyone to join her, and the burly Canadian man who soon began talking about the trek he planned to Everest Base Camp was an unlikely boyfriend. Connie could only trek as far as the nearest morphine fix.

A cassette of bluegrass music was playing, and others joined in with the harmonica and guitar. Luke, the conscientious journalism student, liked to hear travellers' tales and he listened to Laurent.

'You get a better education out of six months travelling than five years of polisci and psych,' the Canadian was saying. Luke agreed. Laurent had dropped out of the University of Winnipeg, got his mining papers, and for the past four years had taken summer jobs and travelled during the winter.

'This way I will have seen the whole world in another eight years. But Everest, wow, I've wanted to see that since I was a kid. This is going to be the best Christmas of my life.'

'So you're raring to go,' said Luke, liking his enthusiasm.

'And glad to get out of Delhi. What a shit-hole.'

'Well, Kathmandu's a bit of a shit-hole too,' said Luke. 'It's the people here who make the difference. They must be the gentlest people in the world.'

At midnight, when the batteries in the cassette player had run down, Laurent and Connie said goodnight to the others and drifted off to their room.

'Those two just don't seem to go together at all,' Luke said. 'He's got his trip together down to a tee. Money, maps, return tickets, and poor old Connie's down to her last hundred dollars ...'

'There's something tragic about that woman,' Sally said.

'Yeah,' Luke agreed. 'She's got tombstones in her eyes.'

It was 22 December, and in the leafy enclave of the US embassy compound, behind a high brick wall, an assistant hurried into First

Secretary Alan Eastham's office. 'They found the body of a Western man yesterday on the road to Dhulikhel, sir,' he said. 'It could be an American.'

Eastham sighed. Kathmandu was considered a hardship zone by US diplomats posted overseas.

On Christmas Eve a battered military vehicle drove along Freak Street and pulled up outside the Oriental Lodge. Luke was sitting in the lobby when he saw three Nepalese men in suits, one obviously a police superintendent, walk upstairs to the room shared by Sally and Katy.

Has the impossible happened? Luke asked himself. A drug bust on Freak Street?

The raised voices of the girls echoed through the tiny hotel as they followed the police onto the landing. The faces of the police were shocked and sombre.

'We have to go to the mortuary,' Sally called out to Luke as they walked down the stairs. It seemed that two bodies had been found and the police wanted help in making an identification. Luke climbed into the police Jeep with the others.

The small square building looked like a weather-beaten bunker. Luke suggested the girls wait outside as he followed the moon-faced Superintendent Chandra Bir Rai, who looked more like a guru than a senior policeman, into the building. Two men at the doorway saluted.

On a stone slab, Luke saw a charred corpse. All the clothes were burned off the body, except for a piece of checked cotton fabric around one wrist. Before he had time to absorb the sight, the superintendent was beckoning Luke into another part of the building. This time he saw the blackened corpse of a woman, with deep gashes in her chest.

'Did you know her?' he asked.

'Oh Jesus, it just might be – Connie,' gasped Luke, looking down at the naked, mutilated figure. She was so badly burned even her jewellery was charred. Luke turned away, trying to stop himself from vomiting. He would have to ask Sally to confirm the identification. She had talked the most with Connie Jo Bronzich.

As Luke walked back towards the door, he stopped again at the mutilated corpse of the tall Western male.

'Who's this?' he asked Superintendent Rai.

Looking supremely apologetic, Rai shook his head. It had been found three days before, in a gully about 35 kilometres from Kathmandu. It had not been identified.

From the body's size Luke realized that it was probably Laurent. The throat was cut from ear to ear, so deeply the head seemed decapitated. My God, Luke thought, horrified, it would take five men to hold him down to do that. The blackened skin was peeling back in places, revealing red tissue. The scrap of fabric seemed to have been used to bind the wrists together.

As Luke forced himself to look at the corpse as a journalist would, objectively looking for clues, he hoped it wasn't the slow-talking Canadian. The reasons for the burning were obvious to him. The murderers had tried to render their victims unidentifiable. In the case of the male victim they had succeeded. Luke told the police superintendent that although there was a good possibility that the corpse was that of Laurent Carrière, a Canadian friend of Connie Jo Bronzich, he could not make a positive identification.

'Is it Connie?' the two girls asked, shivering as they stood outside the door.

'Maybe. I can't say one hundred per cent. Prepare yourselves for something awful,' he warned them. Sally walked into the mortuary and Katy stayed outside talking with Luke. There was no need for both girls to go inside.

Huddling in the doorway, looking miserable, was Sushil Mathema, a Nepalese student who worked as the receptionist at the Oriental Lodge. He had been unceremoniously wrenched from his economics class by police, and as a matter of course would spend the next few days in jail in case he was concealing anything. Already he had told the police what he knew. Four days before, Laurent Carrière had come downstairs early in the morning wearing a backpack, saying he was going off to visit Dhulikhel, an ancient town 45 kilometres to the west. He was alone. Two days later, when he hadn't come back, Connie mentioned to Sushil that she was going off to look for him. That was all he could tell the police except that, once, an Indian boy with a small moustache came to the desk to ask for them both.

Sally rejoined her friends. 'It was Connie, all right,' she said. 'I could tell by the earrings.'

Luke put his arm round her and she sobbed on his shoulder. Superintendent Rai came out from the mortuary and walked over to the three young travellers, standing with them in a gesture of compassionate solidarity.

Half an hour later, the old Jeep drove the three students up the ramp of the police headquarters building in Durbar Square. A young man, bowing low in the presence of the superintendent, brought them a tray of biscuits and tea. Luke, Sally and Katy told Rai everything they could remember about Connie. They had last seen her on 22 December, the night before her body was found, when she had asked them if they wanted to join her for a trip to the Pie and Chai Shop.

'She talked about meeting a gem-dealer at the Oberoi,' Sally recalled. 'She said he was Vietnamese-looking – maybe he knows something?'

'Have you ever seen this gem-dealer, Miss Sally?' the superintendent asked gently.

'I'm not sure,' she answered. 'I bumped into Connie on Freak Street once and she was with some people who could have been the ones. She said this guy had offered to drive her to the garnet mines.'

The superintendent gave the travellers a notebook found in Connie's room. They looked through it and came across a name and address in Bangkok. 'This must be the man,' said Sally, pointing to the name: Alain Gautier, 504 Kanit House. The superintendent thanked them for their help.

That night Katy, Sally and Luke went out to Aunt Jane's restaurant, where they had chocolate cake for Christmas dinner and tried to forget what they had seen at the mortuary that day. But they couldn't and they knew they never would. Later at the Oriental Lodge, Sally vomited, and they sat up together all night, counting the hours until they could leave the city which had symbolized the dream of the overland trek to all of them.

Christmas morning dawned cold and foggy as they shouldered their packs and walked through the streets of Kathmandu. At 8 a.m. they boarded the bus which would take them to the Indian border.

The same morning, a white Datsun drove across the bridge over the Bishnumati River and headed towards the sacred hill of the 2,000-year-old temple, Swayambhunath. From its gold spire the eyes of the all-seeing Buddha looked down on the inhabitants of Kathmandu. All around the wooden pagodas on the sandy banks of the river, the saffron robes of the monks lay out to dry.

A Jeep overtook the car and two men in the back motioned them to stop. Superintendent Rai walked over to the Datsun and politely greeted its occupants. He asked for their names and nationality. Charles smiled. He had returned from his deserted Bangkok apartment that morning, leaving Ajay to deal with the locked safe. He got out of the car and shook hands with the Nepalese policeman.

'My name is Henricus Bintanja – Henk, for short – and I'm from Holland,' he announced, explaining that he taught sociology at the University of Amsterdam and introducing his wife, 'Cocky Hemker'. Behind her sunglasses, Marie-Andrée managed a tight smile and a nod.

Rai thought he knew exactly who they were. Following the Australian girls' lead about the gem-dealer with Vietnamese features, he had found a guest matching the description was registered at the Soaltee Oberoi as Henricus Bintanja.

'If you have been to Holland,' the driver of the Datsun was now saying, 'you will already know my wife, Cocky. She's a celebrity – always on television.'

Rai showed them a photograph of Connie, taken from her visa application. Did they recognize the picture?

Both of them shook their heads.

'Is there something wrong, superintendent?' Charles asked.

'We will just take a small look in your car if you don't mind,' nodded the superintendent.

'By all means,' Charles agreed.

Two young assistants made a cursory search of the back seat and boot of the car and handed Rai a pair of baggy jeans.

'Are these jean pants yours, Mr Henk?'

'I've never seen them before.'

'I am deeply sorry, but I must ask you to remain behind in Kathmandu until we complete our investigations.'

'But we are due to be in Delhi in two days.'

'I am very sorry. And now I must ask you to follow me to the police station. Just a formality. I am very sorry.'

'Oh well, superintendent, perhaps it is fated. I welcome this chance to remain in your beautiful country.'

One hour after the bus left Kathmandu with Luke, Sally and Katy, it was stopped at a police checkpoint. The three travellers were asked to accompany police back to the headquarters.

'We have found a man who looks Vietnamese although it appears that he is Dutch,' Superintendent Rai said to them. 'I wonder if you would recognize him as the man you saw with Miss Connie?'

'I'll try, superintendent,' Sally agreed nervously.

Just then some other people came into the room. Sally looked up and saw a pair of black eyes glaring at her from a sallow, cruelly sensuous face. With him was a woman with long black hair and sharp features. Why did that glare frighten her so much? Was it the same man she had seen briefly with Connie on Freak Street?

'I couldn't be sure, superintendent,' she said, averting her eyes from Sobhraj.

'I must say I am becoming impatient with all this,' Charles said, glancing at his gold Omega watch. 'And it is not nice for my wife.'

'You must excuse us, Mr Bintanja.'

'Yes, of course, you are doing your job. But may I now return to the Oberoi?'

'Certainly, yes.' The superintendent bowed slightly as 'Mr Bintanja' left the room.

Sally wished the police had warned her he was already there. The cold dark eyes had bored right through her and she was still shaking from the menace in his gaze.

'Maybe you should watch him,' she said to Rai after Charles had left the room. The three travellers suddenly felt scared, as though trapped in a web of ill-defined conspiracy.

'You could be in some danger here now,' said the superintendent quietly. Because their presence would be required in Nepal for a few more days, he assigned them a police bodyguard.

'When you feel the heat, go straight to the kitchen,' Charles had often said, and on the morning of 26 December, he walked into the office of Superintendent Rai and asked for the return of his pen, which he had left behind the previous day.

Over tea, Chandra Bir Rai asked 'Mr Henk' whether he had read about the cases of the burned bodies found in Thailand a few days before.

'I never look at newspapers, superintendent,' he said. 'And especially not ones in Bangkok. As a sociologist I have observed the Thais to be a bloodthirsty race, not like the sensitive Nepalese. I'm touring Asia with my wife, and we have no stomach for such horror stories.'

After Charles had left the office in a pantomime of smiles and handshakes, Rai weighed the evidence against the man he thought of as Henk Bintanja. He did not display the usual qualities of a criminal. Quite the opposite. He was gracious, and apparently carefree. There was no firm evidence against him. In fact, he had produced receipts from the restaurant at the Soaltee Oberoi with meal times marked on the back, and other witnesses had verified his constant presence in the hotel casino.

There was another suspect. Records showed that Laurent Carrière had shared a room with Connie Jo at the Oriental Lodge and had then flown out of Kathmandu. Could Carrière have killed Connie and the other unidentified victim and then fled?

And yet a farmer from the spot where the man's body had been found had noticed a car turning around late on the night of the murder. The first digit of its number plate was 5, matching the one on the white Datsun rented by Mr Henk Bintanja. There were not many modern white cars in Kathmandu. And the baggy pair of blue jeans found in the boot of Mr Bintanja's car had been identified by the two Australian girls as probably belonging to Miss Bronzich.

Lining the shelves in Rai's office were old Sherlock Holmes books. He had used them to teach himself both English and police investigatory procedure. In this case, the circumstantial evidence was powerful and there was something a little too methodical about Mr Bintanja's hotel receipts. In the morning, he decided, he would bring the couple back in for further questioning and search their room.

Kathmandu closed in on Sally, Luke and Katy. News of the couple found burned in Thailand had already cast a pall across the Asian trail, and now this atrocity in the Kingdom of Nepal, the birthplace of Buddha, had intensified the general paranoia. As the forlorn trio walked to and from Aunt Jane's each day, other travellers seemed to disappear down alleyways as if avoiding them.

Street talk centred on motive. A huge amount of heroin from Thailand had just hit the city and was being pushed in Freak Street. Was the timing a coincidence, or connected with the murders? Day and night in candlelit dives, overlanders, huddled like conspirators in old oil paintings, talked of nothing else.

'Whatever's going on around here, it must be mighty big,' Luke said to the girls.

Sally nodded. 'Connie's notebook made me realize that,' she said. When they had looked through her papers at the police station, the two girls had found a hand-scrawled note: 'Go [?] miles along the road to Dhulikhel' – they couldn't make out the number – 'and pick it up.' There were also some names and addresses of well-known drug dealers.

Still, they kept assisting the police with their inquiries. It was as if Superintendent Rai, sensing this was an incident outside local traditions, sought their advice. Later, in acknowledgment of their help, Sally, Luke and Katy were presented by police with a vial of hash oil.

Charles was not disturbed by the inevitable investigations into the killings. He knew he was invincible. He believed he had perfected a combination of charm and psychology, sleight of hand, strength, and pharmaceutical expertise, that allowed him to dominate any human situation. The Nepalese police, in their traditional breeches and peaked caps, were just a joke, he thought. His day-trip back to Bangkok, using the passport of Laurent Carrière, was enough to confuse them for weeks. They would assume that Laurent had killed Connie.

Several years later, Charles would claim that Connie Jo Bronzich died because her name had been given to him by his criminal employers in Hong Kong. She had been hired, he said, to fly to Bangkok and return to Kathmandu with a consignment of heroin. Two friends, one of them her so-called 'sister', Dor, from Santa Cruz, were to meet her around Christmas, and then carry the contraband back into America. For this they would be paid $5,000. As for the burly Canadian, on his way to see Mount Everest for the first time, Charles characterized him as a courier too who had been engaged in London.

Brutality, however, had reached a new extreme in these murders, the first to involve a knife. They were intended to create a 'big show', Charles would boast, but Ajay 'had overdone it a bit . . . These Indians . . . they stab fifteen times when once would do.'

After Connie's body was identified by Sally on Christmas Eve, US First Secretary Eastham drafted a telegram to Connie Jo Bronzich's parents in Los Gatos. It said a body had been tentatively identified and asked for Connie's dental records. He would wait a day before sending it. Guarded by two marines, her body was in the embassy refrigerator, which was ready to switch to a portable generator in case of a power failure, a common occurrence in Kathmandu.

Laurent Carrière's unidentified body remained on a slab at the mortuary. There was no room in the small British cemetery, the only one in Kathmandu.

Later, the American consul Allan Eastham would describe Connie as 'a nice young kid who had the worst luck anyone could have'. Mysterious deaths, however, had been part of Connie's life for years. Ten weeks before she left California, her estranged husband, John Franklin Bronzich, was found dead at her home. The coroner's report stated the cause of death as morphine poisoning, although his own family did not agree with this verdict. The amount of morphine found in his body was not normally enough to cause death. On the night he died, John Bronzich had been in a car with Connie on his way to a restaurant in Santa Cruz. He was not living with her at the time and, according to his family, had looked forward to the reunion. The couple had a fight, and John jumped out of the car.

The next morning he was found sprawled on the floor in the mobile home attached to Connie's house, dead. There was a syringe on the floor, some small balloons, and an overturned chair. It is not known how he travelled the 65 kilometres from the city of Santa Cruz to Connie's house in the mountains. His back was sprained, and he was wearing a surgical brace, which would have made walking down the long driveway to the mobile home impossible.

At the time of his argument with Connie, she had been dating a man with a long police record as a notorious Santa Cruz drug dealer. Some said there was animosity between Connie's estranged husband and the new boyfriend.

Perhaps it was no accident that John Bronzich's best friend, Frank Santa Cruz, was also found dead at the same address. One night he had come to Connie's house, taken off his boots and fallen asleep on top of her bed. When she woke up in the morning, Connie told police, she saw a strange grin on his face and tried to wake him. He was dead. This time the coroner's report was less positive in its conclusions. The cause of death was listed as 'undetermined'.

At dawn on 28 December, Superintendent Rai led a police raid on Room 415 of the Oberoi Hotel. When no one answered the door, his men forced their way inside. No one was there. Several suitcases were over-turned, their contents strewn about the floor. In the debris, police picked out eleven empty tins of Regulets (chocolate-flavoured laxatives), boxes of coloured pencils and a protractor (part of Charles' passport-forging kit). There was crumpled black nylon lingerie, a portable fire extinguisher, and some cassettes for learning Spanish. Sapphires and amethysts were scattered on the floor. Among the jumble of paperback books was *The Secret of the Aura* by Lobsang Rampa, *A Book of Life* by Martin Gray, a French inspirational writer, and *Beyond Good and Evil* by Nietzsche.

Through the plate-glass windows of the hotel room, Rai could see the city decked out with flags and flower garlands for the next day's royal birthday celebrations. His Majesty King Birendra Bir Bikram Shah Dev was considered the living reincarnation of Vishnu, the Hindu deity worshipped as the restorer of Karma, the moral order. The rising sun tinted the peaks of the Himalayas, which for aeons had encircled the valley as a protective wall. An awesome force had breached this citadel, Rai thought to himself. Now, somewhere out there, a man of prey was at large.

It was Charles' sixth sense again. Just as he used to sniff out the presence of police when he was a little boy stealing from shops – and a hundred times since – so Charles knew that the Nepalese police had been planning that dawn raid. At midnight he and Marie-Andrée had wrapped their necessities in a bed-sheet and thrown them out of the window to Ajay, waiting on the grass below. Then they had tiptoed down the back stairs and into a taxi.

For Marie-Andrée the escape was a further descent into her increasingly delusional attachment to Charles. 'It is a new start,' she wrote in her diary. 'Spiritual, physical connection, tenderness, glow, complicity; everything is shared, and we make only one person ... I belong to him, I feel I am desired, loved for myself, that he needs me, my presence, my smile to live. At last I am happy. I make plans and think only of our baby ...'

Charles used Hakim's passport while Marie-Andrée had a page from the passport of the dead Canadian, Laurent Carrière, which contained an entrance visa to India, inserted into her own passport. That same day the three of them crossed the border into India.

When they reached the holy city of Varanasi a few days later, Charles spent hours watching the bodies burn on the ghats of the Ganges.

Here Charles befriended Alan Aaron Jacobs, an Israeli tourist who had worked as a crane-driver to save for this holiday. He was happy to meet a group of friendly fellow travellers like Charles, Monique and Ajay, and to share a room with Ajay at a small hotel. The next day, after burning a batch of incriminating passports, Charles, Marie-Andrée and Ajay moved on to Goa, the bohemian enclave on the west coast of India. That same day Jacobs was found dead in his bed in the hotel room.

Charles later insisted this was an accident. 'I only wanted his passport,' he said, blaming the death on Ajay. 'That Israeli was the only one I felt sorry for. He'd told me how hard he had worked.'

In Goa, Charles met a party of Frenchmen at Anjuna Beach. He passed round a bottle of malt whisky and entranced them with talk of gems and his childhood adventures in Asia until the sun rose. One of the travellers, Eric Damour, described the experience in his journal as 'A night of excitement without end'.

On 9 January 1976, Charles, Marie-Andrée and Ajay rode south with the French party in their transit van, stopping for the night at a small beach resort. Charles ordered four chickens from the villagers, bought fresh crabs from the fishermen and mixed a whisky cocktail for his new friends, who were sprawled on the beach by a fire. At 9 p.m., the three Frenchmen passed out. Eric Damour and his two friends were thrown into the back of their van, now stripped of all its valuables, and Charles and Ajay put a rock on the accelerator and jumped out, leaving the drugged occupants to be the apparent victims of a car accident followed by looting. But the travellers were saved by villagers, who appeared seemingly from nowhere.

Charles and his friends moved on. In Madras, Ajay left them, saying he was returning to Delhi to visit his family. Charles and Marie-Andrée flew to Singapore, and then Hong Kong on 31 January. There they met an American school teacher, David Allen Gore, and invited him back to their room at the Sheraton Hotel, where he was drugged.

The haul from Gore included cash, cheques and credit cards, with Charles proudly showing Marie-Andrée a letter of credit for $8,000, which he cashed. He presented her with a gold Bulova watch and bought a diamond ring for his new Thai mistress, Roong. For himself he planned to buy a Jaguar, and a luxury apartment in Bangkok.

While he could have moved on to any number of cities, Charles saw no reason why he should. Although he had recently murdered ten people, he did not live in fear of arrest. He was used to being on the wanted list. His gem business was thriving and he planned to keep up such a show of affluence that he would be above suspicion, or immune from its effects. While the murders didn't add to the complications of his external life, he also experienced no qualms of conscience. 'If some ask me whether I feel remorse I answer: Does a professional soldier feel remorse after having killed a hundred men with a machine gun? Did the American pilots feel remorse after dropping napalm on my homeland? No. Society condoned the soldiers, telling them: You have the right to kill; it is your duty to kill – the more you kill the bigger the promotion. Don't I have the same right? In the interest of my own minority?'

The difference was that Charles' minority consisted of one, himself. And to him, morality was a word-game. 'I can justify the murders to myself,' he would often say. 'I never killed any good people.'

And so he planned to return to Bangkok. The very boldness of the act would be enough to dispel danger, he believed, and at the worst, the police could be bought. The only problem was Nadine Gires. How much did she know?

PART IV

Endgame

February 1976 – July 1977

13

Missing Persons

On Friday 13 February 1976, Nadine Gires sat in one of the leather-covered banquettes of the Indra Regent's foyer. She was waiting for a girlfriend. Dark circles under her eyes gave away the impact of her terrifying situation.

Since Christmas, while Remy was at work, Nadine had been keeping away from Kanit House. She had strolled endlessly through shopping arcades, sat alone in cinemas, and whiled away hours at other people's homes. Everyone was trying to help, but nothing was happening. A French engineer, who was a friend of the young couple, had approached a contact from the British embassy with the story of Alain Gautier. The word came back to Nadine that the British wanted proof. She had persuaded a Kanit House maid to let her into the upstairs apartment, where she had slipped into her handbag an exercise book written in Dutch. On the cover was the name Henk Bintanja. The British made their report, she understood, and had sent it on to the Thai police. Since then, Nadine had heard nothing more.

The news from Paris had added to their fears. Dominique Rennelleau had returned the borrowed airfare with a letter saying he had gone to the French police. 'We can do nothing,' they had told him. Yannick had promised to contact Interpol, but, instead, he had disappeared. There were rumours he had gone to live in a monastery. When Nadine and Remy went over the events at Kanit House, they began to wonder about Yannick. At least Dominique and his pipe-smoking friend François were still pressing ahead. They had obtained an interview with Jean Mouton-Brady, a high-ranking official in the Ministry of Foreign Affairs.

Nadine envied Dominique, safely at home in a picturesque village with his family. We could go, too, Nadine thought, but her husband's contract at the Oriental Hotel still had four months to run and Remy refused to resign just because of the man who lived upstairs.

It was all a matter of contacts, Nadine realized. Surely if they kept trying, something was bound to happen. There would be a police raid on the apartment, and all the damning evidence would be discovered. Alain Gautier would be put in jail, and at last she would feel safe again. Meanwhile, the killer was still around. Last week he had telephoned her, as friendly and casual as usual.

'Hello, Nadine, did you have a good Christmas?' he'd asked smoothly.

At first, her mouth had dried up, and she could hardly talk. So, to make conversation, she told him that she needed the commission she was owed because her brother was in trouble. It was just a story. She didn't have a brother. But, damn him, she would get her money and get him arrested. Alain said he was phoning from Hong Kong, but the connection was so clear it sounded like next door.

Reiner, the German boy, told her that Alain had been back to Bangkok twice since Christmas. He had stayed at the Dusit Thani Hotel but told Reiner that he planned to move back to 504.

Four days after the panic-stricken departure of Dominique, François and Yannick, Nadine had opened the *Bangkok World* to see the headline: 'Tourists Murdered in Nepal'. As soon as she read the story about an American girl and a Canadian man left by the road in Kathmandu, 'burned badly and difficult to identify', she knew, with a sick feeling in her stomach, that Alain must have gone to Kathmandu for his holiday – not to Hong Kong. And where was he now? The question plagued her.

The babble of conversation rose in the Indra foyer. Nadine looked up, hoping to see her friend due in from Paris. A tourist party poured through the revolving doors, clutching their carvings of elephants and souvenir shells, browsing like innocent cows around jewellery shops and boutiques of Thai silk. She looked at their soft, kindly faces. They would care, she thought, if they knew. She wondered

about the families far away – in America, Canada, Turkey, France and
the Netherlands – for whom a Christmas had passed without hearing
any news from their children.

'Hi, Nadine!'

She froze, then turned to find Charles standing behind her.

'We've just flown in from Hong Kong,' he said. 'It's so good to be
back.'

She forced a smile. Her heart was beating fast as he kissed her on
the cheek. His skin felt cold. She saw him as though for the first time
and she felt the force field of power that seemed to surround him.
The young businessman on his way up with his endearing confidence, well-cut clothes, gold Omega watch and crocodile attaché
case was smiling quizzically as he spoke to her in his low, insinuating
voice.

'I seem to have surprised you. Are you waiting for someone?'

'Yes, I've been waiting for a friend, a stewardess from Air France,
but the flight crew doesn't seem to have arrived.'

'How was your Christmas?'

'Fine.'

'And things at Kanit House?'

His questions seemed to have a double meaning.

'Fine,' she said.

'Now, Nadine, tell me about your brother,' he said urgently with a
concerned expression, as though it was something that had been
bothering him since the phone call.

'That's why I'm waiting for my friend, Alain. She's bringing me
news from my family,' said Nadine, improvising. 'But ... I have to
send him more money.'

'Don't worry,' he said, 'I left in a hurry last time. There was no
time to pay your commission.' In a quick, hardly noticeable movement, Charles pulled off the wide black belt around his hips,
unzipped it and took out a bundle of $100 notes, counting out three
of them. 'Maybe you thought I wouldn't pay?' he said as she folded
the notes neatly and put them in her shoulder bag. 'And take this, a
bonus. For your brother.' He handed Nadine another $300.

So, she thought, this means that he knows that I know.

'Well, I should find Monique. When we're settled, you and Remy must come up for a drink. Has anyone been looking for me?'

'Just a few customers. I told them we didn't know when you'd be back,' she said in a neutral voice, trying to smile.

'Maybe you thought we wouldn't come back?'

'Maybe, Alain. I didn't know.'

'Why shouldn't we? So many customers owe me money. We got held up in Hong Kong. My business there is growing too quickly.' He looked pleased with himself.

'And how's Monique?' Nadine asked.

'Sick of travelling, I think. She'll be pleased to see you.'

They talked for a few more minutes, and then Marie-Andrée walked across the hotel foyer wearing dark glasses and carrying Franky.

'Here she comes,' he said, waving to her.

Watching her and the way she was clinging onto the dog, Nadine thought how much thinner she looked. Had she known what Alain was doing, had she been involved? She still remembered the expression on Marie-Andrée's face when she had said, 'I don't like that Turk,' and 'I don't like those Dutch. I want them to go.'

The two women exchanged greetings with a kiss on each cheek.

'Why not come back with us in the car, Nadine?' said Charles, sweeping an arm around her shoulders. 'Your friend wasn't on the plane.'

He was right. While they were talking, she had seen the Air France flight crew check into the hotel, and her friend was not among them.

Her heart starting to beat rapidly, Nadine climbed into the back seat of the brown Datsun and sat there terrified. It was like the beginning of one of her nightmares. Since Christmas she had often dreamed she was being chased down the echoing corridors of Kanit House and into the tiny lift where Charles was waiting for her, smiling. But this was really happening. Marie-Andrée sat in front beside Charles, stroking the dog's ears and saying little.

Behind the breezy intimacy of his chatter, Nadine could sense
Charles probing her fear. He must know that I know, she thought.
Thank God I'm wearing sunglasses. To pay the commission so bla-
tantly the moment he saw me again, hc thinks he can do anything
with money. He thinks he can make me forget what I know. The
uncanny tug of his charm made him more frightening, as though he
knew how to lull a conscience into thinking wrong was right.

Charles seemed in no hurry to reach Kanit House. For once he
wasn't swearing at the rigid lanes of traffic. He could not be sure
how much Yannick had talked before fleeing and he noticed that
Nadine was trying hard to appear cool. Damn that *Bangkok Post* with
its picture of the 'Australian Couple'! It must have caused the others
to panic. To leave them alone had been a mistake. Anyway, what
could Nadine do – tell the French embassy? They were even less of a
worry than the Thai police.

Maybe she had already gone to the Thai police, but he guessed
that they wouldn't give a damn. As far as he could tell from Roong,
they had nothing in their files against him. Roong's father was a
policeman, so were her cousins, and her family already treated him
like their own son. Maybe he would marry her one day. He knew
that Asian women put their men before everything else. In Thailand,
only money mattered. Roong's family had taken care of Franky
while he and Marie-Andrée had been away, and because the dog had
torn some upholstery, he would compensate them with some new
furniture. What a pity the problem of Nadine could not be so easily
solved.

Charles had guessed there might be talk about the strange events
at Kanit House at the end of last year, but he wasn't worried. He had
plenty of cash. Soon he would move to a better apartment and
expand his international gem business with the German boy, Reiner.
He would put up a bigger front, now, to blind the Thais to any
rumours. With the lifestyle he planned, no one would ever believe
that someone like him would kill hippies for pocket money.

Charles had already found a replacement for Yannick. Jean
Dhuisme was a tall, grim-faced Frenchman he had met one night

at the Grace Hotel. Because of a failed property deal, Dhuisme was desperate for money and had already agreed to fly home to Paris and return to Kanit House with parties of French tourists. Charles had met Jean during one of his furtive reconnaissance trips to Bangkok a few weeks before. Now he was telling Nadine that he and Marie-Andrée had only arrived back in Bangkok that day, when in fact they had already spent a few nights at a nearby hotel under false names. He had even phoned Nadine, pretending he was still in Hong Kong.

Glancing at her now in the rear-view mirror, silent behind her sunglasses, Charles wondered whether Nadine had guessed from the newspaper reports that he and Marie-Andrée had spent their Christmas holiday in Kathmandu.

When they reached Kanit House and Nadine helped them carry their bags upstairs, she noticed their new, expensive luggage and wondered if the original owner was still alive. Inside, the air was stale and smelled of medicine and tobacco. Charles opened the windows, letting in the warm afternoon breeze. The maid had followed them up to clean the room, the same one who had allowed Nadine to search the flat six weeks ago. Charles ensured courteous service with generous tips.

'Hello, Dang,' he said, picking up Cocky Hemker's transistor radio from the table. 'Here's a present for you.'

As he handed it to Dang, Nadine's heart sank. To persuade the maid to let her into 504 while Alain was away, she had told her that the police wanted him for murder. What a fool she had been! Perhaps Dang hadn't understood. There was nothing in the maid's behaviour to suggest that she had.

'Nadine! Come in here a moment,' Charles called from the adjoining apartment. 'There's some business we must finish.'

It was a cat-and-mouse game being played with the Asian rule of hiding emotion. The Thais called it *tai chuan*, 'cool heart'. As Nadine took a deep breath and walked into 503, she hoped that her face and voice would not give her away.

In 504, Marie-Andrée began to supervise the cleaning up. Since leaving India, she had been travelling using the passport of Eric Damour – one of the tourists Charles had met on the beach in Goa and drugged – counting on the gender confusion caused by Western names in Asia. Not unusually, she had been in a grim self-pitying mood, and in Hong Kong in January had begun to record her daily tribulations in a small, silk-bound diary: 'I'm tired.' 'Depressed.' 'Can't sleep.' 'We are six months together.' 'He's already made love to Roong.' 'I'm sick and very tired.'

A few days ago she had arrived in Bangkok with Charles, incognito – 'We are thought to be on holiday' – and they had gone together to Pattaya. 'More fights, we don't understand each other.'

As usual, Charles left her alone for hours at a time. In an anguished letter she later wrote: 'It is not to Charles my friend, or my love that I wish to speak, but to Charles the psychologist. I want to know first if we have some chance to recover our balance, to understand each other again, and be happy together.' The letter continued for pages, starting with the scene of her arrival in Bangkok and then analysing the succeeding stages of her relationship with Charles. It was a record of her raw emotions. 'Too quickly, Roong moves into our life. I feel suicidal. I do not feel strong enough to fight with him about her. He is leaving me and gives her everything I would like to have. Happiness, time ... and he is very satisfied with her in the bedroom.'

In the living room of 503, Nadine lit a cigarette as she watched Charles shuffle through his papers, wondering what his next move would be.

'You must be very upset about your brother,' he said in a caressing tone of voice. He used his voice like a weapon, she realized. 'It's a worry when young boys make big mistakes. If he's in prison, you know, I could do something. I have a good friend who's on all the penal reform committees. He lives in Paris.' As he spoke, he was unlocking a drawer.

'It's OK, Alain. It's a family matter. We can take care of it.' Why did her voice sound so unnatural?

'This is for you,' he said, turning around and handing her another wad of banknotes, 'for your brother.'

She put the money in her bag, thanked him and hurried back to her own apartment, where she locked her door and phoned Remy with the news that Alain Gautier was back.

On that same afternoon, Herman Knippenberg was ploughing through paperwork at the Dutch embassy. Officially, his working day began punctually at 7.30 a.m. and ended at 2 p.m. without a lunch break, but often he worked late. This Friday afternoon was no exception. The phone on his desk rang. When he picked it up, the voice of Paul Siemons, his colleague from the Belgian embassy, boomed through the earpiece.

'Herman, are you missing any people?'

Siemons was a droll, worldly, larger-than-life character officially listed as an administrative attaché to the Belgian embassy but operating more like a trouble-shooter behind the scenes. The two men had an easy working relationship and often consulted each other when devising strategies to avoid the smuggling of drugs or sex workers into their adjoining countries.

'Why do you ask?' said Herman, startled. So far, he had told no one outside his staff about his search for Cocky and Henk. 'What do you know?'

Paul launched into a colourful account of an argument between a Belgian diplomat, the Baronet Gilles de Giverney, and a French-Moroccan antiques dealer called Albert Goyot that had happened last October at the Grace Hotel.

Along with most diplomats in Bangkok, Herman knew about the incident involving the likeable but haughty de Giverney, who had been incensed by the high price Goyot had paid to secure de Giverney's favourite Balinese-Thai bar-girl. Ever since, Goyot had been making trouble. Recently he had embarrassed de Giverney by taking out an advertisement in the *Bangkok Post* which advised him to contact a lawyer regarding the incident at the Grace Hotel. Siemons recounted the story with gusto.

'De Giverney came to me for help, and we both started checking on this Albert Goyot. I wanted to find something incriminating against him so we could get him booted out of the country. Anyway, we start to hear certain rumours about a mixed-blood Frenchman living in Soi Saladaeng, not far from me, who lures tourists to his apartment and murders them.'

Paul had spent twenty years in the Belgian Congo on undercover operations and his stories were always colourful.

'Any mention of Dutch tourists?' Herman asked quickly.

'Someone said they saw a whole pile of passports in a safe. Two of them belonged to a Dutch couple who had been seen at the Frenchman's apartment.'

'And who lives there? Albert Goyot?'

'Presumably, yes, although there's some confusion. My source who got it from another source said the name was Alain Gautier, but it's probably the same man.'

'Could be. The initials are the same. You know how European names get bastardized in translation.'

Paul's years as an intelligence officer had made him cagey about revealing contacts. Actually, de Giverney himself had picked up the rumour from a journalist at Agence Presse. This man had heard it from a French schoolteacher who was a friend of Nadine's and knew the story from her.

Herman's mind flashed to an earlier report in the *Bangkok Post* of two Australians found burned on the roadside. It was so gruesome he had remembered it. Now he was struck by a fact that had stuck in his mind when he first read the story. The girl was said to be wearing a T-shirt made in Holland.

'Paul, remember the case of those Australian tourists found burned at Ayutthaya? Were they ever positively identified?'

'I'm not sure.'

Herman told Paul about his missing travellers, Cocky and Henk, and the letter from their relative in Amsterdam, John Zant, who had mentioned a meeting with a gem-dealer in Hong Kong, a gem-dealer living in an apartment in Bangkok who had invited the two to stay with him.

'This Goyot character deals in gems,' Paul said, 'and he's always travelling.'

Herman told his colleague that he would phone him back and put in a call to the vice consul at the Australian embassy, who was positive that the two bodies had never been identified. In December two young Australians had been touring the same area where the burned bodies were found. Nice kids, they had written their names down on pieces of paper for the local children and then just disappeared. No one heard another word. When the burned bodies were found on the road, the police connected the *farang* names.

'So we thought the worst had happened,' the vice consul explained to Herman. 'Then the kids came walking in here just a few days ago, alive and well.'

When Herman put down the phone, he asked his secretary to comb all the English-language newspapers for references to dead or missing Westerners, starting from 8 December, the date Cocky and Henk arrived in Bangkok. Then he phoned Paul Siemons with the news and told him that he would pay an official visit of inquiry to the Thai police.

'*Pfft!*' Paul spat through the phone. He was frequently giving vent to his views on corruption and the Thai police, and now he was concerned for the safety of his source, the young French couple, who still lived in the same apartment block as the suspect. 'You be careful,' he warned Herman. 'I understand that this Gautier has a Thai girlfriend who is a daughter of a high-ranking police officer.'

'I'm not saying that the whole Thai police force is above reproach, Paul, but I do have some contacts with police officials who are,' said Herman. He was thinking of Pao Sarasin, the Deputy Director of the Central Investigation Bureau. This official was also Chairman of the Central Narcotics Board, and Herman had met him on a field trip to the Golden Triangle. 'Pao Sarasin's cousin is social secretary at our embassy, and she can have a word in his ear ... the way things are usually done in this country.'

'Yes, that's why you must not involve the police.'

'But we must involve them,' insisted Herman. 'It's their job and their country.'

Siemons remained unconvinced but agreed to compile a report on the rumours of the mysterious French gem-dealer.

In California, eleven days after posting her letter to the President, Emma Knowlton received a message from another source, one that had more impact on her than any of the official letters which were to follow. In the early morning of 18 February, Teresa's birthday, Emma woke up and saw a light in the kitchen. 'I couldn't understand why the light was on,' she would later recount:

I got out of bed, picked up my clock, and saw it was 1 a.m. I went to turn off the light. Teresa was sitting at the kitchen table like she usually sat, and she just looked beautiful, her face, everything. All her beautiful colouring. I looked at her, and I screamed.

'Oh, Grandma!' she said.

'Teresa, where have you been! I've been searching all over for you,' I said.

And she started to cry, and she said, 'Grandma, I want to come home. Bring me home, Grandma. I've got to come home.'

And I found myself at the edge of my bed. I picked up the clock, and it was still 1 a.m., and the light was on in the kitchen. I ran out there, but she wasn't there. And I knew then, she was dead.

14

The 'Gautier Affair'

At 11 a.m., Friday 20 February, Herman Knippenberg was talking to senior officers at Thai police headquarters about his reasons for requesting information about the burned corpses found at Ayutthaya. The air-conditioning had broken down, and the legs of his light-weight trousers kept sticking to the vinyl-covered armchair.

'Since the two bodies are still not identified there's a possibility that they are our missing Dutch couple,' Herman explained.

Major General Suwit Sothitate, a commander of Crime Suppression, stood up behind the desk and began leafing through a thick file of documents. He was a short man, with a pleasantly wrinkled face and a receding hairline. Over his left pocket were layers of rainbow-striped decorations. General Suwit told Herman that the files of the Ayutthaya case were still in the possession of the provincial police of Ayutthaya where the bodies had been found, but that Crime Suppression would send for them and assume full responsibility for the case.

The other policeman, Major General Pao Sarasin, sat on the edge of the desk in civilian clothes. He was tall and distinguished and reminded Herman more of a diplomat than a policeman. Pao said that the two bodies were now in the police mortuary, and when the dental records of the missing Dutch couple arrived from the Netherlands, they could be checked against the bodies.

When Herman left the office he was reassured. Two top-ranking police officials were personally involved, and Crime Suppression was an elite unit of the Thai police, with many of its officers trained by Scotland Yard. He believed that once a positive identification had been made of the bodies, the police would act decisively.

When he returned to his office shortly after noon, he found a thick envelope on his desk marked 'Personal and Confidential'. He told his secretary to keep out any visitors, closed the door and lit a cigarette. He began reading Paul Siemon's report headed, 'Double Murder on the Road to Ayutthaya: State of Investigation.'

This remarkable document contained a detailed description of an Alain Gautier of 504 Kanit House – 'strong personality, dominates his friends to the point of challenging everybody, megalomaniac, likes to change physical appearance.'

It listed as accomplices: Girlfriend No. 1, 'Monique Leclerc, a trained nurse who has drugged several guests with help of syringe', and Girlfriend No. 2, 'of Thai nationality, daughter of highly placed police official'. The report quoted unnamed sources claiming to have seen the Dutch couple in the apartment and another witness who saw Gautier come back in the early hours of 16 December covered with dirt. It also listed incriminating evidence said to be still in the Kanit House apartment: two Dutch passports, the belongings of various victims, and a travel diary written in Dutch.

Herman stared through his office window, absently watching the pet geese roaming the embassy lawn. He decided that it was time he met Paul's sources for this important lead.

Paul was being secretive about their identities. His note stressed that the police should only be called in at the last moment when all the proof was assembled. There must be no danger that the inquiry would collapse, as had so often happened in Thailand, leaving the witnesses in a dangerous situation.

Yes, it was a remarkable document, and Herman was filled with renewed admiration for his extroverted colleague, even if Paul sometimes got swept away, as he had with the improbable allegation that Gautier was somehow linked with a double murder in Kathmandu last Christmas.

In a sunny ground-floor apartment near Pigalle in Paris, the mother, brother and stepfather of Stephanie Parry were eating lunch in silence. At first, after Stephanie had failed to arrive for Christmas, her mother had phoned her sister Sylvy, who lived on Ibiza. That was when she heard for the first time that her daughter had gone to Bangkok. Now six weeks had passed and each day the family meals were silent and her mother's face more drained. Stephanie's brother, a handsome bearded boy, put his hand on his mother's arm as she sat at the table.

'Come on, mother, she'll be back,' he said comfortingly.

'She won't be back,' she said, looking unseeingly in front of her. 'I know that now. She's dead.'

The Australian embassy had none of the old-world elegance of the Dutch. It occupied a floor of an office building on Silom Road, and its walls were decorated with large colour photographs of orange deserts and pastel eucalyptus forests, koala bears and a portrait of Queen Elizabeth.

On Saturday 21 February, Vice Consul John Carrick was waiting for Herman. He had opened the office this morning at Herman's request to provide him with his own files on the Ayutthaya tourist murders.

'How are you going on the case?' the Australian asked, pouring them both a cup of coffee.

Herman summarized the rumours of the murder suspect who drugged and robbed tourists.

'I'll be damned,' said the vice consul. 'We had a case like that a few months ago, but they survived to tell the tale.'

Herman asked for the details, and the Australian produced a four-page statement from the two victims, Russell and Vera Lapthorne, the young Australian professor and his wife who had been drugged the previous September at the Railway Hotel at Hua Hin. They described their encounter with a French psychiatrist who called himself 'Jean Belmont' – 'wide mouth, muscular arms and legs, broad chest, thin waist, and otherwise slight' – and a woman he introduced as 'Monique' – 'very thin, narrow pointed nose, wore green eye make-up, plucked eyebrows, slight build, quite attractive in appearance'. The couple had a white puppy, Franky, which Monique loved to hold in her arms.

Herman looked at the photos of the burned bodies found at Ayutthaya and the close-ups of the victims' faces which had been taken at the police hospital. He felt sick.

The next Tuesday, 24 February, Herman combed through the records of the Thai Immigration Department. Five flights had arrived from Hong Kong early on 11 December, the night Zant said Cocky and Henk came to Thailand. He checked each passenger list. On Air Siam's flight VG903 which had landed at Don Muang Airport at 1 a.m., he found the names of Bintanja and Hemker. In another departmental cubbyhole he checked through the white cards completed by all arriving passengers. Their cards were still in the 'Active' file. This meant that they had not yet left Thailand.

For once, a bureaucratic bungle had worked against Charles' devious plan. When he and Marie-Andrée had flown to Kathmandu using the identities of their dead house-guests, immigration paperwork would normally have removed Cocky's and Henk's cards from the active file. But the system had not worked. As their proposed address in Thailand, the Dutch couple had written the Hotel Malaysia. The guest register there showed no record of them for those dates. It was beginning to look as though the Frenchman mentioned in John Zant's letter had kept his promise and met Cocky and Henk at the airport.

That afternoon Herman visited the vice consul of the French embassy to try to sort out the confusion between the identities of 'Albert Goyot' and 'Alain Gautier'. Of the latter there was no record, but Albert Goyot had made a bad impression on the consular staff when he had applied for a new passport, stating that his current one had been stolen in January at Pattaya. When asked why he had not reported the theft earlier, Goyot had explained this was unnecessary because he was intimate with high-ranking members of the Thai police and immigration departments.

As proof of his identity, Goyot had handed in an expired passport. The visa stamps revealed a pattern of travel between Hong Kong,

Bangkok, Singapore, India, Nepal and Japan. Herman was excited. When had Goyot arrived in Bangkok? From the direction of Japan, he was told, Goyot had landed at Don Muang Airport on 10 December, one day before Cocky and Henk.

Cocky's and Henk's photographs and dental records arrived from Amsterdam the following Monday. The Dutch X-rays would have to be checked against the bodies.

On Wednesday 3 March, Herman was driven to the mortuary to meet Dr Twijnstra, a warm-hearted, middle-aged dentist. She was a Dutch missionary at the Adventist Hospital and a friend of Herman's wife, Angela, and had gladly agreed to assist her embassy. Herman worried that Twijnstra might be overwhelmed.

When he arrived, the soft, sweet smell of Lysol filled Herman's nostrils as he followed his Thai driver, a rugged ex-policeman, down the bare corridors of the hospital. Gingerly he opened the swinging doors to the mortuary to find shelves stacked to the ceiling with bodies in various states of decay.

'Over here, Mr Knippenberg,' a woman's voice called out to him. 'We've found them!' He saw the grey head of the dentist bent over the mouth of the male corpse. She was poking at the teeth with her instruments. 'The bicuspid's gone, and the molar's moved forward,' she announced, her professional manner unshaken by the surroundings. 'It matches the X-rays from Amsterdam.'

Not only were the naked bodies so charred and shrivelled that it was difficult even to distinguish the sex, but after the autopsy they had been crudely stitched together. A strong smell of burnt flesh merged horribly with the Lysol. Herman's driver fainted and was carried from the room. Knippenberg consulted briefly with Dr Twijnstra and then left her alone to complete her examination while he spoke with the police pathologist. As Herman checked the items of clothing, he saw that the woman's bra was made in Holland. This was the item that had been wrongly translated in the newspaper as a T-shirt. A Dutch bra was even more suggestive of Dutch nationality than a Dutch T-shirt. Not that there were now any doubts about the nationality of the corpses. But he wanted to present a watertight case to the Thai police.

On Friday morning, 5 March, the Mercedes Benz from the Dutch embassy turned off Rama 1 Road in the heart of Chinatown and pulled up next to a dilapidated complex of wooden barracks. Herman followed his Thai assistant through a maze of corridors and staircases, past rooms of policemen hunched over old-fashioned typewriters, slowly tapping keyboards, or sitting around dusty desks playing cards. Herman noticed a few frightened-looking young men in handcuffs were being questioned by the police. His assistant knocked cautiously on a door.

Herman was ushered into a grim office where General Suwit rose from an enormous desk to greet him and, as he had before, patted him on the back, offered him some cigars, and asked him how he was enjoying Thailand.

After these preliminaries, Herman informed his host that the two bodies had been identified as the missing Dutch and handed Suwit a letter which began, 'Dear General Suwit, in the course of your police investigation into the murders of Mr Bintanja and Miss Hemker, the following pieces of information may prove useful to you.'

Over the next six pages Herman had meticulously summarized all the evidence he had gathered in the previous weeks, including all he knew about the 'strange events at a Bangkok apartment occupied by a Frenchman called Alain Gautier or Albert Goyot', and the results of his 'discreet enquiries' into Monique Leclerc and Roong. In conclusion, Herman noted that 'the Dutch Ambassador, His Excellency Dr Van Dongen, is confident that Crime Suppression will do its utmost to bring the murderer(s) of Mr Bintanja and Miss Hemker to justice.'

With the letter were several exhibits, including a photocopy of the Air Siam flight manifest showing the arrival of Cocky and Henk; a photograph given to him by the French embassy of the suspect, Albert Goyot; a copy of the letter from John Zant asking for help in tracking Cocky and Henk; and a copy of Paul's report from which all derogatory remarks about the Thai police had been eliminated.

After studying the letter and the enclosures, Suwit told Herman that Crime Suppression would immediately begin investigating Albert Goyot and the Thai girl, Roong.

'My ambassador believes that the reputation of Thailand will be enhanced if you arrest a killer preying on tourists,' Herman said, ever the diplomat.

The general's round face beamed behind his glasses as he walked his visitor to the door. 'But the timing of your request is so unfortunate, Mr Knippenberg,' he said. 'Our best officers are caught up investigating a whole series of political murders.'

Herman read between the lines. He would continue with his own work on the case.

Herman's task was over. He had cabled The Hague that the bodies in the mortuary had been officially identified as the missing nationals, and he had sent them Dr Twijnstra's dental autopsy reports. But Herman had no intention of dropping his pursuit of the killers until they were locked up in a Thai jail.

The conclusions of the first autopsy reports stayed with Herman as he left police headquarters and hurried out into the steamy heat of Chinatown. 'Cocky Hemker: Cause of death: Cerebral haemorrhage caused by being hit over the head with a hard item. She was set fire to while she was still breathing. Henk Bintanja: Cause of death: This man was strangled so that the blood circulation to the brain was interrupted. He was set fire to when he was still breathing.'

Herman stretched out wearily in the back of the car as it came to a halt on Rama Road near the Giant Swing, a peculiar structure like a giant gibbet. Someone had told him that Buddhist novitiates had swung from it during ceremonies. The practice had been discontinued only forty years ago after several fatalities. To the Thais, death seemed to be of no great consequence. Newspaper pictures of criminals before the firing squad showed them smiling. A Thai friend had once explained to Herman: 'For Buddhists, to die is like getting on a bus and then getting off again at another bus stop.'

Back at the calm oasis of the embassy, Herman phoned Paul Siemons.

'I really want to meet those informants. Take me to Kanit House as soon as you can arrange it.'

'Dear boy, I thought you had dumped the case into the lap of the police,' said Siemons.

'I did. But Suwit said something about political murders taking precedence in their investigation. I got the impression they have bigger fish to fry. He seemed to suggest that I keep working on it.'

'Let's fry our own fish then, Herman.'

On Saturday 6 March, Charles kissed Roong on the lips and told her he would come back to see her soon. From her room on the eighth floor of the Regent Hotel at Pattaya, the pert Thai teenager watched him stroll along the path through the garden. Roong knew he was going to visit the Siam Bay Shore, another of the resort's luxury hotels on the beach, where Monique would be waiting for him. She didn't like it, but how could she ever argue with him?

When Roong had first met Charles at the Indra coffee shop, it was Monique she had noticed first. Accustomed to serving plump American matrons in tour groups, she had come to the conclusion that all *farang* women were overweight. But this one was thin, with lovely breasts. The two girls had smiled at each other. The next day Charles had come back alone and asked Roong to dinner.

'But your wife?' she asked.

'Oh, that's just my secretary,' he told her.

Charles began seeing Roong almost every day. He was so kind. At seven in the morning he would turn up at her parents' home, a small wooden house on stilts near the airport, and drive her to school. She wanted to be a teacher, so she was attending a course each day before going to work at the hotel.

'Darling, you look so tired,' she would say to him. 'You don't have to do this.'

But Charles said he loved her. 'I want to look after you, my little baby, always.' Roong's mother and father loved Charles, and her mother liked to cook him breakfast.

But here she was, dressed, made-up and ready for a nice walk with her boyfriend along the beach, and he was keeping her waiting. They would have a drink and a snack. But she must remember to avoid lobster, which made her skin erupt. Roong phoned the Siam Bay Shore and left a message for him at the desk.

It was only six weeks since she had made love for the first time in her life, to Charles of course, and it was a day she would never forget. He came to her home late one January afternoon. She had been fired from her job in the coffee shop for spending too much time off work. He drove her and Franky to the Dusit Thani Hotel. She had been minding the puppy while Charles and Marie-Andrée went on a Christmas holiday together. Roong stayed with him in the expensive suite and spent the whole day shopping. He wanted her to stop dressing like an old maid and bought her two new pairs of tight jeans, a short yellow dress, three blouses and two pairs of shoes, and then presented her with a beautiful sapphire ring.

It was in the afternoon when they were lying around the suite that something happened which convinced Roong that her boyfriend had a heart of pure gold.

Gems and money were spread all over the room. Customers were coming up, and Charles was asking everyone to call him Eric. Franky, still excited at seeing his master again, sprang onto the coffee table, knocking over some of the stones. The puppy sniffed the diamonds and, before she could stop him, swallowed three of them, big ones, expensive ones. She grabbed him and started slapping his nose. Charles stopped her, laughing, 'Haven't you been feeding him, darling?' She tried to force the dog's mouth open. 'Darling, stop it,' he said. 'Franky didn't know what he was doing.' Charles told her they would lock him in the bathroom until he gave them back. What a kind man he was.

Later, when Roong had felt tired and wanted to sleep, Charles gave her some pills to wake her up. They did. Then he had made love to her.

It was all right to sleep with him, she told herself as she retouched her eyeliner, still waiting for him to arrive. She planned to marry him. He would be a rich and kind husband. Soon the other girl, Monique, would be leaving. He was with her now, that was why he was late.

There was a knock on the door. Roong opened it and Charles walked in. He took her in his arms.

'My little wife, don't be angry,' he said. 'In a few days Monique is going back to her own country.'

'You call me your wife, but you live with her,' Roong sulked, wanting to punish him for leaving her alone so long. With his arm around her waist, Charles led her to the mirror.

'Your eyes, darling. See? They're like mine. Monique is not Asian. How can I love her? Darling, let's get married as soon as we can. Do you think your parents will allow it?'

'They love you.'

'Let's go and ask their permission.'

'Charles, you make me very happy. When?'

He was rich, kind, successful. Her whole world had changed since the day they had met.

'Next week. Friday. I will come to your house and ask your family to allow the engagement. You can explain the Thai customs to me.'

She took out a diary from her handbag and circled the date, Friday 12 March.

That night there was a banging on the door of the room. Charles motioned Roong to keep quiet. The banging grew louder.

'I know you're in there,' a woman's voice shouted.

The two said nothing and Roong held her breath. Now, outside on the landing, Marie-Andrée was crying. She had intercepted the message from Roong to Charles at their hotel. She hadn't even known his Thai mistress was in Pattaya.

'All right, Alain. I've had it. It's over now,' she shouted, banging her fists on the door. She was sick of everything. She wanted to go home. She had already cabled her old boyfriend, Jules Dupont, the accountant, and asked him to come and help her, to take her away.

She didn't have the strength to do it alone. She didn't trust herself any more.

'I'm going to jump,' she yelled through the door. 'I'll kill myself.'

Two Thai men stood on the landing below, watching her. Marie-Andrée opened the window.

Inside the room, Charles sighed and got out of bed.

'I must go to her, Roong,' he said, putting on his underpants and jeans and picking up his shirt. 'She's desperate. These girls from Quebec. Never again! They're so stubborn. She might even do it!'

Marie-Andrée was standing on the balcony. Charles opened the door. A few tourists were looking up. He grabbed her.

'You fool!'

Shutting the door of Roong's room, he lifted Marie-Andrée and carried her down a few steps, waving away the gawking Thais.

'Darling, I've told you why I'm playing this game with Roong,' he said softly in her ear, putting his arm around her shaking shoulders. Couldn't she understand? Roong was the key to their future security. For a long time they sat together on the stairs. Then he walked her down to the car, and they drove back to the suite at the Siam Bay Shore.

'My darling,' he said, caressing her, 'I've got so much money now. In a few days I'll take you to Paris. We can start again.'

She was sobbing against his shoulder. Paris in the spring with Charles. How could she ever leave him?

In his office at 7 a.m. on Monday morning, 8 March, Herman Knippenberg spread out the contents of the package on his desk. He had an hour before the phone calls began – time to study the photographs which had just arrived. They were just ordinary holiday snapshots: the pretty girl leaning over the rails of a ferry, the breeze fluttering her long fair hair; the bearded man posing stolidly at the bottom of ornamental steps, his hands on his hips. There were porcelain buddhas, rickshaws, paper dragons, Chinese food-stalls, a view from the hills of Macao, a glimpse of the Chinese border. Only days before they were murdered, Cocky and Henk had sent the film home to their relatives in Amsterdam. The prints had just arrived in the embassy pouch. Herman made a note of all clothing, luggage and accessories which might provide evidence.

'Good morning, Herman.'

He looked up to see de Giverney standing in the doorway. His cravat was tucked neatly into his silk shirt. Indifferent to the heat, he wore brown corduroy trousers.

'You've been busy?' de Giverney asked with a smile. He had just returned from a holiday and wanted to catch up on the drag-net closing around his old foe from the Grace, Albert Goyot. When Herman had finished briefing him, de Giverney mentioned he had an appointment that afternoon with a Dr Phillippe. Herman handed him a photograph of Albert Goyot he had obtained from the French embassy.

'Show this to him. He treats all the French in Bangkok. Maybe he will recognize this Goyot.'

Later de Giverney phoned him with news. The doctor did not treat Goyot. He had never heard of him. But he did have another patient, an ʿAlain Gautierʾ, who was always bringing women friends to him for treatment. 'Physically speaking,' the doctor had said, 'Alain Gautier is a perfect specimen of the human male.'

Of more relevance, Gautier had a girlfriend called Monique. They lived at Kanit House in Soi Saladaeng.

'OK. Alert Paul. Tell him it's imperative we meet with his witness tonight.'

The sun was low in the sky. It was early evening, and the dishevelled coconut palms dotted unevenly down Soi Saladaeng were black silhouettes. Paul's white Mercedes with its dark-tinted windows cruised past the baskets of ginger root and hundred-day eggs stacked on the pavement in front of the shops. Behind the high walls and the rich vegetation that fell over the jagged broken glass on top of them, residents were relaxing at home as servants prepared the evening meal. Apart from the tinkle of the drink-seller's trishaw, the street was deserted. For a moment it seemed like a country town.

The three men in the Mercedes looked up at the top floor of the building and to the apartment at the end which their source had described. A light was on, and the shadows of human movement flickered behind the blinds of 504.

'Don't park too near the building, Paul,' Herman said. 'Someone might notice the consular plates.'

Paul grumbled about a 'boy-scout mentality' as he backed the car down a side-street, out of sight of the upstairs apartment. 'I don't give a damn if they do see us,' he said. 'Then we can take care of them ourselves.'

The three men laughed, even de Giverney in the back, who had been very quiet until now. But Paul was serious. He didn't trust the Thai police. And he had his own views on the administration of justice. It usually worked best when you took it into your own hands. Get it done and apologise later.

He picked up his blue service pistol, a Belgian FN 7.65, from the seat and checked the chamber.

'I say we place Gautier under citizen's arrest,' he said. The two younger men protested. De Giverney recoiled at the prospect of drama, and Herman wanted this one played according to the rules.

'Bah! What an idealist,' Paul grumbled, sticking the pistol inside the band of his trousers, where it was hidden by his loose sports shirt.

Herman turned around to the back seat. 'You go, Gilles. You've got the best cover story.'

The plan was that de Giverney would go up and knock on the door of Nadine and Remy's apartment. They didn't know him, but he could introduce himself as a friend of the journalist from the Agence Presse who had first tipped him off about the strange events in the apartment upstairs.

'Don't worry if "Gautier" catches you and throws you over the balcony,' Herman said, trying to lighten the atmosphere with his earnest Dutch humour. 'Just try to land in the swimming pool.'

As de Giverney climbed out of the car, he looked down at his colleague with an expression of disdain which must have taken centuries to perfect.

'And if you miss ...' added Herman cheerfully, 'Paul and I will personally read your posthumous citation.'

De Giverney slammed the door.

Nadine and Remy walked arm-in-arm down the corridor of Kanit House to their apartment. That afternoon they had both been to the dentist, and they were on their way to a James Bond film when Nadine realized she had left her purse at home.

Since Charles and Marie-Andrée had moved back, they had kept away from them as much as possible, making all kinds of excuses. Each night they would think of something different to do, and Nadine often stayed with friends on the nights Remy worked late. As Remy put the key in the lock, they heard footsteps in the corridor behind them.

A tall, elegantly dressed but anxious-looking man asked if they were Remy and Nadine Gires.

'Why do you ask ?' Remy said, looking up at de Giverney.

'May I come in? I must speak to you,' de Giverney explained. 'We haven't got much time,' he said as they stepped inside. 'I'm with a Belgian diplomat and an official from the Dutch embassy. They want to debrief you about Alain Gautier. They're afraid he might spot you with us. We've heard terrible rumours ...'

Paul Siemons' living room was as idiosyncratic as its owner. Two African grey parrots with their distinctive red tails squawked from a corner cage as they looked down on the collection of guests and Paul's valuable collection of Buddha statues. He was often advised in his choice of Thai antiques by de Giverney, who was an expert on the subject.

Nadine, Remy and the three diplomats were sitting around the dining room table with a quart of Black Label Johnnie Walker. De Giverney passed round unfiltered Belgian cigarettes.

First, Herman showed Nadine the passport photo of Albert Goyot. She didn't recognize it. 'At last we can get rid of this silly red herring,' Herman said.

'But I could kiss this Goyot,' Paul boomed. 'He put us on the scent!'

Herman was showing her the holiday snapshots of Cocky and Henk in Hong Kong and Macao. 'Yes! That's them!' Nadine said. 'That's the Dutch couple I met in the apartment.'

'Are any of these belongings still in Gautier's flat?'

'Sure,' Nadine said, 'that brown handbag she's carrying. I saw it up there around Christmas when I stole the diary.'

'A diary? You stole a diary?'

'Yes, a diary in Dutch. I handed it over to the British embassy.'

'But we heard nothing about it!' Herman exclaimed, and began to pace up and down the room, his boyish face flushed, smoking distractedly. 'It doesn't make sense,' he said. 'You mean they've had that evidence all along and didn't inform our ambassador? Outrageous! What happened after that?'

'As usual with embassy people, nothing, if you'll forgive me,' Nadine said.

'She's right! Nothing! Just writing reports,' Paul snorted. 'Let's make a move ourselves, Herman. There's no doubt he did it. We can make a citizen's arrest, and if he tries to resist . . .'

'Calm down, Paul. We're guests in Thailand. We must move through the proper channels, give the police a full report – names, dates, witnesses, evidence – make it watertight! They will be forced to act immediately.'

'Bah! Herman, you're a baby,' said Paul, hauling himself out of the armchair. 'Bright, but still an idealist,' he continued, lighting a cigar and pursing his lips. 'And it's only because of inexperience, so I forgive you. There are two hundred thousand police in this country. What does that add up to? Two hundred thousand crooks! Now, Herman, don't burst into tears, but I'm afraid that's the way it is.'

Ignoring his host's teasing, Herman showed Nadine the report that the Australian embassy had made on the chocolate-milk poisoning case at Hua Hin. Nadine scanned it and laughed with relief.

'That's them!' she said. 'They changed their own names, but not their dog's. That dirty little Franky is still upstairs.'

'How many more has he killed?' asked Paul, suddenly serious.

Nadine told them about the night they opened the safe with François, Dominique and Yannick. 'We saw so many passports,' she said, 'French, Indonesian, American.'

And so it went on: detail after detail, until it was almost dawn. Paul poured a final round of cognac. They agreed to meet again the following night.

'We'll organize all this information into an official report for Crime Suppression,' Herman said, allowing himself to feel some hope that justice would be done. 'We'll plant a bomb under them.'

'Bah!' said Paul pleasantly as he led Nadine and Remy out to the car to drive them home. 'The only bombs that would move Crime Suppression to action would have to be nuclear.'

It was almost dawn, and the streets were cool and empty, scented briefly with frangipani. To Remy and Nadine, as they walked up the stairs together, Kanit House now seemed slightly less dangerous.

Herman was furious when he arrived at his embassy the next morning. He had just come from a row with high-ranking British diplomats. At first they were vague about having any Dutch diary and kept offering him cups of tea. 'I understand you have evidence relating to two Dutch murder victims,' he had said repeatedly. The British had still not been forthcoming. Herman threatened to make a fuss at a high level. He was bluffing – he knew his own ambassador would probably not back him – but it had worked. The bumbling British had suddenly found they did have something. A diary written in Dutch.

'We made a report about this,' the British consular official said. 'Would you like to see it? The Thai police already have a copy.'

Embossed with the British royal coat of arms and labelled 'Confidential', the report that Herman now had on his desk had been in the hands of the Thai police since 6 January, eight weeks before.

Apart from confusing the sex of Dominique Rennelleau, referring to him as Yannick's girlfriend, the British aide-memoire was remarkably accurate.

1. A contact, the reliability of whom is unknown, reports that he has two friends of French nationality named Nadine and Remy GIRES. Remy is the Head Chef at the Oriental Hotel. They live in flat 307a Kanit House, Saladaeng Road, off Silom Road, telephone No. 861284 ext. 307.

2. Some weeks ago, because they live in the same block of units, the GIRES became friendly with the occupants of Unit 504 of the same address as above. The apartment is occupied by three persons: Alain GAUTIER, believed of Vietnamese race and nationality; his girlfriend Monique, believed to be a French-Canadian and a nurse by profession; and a person named AJAY, believed to be of Indian extraction and nationality who is fond of pointing out that he is armed with a flick-knife.

3. GAUTIER claims to be a stone-dealer by trade and to make a legitimate living thereby; however, the GIRES made the acquaintance of a young French couple, mutual friends of the GAUTIERS, their names being Jan Jacques YANNICK and his girlfriend Dominique who were staying with GAUTIER a few weeks ago. According to YANNICK, he informed the GIRES, while staying with GAUTIER, he had seen several passports and documents belonging to persons YANNICK believes to have been murdered recently, including a couple believed at the time to be Australian, who were found in a ditch alongside a highway 58 kilometres south of Ayutthaya, details of which appeared in the *Bangkok Post* dated 18 December 1975. According to YANNICK, this couple were not Australian (in fact the Australian embassy denies all knowledge of them) and they were, according to GAUTIER, Dutch. The man's name was Henk BINTANJA.

Herman paused and lit another cigarette. He found his hands were shaking. The English had evidence – a diary, witnesses, bodies, names, addresses – and still they did not bother to notify their colleagues at the Dutch embassy. Even if they could not bring themselves to take action on humanitarian grounds, Herman felt that they should have informed the Dutch as a matter of courtesy – after all, they were both Common Market countries. 'Those bloody British!' Herman fumed, and finished reading the report.

YANNICK, after informing the GIRES of this and relating his suspicions that GAUTIER had been responsible for not only these murders but for others including the two European girls found in Pattaya recently, a Turkish murder and possibly the two murders of young Europeans in Nepal, left with his girlfriend suddenly for Europe. Since then the GIRES claim to have sighted in the GAUTIER flat clothes belonging to the Dutch couple, their diary in Dutch, an extract of which has been photostatted, their tape recorder and their passports together with clothes and passports belonging to others, up to 10 in number, kept in GAUTIER'S safe.

Herman opened the battered exercise book accompanying the report. It was Cocky and Henk's travel diary, written in Dutch. The British had not bothered to have it translated. As Herman read the young couple's painstaking account of their meeting in Hong Kong with a French gem-dealer, who sold them a ring and promised to collect them at Don Muang Airport in Bangkok, he felt that a message about the murder had been sent from beyond the grave.

15

Teamwork

It was 3 a.m. on Wednesday 10 March, and 'the team', as they had begun to call themselves, sat back exhausted at the round table in the home of Paul Siemons. The night sky was lightening and a thick, detailed dossier was laid out across the dining-room table. It contained everything Remy and Nadine could remember about Charles and his house-guests.

'It's all wrapped up,' Herman announced. 'Names, dates, witnesses' statements – everything. What more could they want?'

'Money,' suggested Paul.

Herman ignored him. 'Maybe photographs. If we handed them pictures of each of the suspects, it might stop them from arresting the wrong people. We all look alike to the Thais.'

'From my window I get a good view,' said Nadine. 'Just lend me a camera.'

Paul and Herman had come to admire Nadine over the long hours of debriefing sessions. Her memory was precise. She had honesty, good humour and daring.

Herman took the file to General Suwit that morning and was promised that a police raid on Kanit House was imminent. That afternoon, with rising excitement, he watched as five unmarked police cars pulled up on the Dutch embassy's driveway. The staid atmosphere of the compound was disturbed by the crackling of walkie-talkies. Then two Thai police officers were announced to see him.

A model of courtesy, Colonel Withan introduced his deputy, Captain Sawedt Pattanaky, explaining that General Suwit had handed him the files on the case only a few minutes before he had left Crime Suppression headquarters. Step by step, Knippenberg led the colonel through the details of the case, from Cocky and Henk's first meeting with the gem-dealer in Hong Kong in December to their murder in Thailand eight days later.

'Colonel, we believe you will find this in number 503,' he said, handing the colonel the holiday snapshots and pointing out Cocky's brown handbag.

Only a few hours before, Nadine had rushed to Herman's office with the camera she had used to take photos of all the suspects. 'Here's the camera, Herman,' she had said. 'I don't know how to take the film out.'

To assist the police, Nadine had drawn two diagrams: one a cross-section of the building, marking all entrances and exits, the other a floor plan of apartments 503 and 504. Attached to the diagrams was a list of items 'to which special attention should be given', most of them believed to be belongings of Stephanie Parry, the Dutch couple and Vitali Hakim. A note indicated that 'as a rule, *all* objects within units 503 and 504 are of the utmost interest since most have been stolen'.

1. a safe and its contents, most probably: about 10 French passports and one Indonesian passport
2. a rubber or plastic pipe normally used as gas-pipe but possibly with a smell of petrol
3. medicine
4. syringes
5. a brown-coloured handbag
6. cheques and traveller's cheques
7. travel alarm clock
8. about 500 precious stones: sapphires, rubies, diamonds
9. seal for imposition of visa from Thai Immigration Office
10. postcards with Dutch writing
11. attaché case

Like a student handing in his PhD thesis, Herman Knippenberg presented the file to the colonel.

'Most thorough, Mr Knippenberg,' the colonel said, glancing at the documents before sliding them quickly into his briefcase.

'But you have forgotten one thing,' said Captain Sawedt Pattanaky, who spoke English fluently.

'And what is that, captain?'

'The motive.'

'Motive?'

'You say to us that this man has killed many people, but you do not say why.'

'How should I know? There could be many reasons. Arrest him first. Then you can question him and tell me. When are you going in?'

'Tomorrow morning at six o'clock. Would you care to come along as a guest?'

'I will come if I can.'

At 9.30 p.m. that night, Herman Knippenberg called Colonel Withan to say he could not participate in the raid personally but would remain at his office in 'strategic reserve', assisting the police by phone if necessary. Herman did not mention that his ambassador had vetoed an active role.

'We have made the decision to postpone the raid,' the colonel said.

'Why would you do that?' Herman asked, making no attempt to disguise his dismay.

'To guarantee the safety of your witnesses, Mr and Mrs Gires. We need more time for preparation.'

Herman had been in Thailand long enough to read beneath the Delphic surfaces of official statements. Police pride may have been hurt by being presented with a fait accompli. Perhaps they wanted to watch the apartment on their own, he thought, to get Gautier on another charge so they could take the credit. Anything was possible. Herman tried to think of a way he could goad them to action.

*

On the Thursday morning, 11 March, Marie-Andrée phoned Nadine
and invited her to come shopping. 'Alain says I can go back to Canada
in a day or so,' she said happily. 'Can you come and help me choose
some presents?'

'Sure,' Nadine agreed. In some ways she still felt sorry for this
woman, trapped by her love, her weakness and her lack of initiative.
She was still unsure how much Marie-Andrée knew about the fate of
her house-guests.

They took a taxi to Siam Square, the complex of shopping arcades
around the Siam International Hotel. Some shopfronts were still
under construction, and the workmen were cooking their lunches
over fires on the pavement and drinking soda from plastic bags. The
shops were well stocked with Western goods from Hong Kong, and
dresses and shirts with famous Paris labels were displayed in the windows of the boutiques. The two women, strolling along together
window-shopping, stopped to look.

'I don't need to pay so much extra for these French clothes. I'll be
in Paris soon with Alain,' Marie-Andrée said.

'You're going to Paris? With Alain?'

'Yes, he's going on business. He's been talking about a trip for
months, and I'll fly on to Canada from Europe.'

They stopped in front of an evening-wear boutique, billowing
with the pastel lace flounces of formal wear. Cream and white, layer
upon layer of pink on baby blue, the lace creations almost stood up
by themselves. Old Chinese women in baggy black trousers walked
past with their shopping bags and bamboo hats.

'They're like wedding dresses, aren't they?' Nadine said. But
her heart was thumping. Alain was about to leave the country!
That could be the end of any hope of justice. 'So you're not going
to marry Alain and settle down?' she asked, trying to sound normal.

'He says he wants me to have his baby,' Marie-Andrée said. 'He's
often spoken of it. But how could I? It would be a monster.'

Nadine was shocked by Marie-Andrée's frankness.

'What about Roong?' she asked.

'He says he's getting rid of her too – with psychology! Who cares? He's always using psychology. You know, sometimes I wonder if he's really human.'

'Mmm ...' said Nadine noncommittally. She had wondered the same thing herself.

'Anyway, soon I'll be out of all this. Just a few more days ... I can't wait to get back to Canada. Do you want lunch?'

'No thanks, Monique,' she said, looking at her watch. 'In fact I'll have to leave you now. I forgot that I had an appointment.'

Nadine grabbed a taxi straight to Herman's office.

'They're about to leave the country for Paris,' she blurted out as soon as they were alone. He could see she was exhausted and close to breaking down, and feared her double role was becoming dangerous.

After she had left, Herman telephoned General Suwit but was told that both he and Withan were 'busy at a meeting'. Undeterred, he called Pao Sarasin with the information.

'In that case, we must stop them.'

'I agree, absolutely, General.'

One hour later Sarasin called Herman again.

'We will raid this evening,' he told him. 'The men are on standby. Colonel Withan has orders. Our cover is a narcotics raid.'

Herman smiled grimly. He would believe it when it happened.

At 4 p.m. Remy opened the front door of his apartment to his wife and Paul Siemons, both loaded with cameras, accessories and a tripod.

Paul set up the photographic equipment, with its long telescopic lens, at the window. 'This is what I enjoy, the moments before the kill,' he said as he adjusted the equipment.

'Are you nervous?' asked Nadine.

'Bah! What do you think I did in the Congo all those years? Write memos?' Paul Siemons was happily back in his element.

The phone rang. Paul picked it up. It was Herman calling from his embassy desk, where he was in contact with the Thai police. The raid squad was on its way.

'How many men?' asked Paul.

'Ten, fully armed, but only one in uniform. They'll be looking for all the evidence but telling Gautier it's a drug raid to keep the heat off Nadine and Remy. They're putting a ring round Kanit House now. The police have cars and sharp-shooters watching the stairs.'

'Hold them off a bit longer, Herman. We think only the girl's upstairs now.' Paul put down the phone and turned to his hosts.

'Nadine, you'd better get out of here.'

She hugged Remy, who looked terrified. 'Enjoy yourselves. This is the moment we've all been waiting for.'

Just as she left, the phone rang again. It was Herman, operating from a battery of phones on his desk and the police walkie-talkie. It was a challenge coordinating the information between Paul and the raiding party.

'The colonel's impatient, Paul. Anything happening?'

'Nothing yet. Tell them to wait.'

'They're already in a house next door and raring to go.'

'*Pfft!* Schoolchildren. They think it's the cinema. Wait a minute! Here comes someone. It's Gautier and another man.'

'Ajay?'

'No, someone else.'

'His name is Jean,' Remy whispered.

'Ajay's still not here, Herman. Tell the boys to wait. If we don't get the Indian now, we'll never get him!'

In his office, Herman put down the phone and lit another cigarette, wishing he was on-site with Paul. His walkie-talkie crackled to life. It was Captain Sawedt, with his excellent English. The police must move immediately, he said. Under Thai law, they could only enter a home between sunrise and sunset, otherwise a warrant was required.

'Please, a few more minutes,' Herman pleaded. 'Let me check again, captain.' He phoned Kanit House.

'They're coming soon, Paul. I can't stop them.'

'Nothing like premature ejaculation, eh?' Paul boomed, his cigar smoke beginning to suffocate the small apartment. 'Wait a minute,

Herman. Someone's coming. It's Ajay! Off you go!' He hung up and rushed to his cameras.

'They're all in the bag, colonel!' Herman shouted through his walkie-talkie. 'Good luck!'

An hour later Paul called the Dutch embassy. Everyone from number 504 had been taken to the headquarters of Crime Suppression. Marie-Andrée was overheard complaining to Charles that the neighbours were staring at them.

Herman was elated. He sat at his desk chain-smoking for the next two hours, waiting for the phone call confirming that the suspects had been arrested and charged with multiple murder. At 7 p.m., tired of waiting, he phoned Captain Sawedt. The news astounded him.

In 504, moments before the raid began, Ajay had looked out the window and noticed a group of Thai men hurrying purposefully across the courtyard.

'There are some people down there that look like police' he said quickly to Charles.

'Don't say anything to the others yet,' Charles said. For once his inner radar had failed him. 'Stay cool and smile. They are only Thai police.'

When ten men burst through the door of 504, pushing Ajay aside and brandishing machine guns, Charles was at his desk casually sorting through gems.

'Where is Alain Gautier?' demanded the officer leading the raid.

'He's in Hong Kong on business,' Charles said, getting up from his desk and greeting them all with a polite smile, as though this was a fresh party of customers. 'Who are you?'

'Police – Narcotics – and you?'

Charles told them he was David Allen Gore and showed them a US passport in that name which had his own picture inside. It was the one he had stolen in Hong Kong six weeks ago from an American schoolteacher.

'I'm a college professor from Puerto Rico,' he said pleasantly to the colonel as the men branched off into other rooms. 'But now I deal in gems – it makes more money.'

Ajay and Jean sat at the bar stools and Marie-Andrée stood near the couch hiding her terror behind an expression of sullen disdain. They were trapped. She couldn't believe it. The police began rummaging through her wardrobe as though she was a common criminal.

'Try to look more relaxed,' Charles whispered to her quickly in French, 'and remember to call me Allen, not Alain! Everything will be OK.'

For the next hour and forty minutes the officers from Crime Suppression searched the apartment. As complications arose, Charles smoothed them over.

There was a Canadian passport in the name of Marie-Andrée Leclerc. In another passport, one in the name of Eric Damour, was a photograph of the same woman.

'True, it seems like the same woman,' Charles agreed, 'but really, the one wearing sunglasses doesn't look at all like the other one. Miss Damour was actually a French girl, a customer of Alain Gautier's who bought some gems on credit and left her passport as a deposit. She's in Pattaya now and will be back in a few days.'

'Who is this man?' asked another of the officers, holding up a passport of Vitali Hakim. Just another customer who had left his passport as security, Charles explained. When a dress, which had belonged to Cocky Hemker, was produced from the bedroom in the adjoining apartment, Charles smiled and held it in front of Marie-Andrée.

'See – it's hers.' As for the pair of handcuffs, they were used as a security measure when Mr Gautier transported diamonds, he explained.

But what about the safe? Unfortunately, the key had been lost.

Colonel Withan ordered some of his men to carry the safe to a car, and everyone in the apartment was taken to the offices of Crime Suppression for further questioning. Outside the compound in Soi Saladaeng, a fleet of police radio cars manned by armed officers took off behind the car which held the suspects.

In the front seat Charles grinned at the policeman who sat beside him. 'Well, sir, it looks as though you were prepared for a really big show. Do you mind my asking who it was that made a complaint about Alain?'

'I can't say,' the policeman replied tersely.

'I'm sure I know,' Charles continued. 'Alain told me that he'd had a fight with some customers over some diamonds he sold them. They accused him of stealing them back, I think. The gem business gets dirty sometimes. Anyway, I'm sure we'll be able to clear this matter up.'

Sure enough, after questioning, the occupants of Kanit House were allowed to return home. All of them agreed to return to Crime Suppression headquarters at 9 a.m. the following day.

When Herman Knippenberg arrived home that night he was pale with fury. He had been told on the phone that 'nothing incriminating' had been found and that the suspect had a valid US passport in the name of David Allen Gore. The visa stamps in the passport showed that Mr Gore was out of the country at the time of the murder of the Dutch couple.

'You make a farce of the investigation!' Herman exploded, losing his diplomatic cool as he spoke to Captain Sawedt. 'This man has killed in cold blood – for God's sake change your mind. Arrest him!'

'There's no need to worry,' came the soothing voice of the captain. 'Gore and the others will certainly return to police headquarters in the morning because their passports have been confiscated. Our technicians will open the safe, and then we'll see if there's anything incriminating.'

'Don't you see,' said Herman, struggling to stay composed, 'they'll only come back tomorrow if there is nothing incriminating in that safe. And that's not the point. We know the man's not David Allen Gore! Are you going to let him pull the wool over your eyes?'

'The instructions for their release were issued by General Suwit,' Captain Sawedt said coolly. 'The grounds were lack of evidence.'

Sitting out on the balcony of their apartment with her husband, Angela Knippenberg's clear blue eyes and the slightest of frowns showed she shared her husband's consternation. Herman brooded on what had been said.

'I can't believe this is really happening,' he fumed. 'After everything we've done – the whole of so-called Crime Suppression is going to sit back and be outsmarted!'

His own ambassador was far from supportive. When Herman had told him about the fiasco, His Excellency Van Dongen had replied that there was something odd about the case. The police had not acted before when they received the report from the British embassy. They must have a reason.

Herman went to bed but couldn't sleep. Sure, they had a reason. It had been laziness, inefficiency. And now it was naivety. How could a French-Vietnamese masquerade as an American-born school-teacher?

He jumped out of bed.

'The Americans! That's it!' he cried, waking Angela.

Rushing to the phone, he dialled Ralph Nider at the US embassy and, after filling him in on the background of the case, asked him to send someone to police headquarters in the morning to investigate the passport held by the man claiming to be David Allen Gore. Nider agreed. In addition, two men from the US Drug Enforcement Agency – a department already in close contact with Crime Suppression – would be present in the morning to interrogate the suspects.

Herman was relieved, but before he could hang up, Nider presented him with a question.

'I wonder, Herman, if there could be any connection between the Gautier affair and a missing US national of ours, Teresa Knowlton?'

The US embassy, Nider explained, had received a notice from the State Department to put a trace on Knowlton. She had disappeared in Thailand last October. A comparison of photographs had shown that she might be the girl found at Pattaya whose body had been pictured in the *Bangkok Post* in November. Herman remembered the picture of a woman in a bikini lying on the sand which he had happened to see at Crime Suppression one morning, and he told Nider that he would ask his informants whether Teresa Knowlton had ever been seen at Kanit House.

He had just got back to bed when the phone rang again. It was de Giverney, who was calling from the Grace Hotel. He had just met a man at the bar. As Herman listened to the tale of a man buying $3,000 of diamonds from Gautier and then being drugged and robbed, he asked: 'Is he there with you now?'

'Sure,' said de Giverney.

'OK, Gilles, make sure he turns up at Crime Suppression at 9 a.m. tomorrow to lodge an official complaint. We can use him to blow the Gore alias apart.'

As Herman finally fell asleep, he was satisfied. The trap for Gautier was set once again.

The next day, everything started to come together. At lunchtime, Herman visited Crime Suppression and spoke to Colonel Withan, who told him that the suspects were still being interrogated. Nothing of interest had been found in the safe, however a variety of suspicious drugs had been removed by police from the apartment and these were now being analysed. Herman had heard already from the American officials that the Thai police had been asked to hold 'Mr Gore' in custody, pending an investigation of his passport. Now Colonel Withan showed him a photo in a passport of one 'Eric Damour' which looked remarkably like Marie-Andrée Leclerc.

That evening Herman and Angela sat out on their balcony once more, attempting to calm down after the rigours of the day. But the phone rang again. It was de Giverney, who told Herman that a French embassy official had mentioned a missing person's request to trace a young woman called Stephanie Parry. So here potentially was another victim. Surely, thought Herman, there was no way Gautier could escape now.

At 9.30 p.m. a servant again called Herman to the phone. It was Nadine.

'How do you feel?' asked Herman kindly, feeling confident an outcome was nigh. 'It's all over now.'

'Herman,' she said frantically, 'there's a light on in 504.'

'Don't worry, Nadine, it's all over. That's probably Crime Suppression or the DEA, having a poke about for more evidence.'

'Should I go up and see them?' she said, sounding relieved.

'Why not? Well, maybe phone first, just to make sure. Maybe you can help them.'

A few minutes later Nadine phoned again, and this time she sounded even more panicked.

'Ajay's up there,' she told him.

'My God! He's supposed to be in jail with the others.'

'He recognized my voice, Herman, and he asked me to come up now. He said it was urgent.'

'What did you say?'

'I said Remy was already asleep and I felt tired – but he still wants me to go up.'

'You should,' he told her.

'But why?'

'If you don't it might make him suspicious. He'll know you had something to do with the raid. Listen, just tell him you spent last night with friends and only just got home tonight with Remy after going to the cinema. You saw a light and decided to phone.'

Herman told her he would allow fifteen minutes for the visit, and another five for her to walk downstairs.

'If you haven't called me back by then I'll come over there with Paul.'

Herman's face was white when he put down the phone. After checking his watch, he called his Belgian colleague to alert him. He told Angela what had happened and instructed his driver to park the car in front of the house and stand by. Then he walked upstairs to his study.

From the bottom drawer of his desk he took out a flat green metal object which looked like an oversized cigarette lighter. It was a King Cobra, a secret firearm developed by a US intelligence agency. He clicked it open and loaded it with three bullets. He put it in his shirt pocket, walked downstairs and began pacing up and down near the phone. As the minutes ticked by, Herman's doubts grew about the wisdom of his instructions to Nadine. He had been thoughtless, swept away by the excitement of the moment like a schoolboy playing spy games. Throughout the whole investigation he had been so sure about what course of action to take, but now, as the minutes ticked slowly past, the stupidity of what he had just done dawned on him.

Angela had never seen her husband look so shaken.

'What will I do if anything happens to Nadine?' he began, as she put her arms around him.

They would learn later that at lunchtime that day, Charles and the others had walked out of the offices of Crime Suppression, leaving Ajay behind to take care of details. Later, when the story became public, the possibility of a bribe was rumoured.

A few hours later, a Toyota driven by Tommy, a Thai-born gem-dealer based in Chanthaburi, had headed south along Route 4 towards the Malaysian border. Sitting next to Tommy was Charles, an attaché case on his lap. He was sticking a photo of Marie-Andrée inside an Italian passport. That afternoon he had picked up a bag full of passports from his former girlfriend, Ann. In the back of the car with Marie-Andrée, his tall frame hunched uncomfortably, was Jean Dhuisme, now being swept along in an adventure he did not understand.

Back at Kanit House, Nadine knocked on the door and Ajay opened it looking more like a penitent schoolboy than the brutal killer she knew he must be.

They stood among the wreckage of upturned files, strewn clothes and dirty dishes, in apartment 504. Franky whined, sniffing among the debris.

'Ajay, what's happened here?' Nadine asked, as if surprised by the chaos. He told her that Charles and Marie-Andrée had got into trouble over passports and had left for a short holiday.

Outside, Remy crouched by the door, checking the scene through the keyhole. He listened as Ajay told Nadine that the police had raided the apartment because a customer had complained that

Charles had sold him some diamonds and later stolen them back from him.

Making her excuses, Nadine left as quickly as possible. She and Remy returned to their apartment to phone a relieved Herman, who told them he had been just about to jump in a car.

In the little stilt house near the airport, Roong sat alone in her best dress, heavily made-up, waiting for Charles. He had told her he was coming to ask her parents for permission to marry her. A banquet had been prepared, which now lay cold in the kitchen. Where was he? At midnight, she took a taxi to Kanit House. After Ajay told her what had happened, she stayed the night on the sofa. In the morning she was still crying when she left, carrying Franky in her arms.

Over the ensuing days, Ajay moved from Kanit House to a small hotel, taking with him cameras, a television set, cassette players and any other equipment he could sell. Smartly dressed and polite, he consented to be interviewed by Bob Jacobs, a consular official at the US embassy, where he denied ever having met Teresa Knowlton. A week after the police raid, Ajay and Roong flew from Bangkok to Penang to meet Charles.

Charles had been busy creating the usual havoc among overland tourists. He had drugged and robbed three Australians and been picked up by the Malaysian police for trying to cash stolen traveller's cheques at the Hilton. As usual, he talked his way out of it.

Ajay and Roong then flew back to Bangkok, and Marie-Andrée, Charles and Tommy flew to Karachi, where they met Mary, an Australian nurse who Charles claimed had provided the cologne used in his escape from the prison van in Greece the previous year.

Mary was renting a beach house and selling jewellery and drugs to tourists as well as helping the local fishing population with medical problems. After a few days with her, Charles and Tommy flew on to Europe, leaving Marie-Andrée to stay alone with the Australian girl. After ten days Marie-Andrée received a ticket to join Charles in Europe. Later she would not be able to explain why she had not used this intervening time to run away from Charles.

All the while, Herman Knippenberg was following up leads, contacting other embassy personnel, and recording Ajay's every move. He'd been devastated by the failure of the raid, to the point where well-meaning friends were now warning Angela that Herman's obsession with the case was ruining his career. He was even instructed by his ambassador to take at least three weeks holiday. Yet right up to the last hours before boarding the plane to Sumatra, Herman and Angela were preparing an in-depth account of the Gautier investigation. A copy of this document, later to achieve local fame as the 'Knippenberg Report', was delivered to every foreign embassy involved.

'I hope it will give them all something to think about,' said Herman to Angela as they fastened their seatbelts and flew off for the holiday that he had been forced to take.

Almost four weeks after the raid, on 6 April, Nadine received a postcard from Switzerland. It was from Charles: 'I haven't forgotten you and will see you again soon. I hope, my dear Nadine, I will be able to show my gratitude. Love, Alain.'

When she passed this on to Paul Siemons, he told her he would cable his Interpol contact in Geneva and begin a new attempt to have Charles arrested.

A few days later, Nadine was asked to present herself to the French embassy. The news had finally filtered through that Alain Gautier might be responsible for the disappearance of one of their nationals, Stephanie Parry. An official went so far as to hint that Nadine must have been in league with the gang at Kanit House.

'Haven't you read the Knippenberg Report?' she asked, astonished.

'Yes,' the official replied, showing her to the door. 'It's in the wastepaper basket. You realize you spelled Parry's name as "Paris". If you can't even get the names right, how can we take you seriously?'

*

On 12 April, a Reuters correspondent filed a report from Kathmandu headed 'Trouble in Kathmandu's Freak Street'. Linking the murders of Cocky and Henk in Bangkok and the two murders in Nepal to a 'heroin trafficking ring', the report said: 'Police investigations have made little progress but there is little doubt that the killings were drug related and were carried out by foreigners.'

Quoting an unnamed US official, the report concluded that 'organized groups were trading hashish for heroin in Bangkok on a courier system and the murders are believed to be linked with this racket.' While the identity of the official quoted in this report has never been revealed, references to the machinations of the Asian drug trade and its links to the crimes were corroborated by the rumours on the street in Kathmandu, as well as the unusually consistent story later told by Sobhraj himself. The fact that Connie Jo Bronzich, Vitali Hakim and Stephanie Parry were clearly involved in heroin trafficking supplies yet another piece in a jigsaw of relationships that even forty years later is yet to be clarified.

The next day, 13 April, Emma Knowlton was informed in a telegram from the US embassy in Bangkok that the body of her granddaughter Teresa had been identified, and that she had apparently drowned off Pattaya Beach.

The day after Herman and Angela returned to Bangkok from their holiday, Nadine phoned them with the news that the manager of Kanit House was planning to sell the contents of the Gautier apartments to make up the unpaid rent.

'But the evidence!' cried Herman. 'I have to stop them.'

He and Nadine both knew that Cocky's brown bag and every other item on the list they had given the Thai police were still in the apartment. Having been assured by the police that they had no further use for whatever was left at Kanit House, Herman organized an inspection team of his own.

On the afternoon of 27 April, five diplomats and Remy, Nadine and Angela entered the two adjoining apartments rented in the name of Alain Gautier. As soon as Herman turned on the light in the mildewed guest bedroom of 503 he saw the bag that Cocky was carrying in the holiday snapshots. In the next few minutes he found a purse full of guilders and cents, a sewing kit and tape measure made in Holland, and a hand-painted fan from the Chinese Emporium in Hong Kong which had been mentioned in the couple's diary. Hanging in the wardrobe was the orange jacket Cocky was also seen wearing in the photographs.

Over the past weeks, following a tip-off from Paul, two agents from the US Drug Enforcement Agency had been pursuing their own inquiries into the activities of Alain Gautier. One of their key sources in Bangkok had maintained that the suspect was involved in narcotics, and a telex from the DEA's Paris office said that French police believed drugs were the likely motive. Now the team began to rifle through the desk in the living room, looking for clues to connect the occupants of the apartment with the heroin trade. They were shocked by the number of documents, letters and pieces of paper lying around which had once belonged to the hundreds of travellers who'd had the misfortune to come into contact with Sobhraj.

In the two bathrooms and underneath the cocktail bar was a jumbled arsenal of tubes, capsules, syrups, pills and powders. Prominent among the fifty-one brand names were drugs to produce both euphoria and unconsciousness, as well as diarrhoea, nausea, sleep and hallucinations. Ten kilograms of itching powder completed the collection.

Turning his attention to the bookcase, Herman began methodically examining each volume until he discovered *Oil Politics*, which he remembered from the Australian couple's statement they had been reading at Hua Hin on the night they drank the drugged milkshakes. In another book, *Foundation of Buddhist Meditation* by Kalu Rinpoche, the name of its former owner was neatly written on the flyleaf: 'Teresa'. Nadine had remembered Monique mentioning an American girl who had talked outrageously about sex, but this was the first hard evidence that connected Gautier to Teresa.

In the desk among a pile of papers they found a letter written in Turkish beginning 'Sigge, Ved'. When it was translated, it turned out to be an introductory letter about the courier Stephanie Parry from Ved's partner in Spain. 'You should both leave Bangkok at different times and return to Europe via different routes,' it instructed.

In the bedroom, Angela Knippenberg was sorting through the belongings of Marie-Andrée. In a handbag she found the small day-book recording the couple's movements since January and its owner's bleak mood, plus the letter addressed to 'Dear Charles the Psychologist' scribbled on several sheets of airmail paper. On the last page Marie-Andrée had scrawled her feelings during the days before the police raid: 'He is the only man who can help me for I love him so much that I can only make one being with him. I can only exist because of him, I can only breathe because of him. And my love is increasing.'

When Angela showed the letter to Nadine she recognized 'Monique's' handwriting immediately.

Also in the handbag was a pile of photographs, most of them of Charles and Marie-Andrée. One of them showed Charles lying on a bed naked, with an erection.

'What's he got to be proud of?' Paul snorted.

All sorts of motives were discussed by the group in the room, but no single explanation seemed to fit all the murders. Nadine had never forgotten the photograph that Sobhraj had kept which showed two severed heads on display during the Vietnam War. Finding it in the stash, she showed it to the others, commenting that Alain Gautier was 'sick in the head'.

By the end of the afternoon, the search party had begun stacking all the files and pieces of paper from the desk into cardboard boxes which would, in the following week, be sorted through by the Gires and the Knippenbergs. There were business cards, driving licences, and countless other documents Sobhraj compulsively hoarded. Among these was a travel itinerary in the name of André Breugnot, the 'pudgy Frenchman' Charles had murdered in Chiang Mai and would later claim was a heroin operative. It showed a flight schedule for the months of September/October 1975 including Paris, Amsterdam, Hong Kong, Bangkok and Copenhagen.

It was nearly dark when the investigating group left Kanit House, each carrying a bag bulging with documents and drugs. A mauve haze hung over the city. Stopping for a moment on the walkway and staring down at the turquoise patch of the swimming pool, Herman thought about the victims who had been led along this path, like Cocky and Henk, to their deaths. He glanced at Paul standing beside him, his face for once poker-like and his spirits subdued. There was nothing more anyone wanted to say about Alain Gautier.

Ten days later, on 6 May, *Thai Rath*, a mass circulation Thai-language newspaper, announced that 'Gautier and his gang have been caught in Singapore.' The source of the story was unclear and there was no by-line, but after listing the details of the deaths of Cocky and Henk, the report said that Gautier had confessed to killing the Dutch couple. 'Gautier had been ordered by the biggest narcotics smuggling gang in Hong Kong to kill the two young Dutch who were treacherous to the big boss.'

The next day a follow-up story appeared. The same newspaper reported Hong Kong police as concluding: 'The murder happened because of the double-crossing between the narcotics and diamond-smuggling gangs.'

These news items set off a frenzy of activity at the *Bangkok Post*, the local showpiece of Western investigatory journalism. The *Thai Rath* story could not be confirmed. The Singapore police knew nothing of the arrest of anyone called Gautier or of any confession. In fact, Charles was currently in Europe, setting up appointments with large and prestigious gem firms.

Now the editor of the *Bangkok Post*, Graeme Stanton, contacted the Dutch ambassador and was finally put in touch with Herman Knippenberg. 'The team' – Nadine and Remy and the three diplomats – decided that a barrage of front-page headlines would force the Thai police to issue an international arrest warrant.

On 7 and 8 May, the story broke. Under the headline 'Web Of Death', the *Bangkok Post* printed pictures of the five known murder victims and announced that 'a web of murder, robbery and forced druggings has been uncovered by the *Bangkok Post* in extensive investigations'. There was a picture of Charles and Marie-Andrée captioned: 'Gautier and Leclerc'. The newspaper's investigations were in fact sifted from the Knippenberg's living room floor, where Stanton and Knippenberg had spent days combing through Herman's copious files and the boxes of evidence to put the newspaper story together.

Now the reports were syndicated all over Asia. One morning a commercial attaché at the French embassy in Singapore cut out a story of the killings from the local newspaper. He had met 'Gautier' several times and bought gems from him. On Charles' last visit to Singapore, the attaché had introduced him to a high-ranking French police officer, then holidaying in Asia. The commercial attaché put the newspaper cutting in the embassy pouch and addressed it to the policeman in Paris.

That April 1976, Charles, Marie-Andrée and Tommy were also in Paris, staying at the home of Jean Dhuisme. Charles was enjoying profitable meetings with the gem customers he had met in Asia. Tommy had brought with him the pride of his family's collection, a dazzling set of sapphires and rubies. Working out of plush offices in the Place de Vendôme and the Champs-Élysées for several weeks, they displayed their exquisite wares and took orders from the most famous jewellers of Paris.

Selling gems was not all that occupied Charles that spring. He had learned that Chantal, his former wife, was also in Paris. Her mother was dying and she had come from America to be with her. Parking a brand-new white Citroën C2200 outside her family's house, Charles watched to make sure no one else was at home, just as he had done that morning four years ago when he had kidnapped his daughter, Madhu.

Chantal was visibly shocked when she opened the door to see her ex-husband smiling in front of her.

'You can't come in,' she said immediately.

'Not even for coffee?' he asked smoothly, the perfect gentleman.

She let him in and the two of them talked in the hall.

'I was a fool to lose you,' he said. She blushed and asked him not to interfere with her new life.

'Madhu, is she all right?' he pressed her, playing the role of a concerned father. 'Is she going to school?'

While Chantal noticed that he kept glancing through the window, she couldn't help responding to his grace and charm. He offered her money from a wallet bulging with 500-franc notes. After he had said goodbye and hurried out to the car, she watched him drive away and felt sad. She knew that he was on the run again.

Alain Benard had not seen Charles and Marie-Andrée for several years, but he welcomed them into his apartment, hopeful that Charles might finally have set his life on the right path.

'Take one for your mother, Alain,' Charles said, opening a satin-lined case which glittered with gems. He wanted Benard to see that he had become a big success. But his old friend already suspected that the police could not be far behind.

'Come on, Alain, pick out a ruby for your mother,' Charles urged him again.

Although Benard would have liked to present his mother with a precious stone, he was not going to sort through the gems like a scavenger. No, he felt Charles should have picked one and offered it to him. But Charles was busy. He spent most of his time at Benard's using his phone and setting up business appointments. Marie-Andrée, who unnerved Benard, sat around sullenly drinking coffee. Benard became increasingly uncomfortable. He never lets himself be alone with me, he thought. He never allows me to look in his eyes. Where was the boy he had met ten years ago in Poissy Jail?

Early in May, unaware that by now they were making front-page headlines all over Asia, Charles and Marie-Andrée paid a visit to the home of the high-ranking policeman and his wife they had met in Singapore. The French couple had been impressed by Charles' formidable reputation as a gem-dealer. But as soon as the prefect of police opened his door to them, Charles sensed that something was wrong. With Marie-Andrée he followed the prefect through the gloomy hallway into a living room filled with antiques. The man's wife, normally gay and effusive, greeted them both with a chill in her voice and Charles was ushered into the study alone.

The prefect was embarrassed. Charles had visited him several times since his arrival in Europe. They had spent an afternoon listening to Chopin, and Charles had admired the prefect's collection of rare books. But the man was frowning now as he leaned across his desk.

'Mr Gautier, I must demand an explanation from you,' he said abruptly.

The prefect had ordered thousands of dollars' worth of necklaces and bracelets from Charles, who had agreed to accept a modest deposit and monthly payments.

'If you think I am going to cheat you—' Charles began, knowing this couldn't be about the gems. Already he was laying out a strategy in case the worst had happened.

'No – it's nothing to do with your business,' the prefect said. He took a newspaper cutting from an envelope – the 'Web of Death' story – and handed it to Charles, who glanced at it a few seconds, then gave it back to him.

'I don't need to read it, it's an old piece of slander,' he smiled.

'But it only arrived here this morning!' exclaimed the prefect.

It was simple, said Charles. He had made many enemies in Bangkok because of his low prices. The gem business was run like the Mafia and he had broken the rules. All the others had banded together to ruin his reputation. They had even sent someone posing as a defrauded customer to complain to the Thai police. They had planted false evidence, leaked libellous stories. It was ridiculous. What could he do? In Asia, people had a slack morality. Five, six, seven murders ... how many did they say? When would he have had time to commit them? Why would he kill hippies for a few hundred dollars? And naturally, having done so, would he now spend his time wandering around Paris, visiting policemen?

'I should tell you now,' the prefect said, 'I contacted Interpol this morning. I could have had you arrested in my house, Alain, but your name was not on their files.'

Still not computerised, Interpol had failed to assimilate and properly file the information it had already received on Gautier. On 4 May, as a result of Dominique and François having visited the Ministry of Foreign Affairs, the Paris office had cabled Bangkok seeking further information on him. In the last few days, Stephanie Parry's father had passed on to French police a dossier he had received on 'Gautier' from 'the team' in Bangkok. This even included the name and address of Jean Dhuisme, with whom the couple was still staying, as a possible contact.

Having set the prefect's questions to rest, Charles and Marie-Andrée left the house amid a flurry of smiles and handshakes and drove south. In Charles' pocket was $1,000 handed to him by the prefect as a deposit on a necklace of river sapphires. He had also given Charles a valuable family heirloom, a diamond cut in the old-fashioned style. Charles had promised to have it re-cut in a contemporary style to add to its value.

At the Crédit Municipal in Marseilles, Charles mortgaged the diamond for 10,000 francs and then drove to Villa La Roche to see Noi, his mother.

At about the same time in Quebec, investigators knocked on the door of the modest house in Levis and questioned Marie-Andrée's family. The massive report which Herman Knippenberg had delivered to foreign embassies had had repercussions beyond the headlines in the Asian press. When the high commissioner of Canada had realized that one of his nationals was involved in a murder case, he had immediately notified his country's police. When the Royal Canadian Mounted Police left the house in Levis they had the key to the riddle of 'Alain Gautier's' true identity – although no one realized it at the time.

On 12 May, the Interpol office in Ottawa sent a cable informing all member countries, including France and Thailand, that 'in an emergency Marie-Andrée had instructed her parents to contact "Madame Sobhraj"'. The address was Villa La Roche, Noi's house in Marseilles, where Charles was now staying.

As yet, there was still no warrant for Charles' arrest on charges of murder, but the daily headlines in the *Bangkok Post* and the previous inquiry from Paris Interpol asking for information about the death of Stephanie Parry had finally aroused the attention of Colonel Somphol, the head of Bangkok Interpol. He recorded statements from Herman Knippenberg, Remy and Nadine, and took possession of the boxes of the evidence found at Kanit House. He interviewed survivors of Charles' earlier drug-muggings in India, including the real Eric Damour, one of the Frenchmen drugged in the van in southern India.

On 19 May, Gilles Carrière visited the police in Kathmandu and formally identified photographs of a charred and mutilated body as his brother, Laurent. On the same day, Emma Knowlton wrote another of her desperate (and unanswered) letters to the US embassy in Bangkok, asking for the date and circumstances of her grand-daughter's death, and Paris Interpol cabled the following message to Bangkok:

THE DISCREET VERIFICATION OF ADDRESS VILLA LA ROCHE SHOWS THAT VAN LONG NOI, EX CONCUBINE OF HOTCHAND SOBHRAJ, IS LIV-ING THERE. NOI HAD TWO CHILDREN BY SOBHRAJ, ONE OF THEM, A SON, IS RECORDED IN OUR DOCUMENTS UNDER DIVERSE IDENTITIES ... INCLUDING CHARLES SOBHRAJ. THIS HOSTILE INDIVIDUAL IS KNOWN FOR ESCAPING AND IS UNDER INDICTMENT IN FRANCE ... IT APPEARS THAT CHARLES SOBHRAJ TOOK THE IDENTITY OF GAUTIER, ALAIN. THIS IS CONSIDERED AN URGENT AND GRAVE AFFAIR IN FRANCE.

In Bangkok that same night, Herman and Angela, along with Remy and Nadine, assembled at the offices of Interpol over Chinese take-away. Something of an aristocrat, the urbane Colonel Somphol spoke fluent English and worked comfortably with his guests over the next few hours compiling a detailed description of the three suspects before issuing a formal warrant.

As they watched the information being fed into the huge battery of telexes which linked all member countries of Interpol, the two couples still felt some anxiety as to whether the rest of the world would at last become involved in catching the killers.

The next day, Bangkok Interpol issued an international warrant of arrest for Alain Gautier, Marie-Andrée Leclerc and Ajay Chowdury for conspiring to murder Teresa Knowlton, Henk Bintanja, Cocky Hemker and Vitali Hakim. 'If found inform immediately, extradition will be requested.'

One week later, the bodies of Teresa Knowlton and Vitali Hakim were exhumed from the desolate cemetery near Pattaya and unwound from the sheets of plastic. Vitali's father, Leon Hakim, had flown from Istanbul. As he watched the charred body of his son being moved, its head fell off. Later he was seen weeping in his hotel foyer, heartbroken by the attitude of official indifference which had kept him ignorant of his son's death for more than six months.

16

Old Demons, Old Tricks

At a table in Dipty's House of Pure Drinks in Bombay, on an afternoon early in June 1976, a scruffy European man wearing patched jeans and a torn singlet sat with a bottle of Indian lemonade in front of him. Jean Huygens had taken a bus from Goa, where he lived, into Bombay hoping to find work as a film extra.

As he looked out onto the glare of Ormiston Road, he was hoping one of the casting directors he'd been told frequented Dipty's might stroll in today. The forty-five-year-old Belgian knew that producers were always scouring overland hangouts looking for Western faces, usually to play villains, and he could expect $4 for a day's work, or more if he was given a few lines to say.

Until the end of the 1960s Huygens had led a conventional existence in his native Brussels as foreman of a construction company. Then his marriage had broken down. A year after that, his son had died. Heartbroken, he'd fled Europe and drifted around Asia. Four years ago, he had married an Indian woman and now lived in a hut near the beach in Goa with his wife and two children.

Huygens lit up a cheap Indian cigarette. He was used to them by now. Looking up he saw a prosperous Asian man with a beard and moustache strolling towards him. Perhaps he was a film producer. With his gold-rimmed glasses, pressed trousers and monogrammed shirt he looked like one. He also carried a crocodile-skin attaché case.

'Hello,' said the man in French, 'you look as though you might be able to help me.'

'I'm sure I can,' Huygens said, positive now that the man was about to offer him a job.

'Good. My name's Daniel, and I need passports.'

So not a producer. But still, a source of money. Huygens was delighted.

'That should be no trouble,' he said, his grin revealing the fact that he had lost most of his teeth. 'I know plenty of travellers who need the bread.'

'Good, then you might also be able to help me find a girl to work for me,' said the stranger. 'I want someone without scruples. She could make good money carrying gems across borders for me. There could be money in it for you too.'

'Sure, I can do that,' said Huygens.

'OK, I'm in a hurry at the moment. I'll meet you here at the same time tomorrow.'

The Belgian sat finishing his drink. 'A girl without scruples'? That was an apt description of Barbara, an English girl he knew who scraped a living in Bombay. He watched the Frenchman walking away from Dipty's. Street urchins jostled along beside him, and a man with a dancing monkey and some hash-sellers tagged along, all trying fruitlessly to grab the prosperous man's attention.

Charles was already making plans for South America, where the police were lax and the press, he hoped, less inquisitive. He quickened his pace towards the park near the Taj Mahal Hotel. He knew that Asia was dangerous for him now. Two weeks ago, he had left France with Marie-Andrée and Jean Dhuisme in the brand-new Citroën. It was the perfect getaway car for the job he was now planning. But he was short of cash. It was that old demon of his, gambling.

No matter how much money Charles had made over the years, a pattern had emerged. Repeatedly he had lost it all, having to start from scratch time and again. During this last visit to France he had lost a fortune at a Rouen casino as a miserable Marie-Andrée looked on. But there was more money in Thailand, in bank accounts under false names and with the appropriate documents in the hands of another party. And he knew that in India money would not be a problem for long. He had the perfect set-up. In a few more days he'd be rolling again.

But money was not his biggest problem.

During the trip from Paris it had been a shock to pick up a copy of *Asiaweek*, the cover headline screaming: THE BIKINI MURDERS. Flicking through the pages, he had read a detailed account of his career in Bangkok. There were pictures of himself, Marie-Andrée and the victims. Before he had time to hide it, Marie-Andrée had seen it too.

'They have no proof,' he told her. 'It's just journalists looking for a story.' But he knew he couldn't trust her any more. He was sure she was trying to get away from him. Should he let her go? He would wait until the time was right.

In the meantime, Charles used his usual array of seductions to befriend a young French traveller called Luke Solomon. He invited Luke to join his group for dinner, promising him a night in bed with Barbara, the English girl. During dinner, he had dropped drugs into Solomon's highly spiced chicken curry. Charles later went to his room and, as the young man lay in a stupor, went through his valuables. His passport was useless, too many visa stamps, but Charles took his money. Found unconscious the next day by the hotel maids, Solomon was taken to the local hospital, where on 2 July 1976 he died.

One week later, Jean Huygens found himself sitting on the steps of the Bombay International Telephone Exchange minding Marie-Andrée's black leather bag while she was inside calling her parents in Canada. He was terrified. How had he got himself mixed up with such people? How had a down-and-out drifter who was hoping for a bit-part in a Hindi movie found himself playing the role of a gangster in real life? 'Daniel' was in the gem business, all right. Within the next week he was planning to clean out all the big jewellery shops of Delhi and Agra.

A few days before, Charles had instructed Huygens to couple up with the Australian girl, Mary, and visit the jewellery shops of Delhi posing as customers, appraising the value of the stock. Charles seemed to have known her for years and had picked her up in Karachi on the way from Paris to Bombay.

'I was told to pretend to be a foreign diplomat, shopping with my wife,' Huygens later said in a statement to police. 'This was designed to infuse confidence in the mind of the victim jeweller.'

Charles was obviously planning the biggest and the best robbery of his career. Huygens had watched Marie-Andrée stroll into the State Bank of India and cash stolen traveller's cheques with a fake passport. Mary had done the same. But despite his years of hustling for a living on the back streets of Bombay, Huygens had recoiled when he began to grasp the full range of his employer's 'business deals'. 'Daniel' had ordered everyone to be on the lookout for tourists who could be lured into friendly conversation, then drugged and robbed. Huygens decided he wanted no part in it. It didn't help that he had not been paid the money that had been promised. Nor was Daniel easy to work for. Once when the Belgian had casually picked up a camera in the boot of the car, the Frenchman had snapped, 'Don't touch any of this without my permission.' A jumble of expensive camera equipment lay tossed in the boot, as well as travel documents. They had been stolen from three French travellers at the YMCA, Huygens learned. They had all been drugged.

Huygens had decided to wait for an opportunity to make his getaway. This was it. All the money, passports and other valuables belonging to the accomplices were kept in Marie-Andrée's black leather bag, usually carefully guarded by 'Daniel'. But at this moment that bag was sitting in his lap. And he was alone . . .

Marie-Andrée, too, was hatching plans for an escape, but her position was more complicated. The phone call she was trying to make was to hurry her family into sending a lawyer to Delhi. It was the only way she could begin to extricate herself from the nightmare. She had carefully rolled up three $100 notes and hidden them in her lipstick case in her black bag. Finally, she had got through to her parents on the phone, and now she knew that help was on its way. But when, elated, she returned to the steps of the International Telephone Exchange that June afternoon the Belgian had gone. And the bag had gone with him.

*

It was cool and dark inside the tomb and the Dutch student group welcomed relief from the sun. With a flourish, the guide pressed the flashlight against the wall and, when he switched it on, the stones blazed. The sapphires, jade, topaz, the pinky-red garnets and cornelian, all came alive in the light-beam, revealing an inlaid garden of glowing lotus blossoms.

'It may surprise you much to learn, please,' said the local guide, in the lilting intonation of Indian-English, 'that it took over a thousand elephants to carry the marble slabs to build the Taj Mahal.'

As the guide herded his straggle of students back along the path to the courtyard where their buses were waiting, they didn't know whether to feel disappointed or exalted by the immortal structure, perhaps the most famous building in the world. While they were milling about the great stone gate, a stranger appeared. 'Walk with me,' Charles was saying, his hands around the waist of one of the girls. 'But keep looking ahead.' Still holding her waist, he led her backwards, away from the Taj Mahal.

'It's fantastic!' the girl said, looking along the path between the lawns, the reflecting pools lined with cypress trees and the famous mausoleum glaring under the sun. 'It's following me.'

The Indian guide continued his lecture. 'It may surprise you very much to know, that were the Taj to be built today, the cost would be a shocking seven hundred million dollars!' But few of the tourist party were listening. They were walking backwards, with the same exclamations of glee. The official guide looked on dourly. His spiel had been interrupted by the stranger who had so casually picked up these young tourists as they headed back to the bus.

Charles said goodbye to the girl and her friends, promising to meet them later. Yes, he would clean this Dutch group out that very afternoon. They were exactly the sort of naive tourists he and his new 'family' of accomplices (Jean, Mary and Barbara) had come to Agra to ensnare. Since that 'toothless Dracula', the Belgian, had walked off with Marie-Andrée's black bag the situation had become desperate. Nearly all of their passports, cash and stolen traveller's cheques were inside. Luckily, Charles still had the sapphires and rubies he had stolen from Tommy in Paris. But before he could carry out the biggest jewellery heist of his life – it was all set up – he needed a new batch of passports to ensure an easy getaway to South America. He took a taxi down the squalid, dusty streets to Mahatma Gandhi Road and the Lauries Hotel.

He found Marie-Andrée lying on the bed reading, her eyes puffy with tears. He knew that her emotional state was a danger to him. From the *Asiaweek* article she had learned that there was a warrant out for her arrest on murder charges. Even he was on edge, and she detected the cracks in his confidence. Superstitious, he had taken the loss of her black bag as a bad omen. And she felt guilty. It was her fault.

Marie-Andrée was planning to escape from Charles and yet she still felt trapped by her love for him. Even more so now, since she had met his mother in Marseilles. She felt she understood everything. Her own mother was like a mother should be: jolly, roly-poly and friendly to everyone. But Noi! What a woman! Noi and Charles had fought from the first moment they had met again. She had accused him of deserting his brother, Guy, who was still in a Greek jail. Then she had accompanied her son on a gambling spree where Charles had lost a huge amount of money. Even as they were leaving Villa La Roche to set off on their nightmarish drive back to India, Noi had needled him.

'You're almost thirty-three now, Charles,' she had said. 'Be careful. Christ died when he was thirty-three.'

'I'm smarter than Christ,' Charles had replied, 'and I'll die an old man.'

Marie-Andrée had never known much about his past before. Once she understood, she had felt a surge of pity for him. At least they were fugitives together, and that made it bearable ... sometimes. It was so hot. She sighed and stretched out on the bed, watching Charles' face.

'Darling ...' She reached out to touch him. 'Aren't you frightened a little?'

'Why should I be frightened?' he snapped. 'Listen, we're in Asia, don't you understand? We can get away with anything.'

Through the open window they heard the excited babble of French voices. Charles looked out to see a tour coach in the parking lot disgorging scores of young tourists. A gift! He changed his plans immediately.

'Look,' he said. 'The perfect set-up. If they're booked into this hotel, I can start working on them straight away in the bar or the foyer.'

French passports were so much easier to loosen. He could reshuffle their pages, transferring visas from one to another. Yes, he enjoyed preying on the French.

'I'll drop the Dutch,' he said to Marie-Andrée. 'These are much better.'

Suddenly she cracked. 'Damn you! I'm not staying here another minute! I'm fed up with you. God, why do I suffer like this?'

She rushed to the door, but Charles grabbed her. He didn't trust her to leave the room. She struggled as he held her tightly, clamping his arms around her thin shoulders.

Charles noticed that some of the tourists had stopped near the window and were looking up into the room. Marie-Andrée was still struggling and screaming. Charles dragged her into the bathroom and threw her down into the tub. She lay there a few seconds, dazed, then scrambled up and started screaming again. Charles slapped her across the face and caught her as she fell. Later, he was to say that at this moment he was close to 'cleaning' Marie-Andrée. She was so much trouble.

When she opened her eyes a few seconds later, Charles had lowered her onto the edge of the bathtub and was washing her face with a towel. For sentimental reasons he had spared her. He carried her to the bed, bunching the pillows under her head.

'You know, darling,' he murmured, 'with all these fights we're having, you are making me lose my power over the others.'

Marie-Andrée rubbed her eyes sullenly. Since the Belgian had stolen her bag the tension between Charles and his accomplices had become intolerable. His meticulous but often pointless orders were irritating, opening chinks in the armour of his authority. Now, without money or passports to bribe them with, he had to rely totally on his charismatic manipulations. A 'wife' who was constantly over-flowing with recriminations and bitter insights into his personality was making this very difficult.

'It's the magazine article,' Marie-Andrée moaned. 'The publicity is making me sick.'

'Look, we'll soon be out of this country,' he reassured her. 'And then, South America! With enough bread to go straight, like I prom-ised. And if anything happens before then – well, you can just say that I compelled you to stay with me. You couldn't escape, you knew nothing. I kept everything a secret ...'

Marie-Andrée turned on her side and opened her sci-fi paperback, *Extra Terrestrials*.

From his shoulder-bag, Charles took out his nunchaku, a kung fu weapon popularised by Bruce Lee. He stripped off and stood in front of the mirror, twirling the silver sticks. As a rule the Indian police did not carry guns. If there was trouble, he was sure he could control it.

That afternoon in the bar of the Lauries Hotel, unaware of Luke Solomon's death, Charles skilfully struck up conversation with Frederick, the tour operator in charge of the newly arrived French group, and his wife.

After a few drinks they were soon enthralled by his tales about India. He talked about the mothers who gouged out the eyes of their children to make them good beggars. And the Zoroastrians in Bombay who lay their dead on top of tall 'towers of silence', where the bodies were picked clean by the crows and vultures. And the Hindus, who burned their dead in the holy city of Varanasi, while the priests stood by, plunging sticks into the corpses and folding them over like crepes suzettes. Before long the students were stand-ing around listening to Charles, and the tour leader invited him to join the party for dinner.

Over the next two days Charles befriended dozens of the young French tourists. They were engineering graduates from a college in Tarbes in south-west France. His knowledge of the gem trade fasci-nated them all and when two of the girls showed him some sapphires they had bought, he told them they had been cheated, accompanied them to the shop in question, and ordered its owner to refund the girls' money.

In all his conversations with the students, he impressed on them the dangers of Indian drinking water, quietly slipping laxatives into some of their drinks. He wanted to arouse their anger at Indians, drawing them closer to the fellow Frenchman from whom they could seek advice.

On 4 July, their bus set off to visit the pink city of Jaipur. The students begged Charles to accompany them, but he declined, promising to visit them again in Delhi. Before the group left, he distributed some capsules to his new friends as a safeguard against polluted water. Most of the drugs were harmless but a few were laced with laxatives. He wanted only a few of them stricken with diarrhoea, so the rest would think that their good health was due to his medicines. Charles waved to the group in the bus as it pulled out from Lauries Hotel.

That night his room looked like a dispensary as he and his young accomplices sat round filling up gelatine capsules with a mixture of powdered sleeping pills and laxatives, preparing for the forthcoming reunion with the French students in Delhi. Sixty French students! Sixty passports! Then the jewellery heist and the flight to South America and a new life. Anything was possible.

'A police officer is a citizen in uniform,' read the sign on the wall in the office of New Delhi's Crime Branch, 'and every citizen is a police officer without a uniform.'

Sitting in the dilapidated office behind an ink-stained wooden desk, Deputy Superintendent Naranda Nath Tuli was elated. There had been a breakthrough in the Sobhraj case. Tuli had a fine-boned Brahmin face with searching eyes. For thirty years he had been solving crimes for New Delhi's police force, some of them quite celebrated. But now, if he could cap his career with the arrest of Charles Sobhraj, he could retire and write his memoir.

Tuli still remembered the furore caused by Charles' robbery at the Ashoka Hotel five years ago. Who could forget the tale of the flamenco dancer held hostage above the jewellery shop, and Charles' audacious escape from jail engineered with a faked attack of appendicitis?

This time, Tuli was determined that Sobhraj would not slip away. There was a tip-off from Interpol that Sobhraj had re-entered India. One of his accomplices had been phoning her Canadian family from Delhi. Even before this news, Tuli guessed Charles might be around. Three young French travellers had been found drugged at the YMCA in Delhi and all their belongings stolen by a man calling himself Daniel.

Then came the break. On 2 July, a Belgian, Jean Huygens, had written to the Canadian embassy saying he was in fear of his life. He enclosed pictures of a man calling himself Daniel. It certainly looked like Sobhraj. One morning not long after Huygens had stolen the black bag from Marie-Andrée, Tuli, disguised as a tourist, travelled to Anjuna Beach in Goa to meet with him.

All over the beach, overlanders were passing chillums of hashish and strumming guitars as they lay naked in the sun. Trying to appear at home in the hippie colony, Tuli had dressed in a loud sports shirt. Sipping juice from a coconut, he listened carefully to the Belgian's story. Almost twenty years before, Huygens had taken a detective training course at a night school in Brussels, so the two men, such complete opposites in every way, shared a bond. And they both loved Sherlock Holmes.

Convinced that 'Daniel' was Charles Sobhraj, Tuli flew back to Delhi, alerted his informers, and distributed mug shots of Charles to his men.

Arriving back in Delhi for his date with the young engineers, Charles shuffled his three accomplices around each night between cheap hotels, where they checked in with false identities.

He and Marie-Andrée slept in the Citroën, meeting the others at breakfast to plan each day's activities. Money was running low. Fights kept erupting between Charles and Marie-Andrée, whose white skin was now covered with bruises. Crammed in the dank hotel rooms with luggage and stolen property, the others became increasingly upset by their situation. One morning Mary saw her employer slap Marie-Andrée across the face.

'Go on, hit me again,' Marie-Andrée was screaming. 'I don't even feel it any more.'

'If you don't feel the pain, then why should I injure myself? You make me sick with all your whining,' Charles had answered coldly before walking out, slamming the door behind him.

At 2.30 p.m. on 5 July 1976, the French group's tourist bus turned off the Ring Road in Delhi and pulled up on the tree-lined driveway of the Vikram Hotel. It was a comfortable establishment in the suburbs, not luxurious, which gave discounts to tour groups. When the sixty graduate engineers filed into the foyer, Charles was waiting for them.

'Bonjour, Daniel,' several of them called out to their friend from Agra. As they dispersed to their rooms, some of them stopped to talk to Charles, who was leaning against the bar. He asked the engineers how they had enjoyed Jaipur. Jean Dhuisme was standing next to him looking uncomfortable. In May, the night before they had left Paris, his wife had burst into tears in the bedroom and begged him not to go. She had a bad feeling about Charles, she said. He had needed money but now he realized that Charles had dragged him much deeper into criminality than he'd ever intended.

In a few minutes the subject shifted to dysentery, as it so often did among travellers in India. Charles shook his head sadly as he listened to the tales of woe. That same night the group was planning to fly from Delhi to Bangkok and Charles warned them that after their last meal in Jaipur the whole group could be subject to severe stomach cramps on the plane.

'Have you got any more tablets?' the students asked urgently. Not really, Charles said, but he had a doctor friend in the city who could perhaps arrange an emergency supply. The students thanked him effusively as he and Jean left the hotel, promising to do their best.

At 8.45 p.m. the Tarbes engineers met for dinner in the Samrat restaurant in the Vikram Hotel. Charles walked through the door followed by Jean, carrying a doctor's black bag. The group leader, Frederick, stood up and shook Charles by the hand.

'Sad to be leaving India?' Charles asked. 'No one else has fallen sick, I hope? Here are the anti-bacterial drugs I promised you. Hand them out now. Take one before dinner and two after.'

Some of the students distributed the capsules to each person in the group. The tour leader and his wife were sitting at a table with the group's treasurer and the two men had taken out a precious bottle of duty-free vodka. Some of the students swallowed the capsules immediately, others put them on the table.

'The sooner the better,' Charles was saying to the cautious ones. 'The medicine must have time to build up resistance to the amoeba.' He wanted most of the students to feel sleepy soon after dinner and go to their rooms, where they would pass out. He could then get inside and steal their belongings. He was also discreetly watching the treasurer, wondering if the case near his feet contained the passports, all sixty of them!

Without warning, Frederick's wife groaned and fell to the floor.

This reaction was as much a surprise to Charles as it was to everyone else in the group. It must be the vodka! The woman looked to be unconscious and her body was twitching.

'Darling, darling, oh God, what's happened? Darling, answer me!' cried Frederick, kneeling beside his wife as the waiters and students gathered around. 'Get a doctor, someone! Has she had a stroke?'

The treasurer looked at Charles.

'Maybe it was the pills you gave her,' he said quietly.

'Impossible,' Charles replied. 'They are quite harmless – quick! Let's carry her to the couch in the foyer.'

Other students began complaining of dizziness and two more fell to the floor. An angry group gathered around Charles.

'Have any of you been taking quinine against malaria?' he asked.

A few nodded their heads.

'It must be a reaction,' Charles reassured them. 'It's only temporary.'

Jean began to tremble, his face betraying terror.

'Relax,' Charles said quickly under his breath. 'The situation can still be controlled.'

By now about a dozen students had succumbed to the crudely mixed capsules of sleeping pills and laxatives. Their friends were dragging the unconscious ones from the dining room to the foyer and laying them on the floor. More students began to accuse Charles.

Then one young woman said she too was feeling dizzy, but she hadn't taken any of the pills.

'Did you take quinine this morning?' Charles asked.

She had.

'You see?' Charles said to those looking on. Again, his accusers calmed down.

But still more students kept collapsing. At least ten of them were lying in the lobby now, unconscious or moaning. Charles advised the friends of those who were sick to take them to the lavatories in the basement and induce them to vomit. He had to concede that he had seriously misjudged the dosage. It was strange because he had taken the precaution of testing a capsule on Barbara first. It had taken more than half an hour before she felt ready to pass out. Even so, he had reduced the amount of powder in the capsules.

Meanwhile the hotel receptionist was frantically trying to telephone a doctor. Ever since the first woman fell on the floor, she had been dialling various emergency phone numbers – a procedure often without effect in Delhi in 1976.

The manager of the Vikram was now kneeling by the side of Frederick's wife, who was still lying on a couch in the foyer, and put a glass of water to her lips using his fingers to prize open her mouth. The woman convulsed and bit down on his thumb, almost cutting it off. He screamed. There was blood everywhere.

By now some of the students were telephoning the French embassy, but no one was answering after-hours. Twenty students were laid out on the floor and on the furniture, moaning, vomiting or unconscious. The Indian waiters were panicking, yelling and screaming at each other.

Charles told Jean to go to the car while he remained in the foyer, still intent on stealing the treasurer's bag. He had no intention of leaving, despite the escalating crisis, without the sixty passports.

Really, this was ridiculous, he thought, smiling solicitously. It was like a street in Saigon after a bomb had exploded. And he could have slipped away. But he stayed. Perhaps his gambling instinct and the prize of the sixty passports compelled him to stay. Perhaps it was an irrational desire to court danger.

Three of the students who had not taken the capsules had just positioned themselves like guards around Charles, who pretended not to notice them, when two policemen approached and asked him to come with them into the management's office.

'Of course, officer,' he said pleasantly. 'What a dreadful thing to happen on their last night in India.'

He explained that he had bought the pills that afternoon from a European doctor called Jean, in Connaught Circus. He could take them to him now. Yes, he agreed, there was obviously something fishy about the capsules.

Walking to the door with the two young policemen, Charles felt a wave of relief. He could use them to unwittingly assist his getaway. But the French students who had been keeping him under surveillance stood at the door. No, they insisted to the police. They had finally contacted someone from the French embassy who said that on no account was the man who had given out the pills to be allowed out of the hotel. The French consul was on his way.

Charles shrugged and sat down in the foyer with the police. Be cool, stay calm, plan ahead, he thought.

Tommy's stones! What if he was searched? He took the packet of sapphires and rubies from his bag. While pretending to scratch an itchy toe, he hid them inside his socks.

At the nearby hospital in Greater Kailash, the students were starting to arrive in taxis. Emergency procedures were put into effect. Some students were shouting hysterically, others were involuntarily relieving themselves, some were unconscious. But there were only six beds available. As more victims arrived, they were put on stretchers in rows in the corridors.

Back in the hotel, Superintendent Tuli walked briskly into the lobby and was immediately hit by the stench of vomit and faeces. He pushed his way through the melee of angry students and shocked hotel staff.

There, sitting between two policemen and surrounded by the tourists, was the object of his investigation. Tuli appraised the bearded, dark-eyed suspect.

'So, it is you again,' he said. 'You are behind this disaster.'

'Not a disaster,' the suspect replied, rising politely to his feet and introducing himself as Daniel. 'It's just a mix-up over some medicines. I can take you to the doctor who did it.'

Tuli experienced a rush of adrenalin. All those bodies burnt and mutilated. And now I've got you cornered, he thought. He knew he was about to experience the peak of his career in law enforcement. This man was a monster.

He loosened the suspect's belt and lifted his shirt. He was looking for the appendectomy scar Sobhraj had got five years before, when he had escaped from the hospital in Delhi.

'This is Charles Sobhraj,' he said, pointing triumphantly at the scar on Charles' abdomen. 'You are under arrest.' He nodded at the officers. 'Put him in handcuffs.'

On an old fishing boat moored in Pattaya Bay, Herman Knippenberg sat in a deck-chair in the shade holding a fibreglass fishing rod. He was not a fisherman and had only gone along for the tournament out of politeness.

Hot and bored, he stared out over the water and began to worry as usual about the Sobhraj case. It was uncanny. The man had managed to outwit so many police in so many countries. What a tragic misuse of such a gifted mind, he thought, still puzzled by the motives for the murders and the lazy trail of evidence left behind. At least Nadine and Remy were safely out of the way, back home in France.

A sharp tug at his line brought him back to the real world. Startled, Herman watched his fishing line sizzling away into the bright turquoise water while the reel clicked fast. He'd never caught a big fish before.

'Quick, come here. Give me a hand!' he yelled to his companions. But it was against the rules of the tournament, so he had to struggle for fifteen more minutes until the 3½-kilogram Jack Crevalle was finally landed.

The following day he drove back with his friends to Bangkok, his record-breaking fish in the icebox. He had just stepped out of the shower at home when the phone rang.

'We've been trying to contact you,' said an official from the Canadian embassy.

'I was out of town on a fishing trip.'

'Yes. So were the police in Delhi. They've caught Sobhraj.'

'Well. That is wonderful,' was all Herman could think to say.

Over the next few days, Charles' four accomplices were picked up. It seemed Marie-Andrée was glad it was over. She wrote out her own statement by hand, much of it implicating Charles and Ajay in the Kanit House murders. In it she stated that she had not seen Ajay since March. 'Charles could have killed him,' she suggested. Ajay has never been seen or heard of again.

At the Greater Kailash hospital, the recovering students shook their heads in dismay when told of the arrest of the man who had given them the capsules. 'Oh, not him, it couldn't be!' they protested. 'We will go to the police. He must be set free. He was our friend.'

The news of Charles and Marie-Andrée's arrest was announced in the French daily newspaper *France-Soir* the same week, and soon after *Paris Match* featured the photograph of the 'diabolic duo' on its cover.

Alain Benard saw the headlines announcing the arrest. At home, he cut out the news story and added it to his voluminous files. A shelf of his library was lined with neat green boxes containing all the documents he had collected relating to his young friend, Charles

Sobhraj. From the earliest disappointed school reports, to this latest news.

Not long after, Charles wrote to him from Tihar Jail.

Alain, perhaps you can understand when I tell you that throughout all this, I have been searching only for a way to live. And that although I was often engaged in illegal activities and sometimes lost my principles, I had a certain respect for the human state. I tell you, Alain, I promise you, I did not kill. I am not a liar. During the few years that Chantal spent with me, she will tell you that she never saw me do any physical harm to anyone. So they are wrong who say that I have committed all those murders for a few hundred or a few thousand dollars. As you know, I have never been short of illegal ways to make money. Why, during a whole year, I didn't commit a murder, and then, in three months ... nine or ten ... murders, all in one blow, in which the profit didn't total more than five thousand dollars? If that were the case, it means I did it not for the money, but simply to kill. So Alain, above all, despite these stupid accusations, I tell you it is not true. They are all liars and now I risk the loss of my head.

So I have said to myself ... 'My little Charlie, this is serious. It is necessary to play a dangerous game. You can't weaken, you can't let yourself cry, or they will hear you and think you are becoming soft. It is necessary to FIGHT!'

Yes, Alain, I remain Asiatic above all. I am obliged to accept the rules of this new game, and to smile, and to go forward. Whoever will live, will see. Isn't that so? So, I prefer to live, and to see.

Benard was no longer a prison visitor. After seeing an inmate being beaten by the guards he had complained to the governor. When nothing was done, he resigned. He was recalling how it had all begun, when he was walking in the park, feeling bored with his life and wanting a challenge. A hot summer breeze blew through the open window of his apartment, carrying up the sounds of the street.

Charles' letter, fifteen pages long, was lying on the long cedar table where in the hopeful early days he had so often sat with Benard, talking all night about his philosophies and ambitions. Whether or not Charles had committed these murders Benard knew he would still stand by, ready to help if he was needed. He was not going to abandon him as Hotchand Sobhraj had done when his son fled with Chantal to Asia six years before, leaving a wreckage of bounced cheques and unpaid bills.

At that time, Hotchand had written to Benard with great acuity about the situation:

Once a blind boy was sitting on a stone near a pond. All the other boys were swimming, chatting and laughing. A priest passed by and saw this boy sitting alone. He saw he was blind and took pity on him. The priest prayed to the mighty God to give him eyes so he could swim too. God agreed and gave the boy light.

The boy jumped in the pond for a swim and began to beat the other boys. 'He's dangerous,' they all said and ran away. The boy came out of the pond and began to beat the priest, who asked God to make the boy like he was before. God did so and said to the priest, 'I saw this boy was dangerous to humans so I took away his light.'

Dear Benard, you have done the same thing with this boy. Let him be in prison rather than let him be freed. This was your great mistake. You thought he would do good when he will be freed. He begged you, and you took pity on him. This is the result of your mercy.

Even now, with Charles accused of multiple murders, Benard believed Hotchand's argument was false. Every human being, including this ill-fated man, had the right to one friend standing by until the end. He sent back the same small red Bible to the Indian jail that he had presented to Charles ten years before at Poissy.

17

In Chains

'It's Mr Charles! It's Mr Charles!' came the cry, growing louder as it echoed along the grubby concrete hallways.

Small boys in ragged clothes were running behind a gaggle of soldiers leading a procession. The star of the proceedings was making his first appearance of the day. In the corridors which honeycombed the courthouse, the whisper rippled through the crush of guards and prisoners as if a great personage was about to arrive. Charles moved through the crowd. He was wearing a beige T-shirt, blue trousers, tennis shoes and a gold Omega watch. Thick steel cuffs circling his ankles were attached to an iron bar twenty inches long, which locked onto the belt of his trousers. His left wrist was cuffed and connected by a long chain to the belt of one of the soldiers, who was being dragged behind his prisoner like a dog being walked in a downpour. But Charles, despite the shackles, moved with lithe grace.

It was 5 July 1977, and inside the compound of Old Delhi's Tis Hazari courthouse one of the more notorious criminal trials of the twentieth century was unfolding.

In the twelve months since Charles Sobhraj's arrest at the Vikram Hotel in Delhi, the publicity surrounding his exploits had made him world-famous. Reporters from the international news services, including Reuters, UPI and Agence France Presse, were gathered in the courtroom to cover the case.

At his side, wearing a red shirt-dress, Marie-Andrée scowled at the staring bystanders. She had been on a hunger strike to protest against her prison conditions and her face revealed a soul in torment.

At the rear of this almost medieval procession was Jean Dhuisme also chained to a soldier, his high forehead creased in despair and his tall frame hunched.

The rumours that surrounded Charles were as impressive as his aura of being in complete control. It was said that a fortune in gems was hidden in his teeth and that the tarnished charm he wore round his neck contained a cache of rubies. He was a karate black belt who could jump twelve feet in the air. Guns were hidden in his cell. He could read minds and hypnotize a man in an instant.

All these myths Charles had encouraged. He had also hinted at the existence of bank accounts in various countries under false names.

Behind Charles and Marie-Andrée, under separate guard, Mary followed, giggling with Barbara, who wore an Indian cotton kurta and a sprig of jasmine in her hair. The eyes of most of the soldiers focused closely on the bodies of these two young women. As soon as they'd been arrested, both had agreed to turn witness for the prosecution. For this reason, neither Mary nor Barbara was allowed any contact with Charles or Marie-Andrée. Charles' ability to flourish in jail, however, meant that letters passed constantly between him and the rest of his gang. Just a few weeks before, after giving state's evidence at the opening of the trial, the two women had been found unconscious in their cells. Both had overdosed with sleeping pills and insecticide. Soon after that, a false beard, moustache, 20,000 rupees and a guard's uniform had been found hidden in Charles' cell.

The third-floor courtroom was packed. An elderly lawyer with silver hair and a high, starched collar of a type not often seen in a lowly magistrate's court, stood up to speak.

'A scurrilous item in the *Times of India* has stated that my client was a member of a notorious gang of international criminals,' the lawyer said to the judge. 'It is an *absolute outrage* and I intend to file an objection in the High Court.'

In the dock, pressed close to Marie-Andrée and surrounded by soldiers, Charles was whispering to a short, plump criminal lawyer with a scar on his face. This scar was rumoured to have been caused by Charles, who had ordered him to be taught a lesson several years earlier. After more whispering amongst the other dignitaries, the opening of the day's proceedings was temporarily postponed. The magistrate sat fiddling with his pen, looking vaguely at the ceiling.

Now Charles walked to the back of the courtroom. He had spotted two new visitors to the proceedings. He'd been expecting us – my boyfriend Richard and me.

When Random House New York had purchased the rights to the Sobhraj story, the publishers had commissioned Richard to write the book about the case within six months. So I decided to leave my job as a New York correspondent for an Australian media organization and join him as a researcher.

Charismatic and articulate, Richard had been a darling of the media. He had smoked pot on television and had written *Playpower*, an early chronicle of the Asian hippie trail. It was one of the reasons he had been offered the book contract. His prosecution at the Old Bailey for obscenity as the editor of his now fashionable underground magazine, in what became known as the *OZ* Trials, had been a cause célèbre of London's literary scene in the early seventies. He had defended himself, and John Lennon and Yoko Ono were among the crowds demonstrating their support.

We had met in 1974 when I was a cadet journalist sent to interview him. With his encouragement I had spent six months of 1975 crossing Asia to Europe on the hippie trail. After that came my posting to New York.

High on our typhoid and hepatitis vaccinations we rushed out and purchased the smallest tape recorder we could find, and a stack of cassette tapes. Then, Richard flew to Paris to meet with the prison visitor and mentor of Charles Sobhraj, who we called 'Benard' in the book. Richard phoned from Paris to say that Benard was a deeply cultured Catholic whose bookshelves were lined with all the philosophy books that Richard himself had lightly studied. He said that they had spent several days together, and that Benard was still open-minded regarding Charles' guilt in what were being called 'the Bikini

Killings'. All the interviews were taped, and Benard had given Richard copies of all the records he had collected of Charles' life.

In July 1977 we arrived in Delhi and moved into a room at the Hotel Imperial. It was beautifully sparse then, in its full glory before it was renovated. For room service, an elderly man slept on the floor outside our door in case we wanted anything. Vestiges of the Raj were still everywhere.

As hippie-yuppies, we made an effort that first morning in the Indian courtroom to project a conservative image. Richard's usually longish hair was cut and he was wearing chinos and a pale-blue shirt, while I too had tried to present sartorial gravitas in a demure linen dress. The heat was overwhelming. Charles sat down on the bench next to us and introduced himself with the air of a gracious host putting guests at ease. I caught my breath.

It was like meeting a movie star. He gave the impression of being a person of substance and, oddly, respectability.

Later I misremembered that I took an instant dislike to him, but my journal showed I had the typical reaction: I was charmed, I wanted him to like me. Yes, his eyes did bore into me, he did exude animal magnetism as though just the two of us were alone together in the universe and we could just settle down for a long intimate chat.

What if I had met him in the lobby of the Hotel Malaysia? I pride myself on having an excellent shit-detector, but I'm not sure it would have worked for me at that age and with such a brilliant psychopath.

'Don't be fooled by all these chains,' he smiled, extending his hand. 'It was much worse in Greece. As for these children –' he gestured at the soldiers who had been forced to follow him dutifully across the room '– just ignore them. Indians are all quantity and no quality,' he said dismissively. We were soon to become accustomed to Charles' racism about his father's homeland. Raised in a privileged first-world country, we loved India with a passion for all its explosive colour and cacophony of eccentricities and extremes.

Throughout the rest of the morning, concocted interruptions continued to delay the start of the day's proceedings. From his seat at the back of the courtroom, Charles surreptitiously handed out notes to a bevy of haggard young French and Americans he had met during their jail time. Recently released, these smitten youths loitered within earshot ready to do his bidding – perhaps slip him a file inside a box of felt pens, take a letter he wanted posted, or bring him a bottle of Coke.

When the court finally convened, Mary was led through her statement by the prosecution lawyer accompanied by the clatter of the court typewriter. After a year in jail she now spoke with an Indian accent. Sometimes, when the stenographer asked her to repeat her statements and answers, Charles would prompt her from the back of the court. It was clear to us that Charles was running the show.

It was still a surprise, however, when Mary suddenly began to retract her statement. She wept, she shouted. She claimed that she did not actually see Charles pour the fatal cocktail of drugs into Luke Solomon's chicken curry and that the police had blackmailed her to incriminate the defendant.

'A beautiful story,' Charles whispered under his breath to Richard, while the prosecution lawyers huddled in disarray. 'Now you can see why I'm not so worried, eh? In the end they will have to acquit me. And the judge is on my side.'

We smiled politely. Surely this was a cheap boast?

Now, a tall Sikh lawyer with a long, black beard walked up to Charles and offered his congratulations.

'We've finished drafting your petition,' he said. 'It's a brilliant argument. I'll take it to the highest court in the land.'

'It's to get my shackles removed,' Charles explained, leaning towards us with collegiate body language. 'Aren't they barbaric?'

The next day Richard arrived outside a small stone cell on the edge of the court buildings, keyed up for his first interview with Charles.

A peeling sign on the wall read, 'Report instances of corruption to the officer on duty'. As Richard waited outside the cell, a senior

policeman tried to sell him a sheaf of documents relating to Charles
for $7,000 plus a percentage of book royalties. The anti-corruption
programme was clearly failing.

Nearby, a giant fig tree spread its comforting shade over the bare
earth and cracked cement of the court compound which was throbbing in the humid heat. The tree had become an unofficial office
area and signs advertising legal services were nailed to its trunk.
Under its protection, stenographers in plastic sandals sat pecking
out affidavits on rickety Remington typewriters. I found a box to sit
on and also took notes, while waiting for the lesser members of the
gang to turn up.

The scene around me was Dickensian in its complexity. There
was such a mixture of clearly delineated classes and castes, and pov-
erty mixed in with the imported British legal system which was
being upheld so rigorously. A plethora of somnolent guards with
their unwieldy rifles were interspersed with cold-drink and snack
sellers whose modest wares were set up on makeshift stands.
Mothers, hoping to see their prisoner husbands, sat on the ground,
feeding babies.

Richard wrote that night in his diary:

Ushered into the small cell I was once again taken by Charles'
warm and relaxed manner, and we fell into an easy discourse.
Rifling through his shoulder bag he began to produce fragments of an autobiography he said he had been writing in jail,
which he gave to me.

'In some ways my whole life has been a protest against the
French legal system which stole so many years of my youth.
All I have ever wanted is to win them back.'

Over the following week, Charles deftly skirted the subject
of murder and reminisced about his early buccaneering days,
regaling me with tales of his great escapes, the search for his
father, and the mad dashes across Asia with his first wife,
Chantal, and their child, Madhu. As he talked, he often touched
me on the arm to make a point; rounding off an anecdote with

a poetic turn of phrase; wisecracking about India; gloating at all the venal weaknesses of those around him.

'As long as I can talk to people, I can manipulate them,' he told me in the soothing voice of a therapist, implying at the same time that our own relationship was immune to such tricks.

After a couple of weeks of Richard and Charles' burgeoning friendship, I could see that Richard (always an enthusiast) was close to losing contact with the real world – the world in which Charles was considered 'evil'. I was researching the other side of the story, talking with the police, families and friends of Charles' victims. One Canadian diplomat with whom I was discussing the case said to me directly, 'He wouldn't have so much power in jail if people like you weren't giving him money.' And that was a painful truth.

Here in Delhi, a topsy-turvy morality reigned, and rupees were certainly at the heart of it. The court processes were like something out of the Mad Hatter's tea party and it felt as though money, or even the scent of it, could open any door. That our project had provided some of those rupees was to become a cause of much angst.

One night while lying in bed at the Hotel Imperial, we heard the grinding of a hand drill on the door to our room, quickly followed, to our astonishment, by a drill-bit poking through the wood. A peephole had been set up. Was it the police who had begun ostentatiously following us? The authorities were obviously keen to foil any escape plans and suspected us of being part of them. In fact, we soon realized that many vested interests were spying on us. Not least Charles.

Every night in our hotel room we transcribed Richard's tapes on our portable Olivetti typewriters. As I listened to the instant rapport that was flourishing between the man I loved and the notorious criminal, it would be an understatement to say that their relationship began to disturb me. It was above all Charles' voice, in turn intimate, manipulative, persuasive and playful, that held so much power over everyone who engaged with him. Richard too was so charming that I had seen new acquaintances become completely enthralled by him.

These two men were opposites in background and moral character, and yet so well matched. Both were autodidacts, always hungry to learn new things. Like Charles, Richard had been sent to boarding school at a young age where he had learnt the tricks of befriending and captivating (mainly with humour) to protect himself from loneliness. He had also briefly been jailed after his notorious OZ magazine trial, amid a flurry of newspaper headlines, an experience he claimed to have found educational and similar to his boarding school. Richard too was a boy from the colonies, capable of shape-shifting between the mansions of the British aristocracy and the radical left-wing agitators of Brixton. He must have provided Charles with a level of intellectual engagement he rarely enjoyed with the tourists and thugs he recruited into his business activities. Was it for this reason that the conversations between Richard and Charles were so astonishing in their detail and range?

Later, Richard observed, 'Sinuously, Charles mounted a siege against my professional detachment, discrediting the opinions of others, and keying his observations to match what he guessed were my personal prejudices.'

These prejudices included Richard's strenuous opposition (and that of his contemporaries) to the war in Vietnam ten years before. Charles portrayed himself as a victim of the Vietnam War and America's other interventions in Southeast Asia.

It was a heady mix of Nietzschean philosophy and *Bad Boys' Own Adventure*. Whether Charles was guilty of any murders or not was still to us an open question. And Richard was not put off by Charles' anti-authoritarian diatribes, in fact just the opposite. Drawing from psychoanalysis, global politics, philosophy and Buddhism, Charles created a cocoon in the little cell, a spellbinding mix of rationalization and extenuating circumstance which justified his entire criminal career.

This enthralment (from which Richard did slowly recover) enabled us to understand how Charles had managed to ensnare such a wide cross-section of people as either co-conspirators or victims in his relentless criminal rampage. In his diary, Richard wrote of those

first weeks, 'I almost felt sorry for the prisoner, shackled and surrounded by soldiers, his future bleak. But now I begin to wonder if I
have become a bandit's groupie, smiling and nodding in complicity
over his self-glorifying tales of crime.'

In truth, the pace of Charles' confidences would have been
impossible for any journalist to resist. The more Richard nodded
and took notes, the more Charles poured forth stories of his traps,
frauds and poisonings. At this stage he resisted all Richard's efforts
to find out more about the murders, even though he had agreed to
discuss these accusations in the contract. He also knew that we were
about to go to Bangkok for more research and hinted that he might
be ready to reveal more when we returned. At the end of each session, almost without pausing for breath, Charles would conclude
with requests for pens, notebooks and biscuits. He was worried
about the prison diet of lentils, and asked Richard to bring him
vitamins.

'He must be joking,' I quipped at the time. 'Let's give him laxatives.' Although we laughed, I had never even been arrested at a
demonstration against the war in Vietnam and had been raised by
Methodists. Now someone was tampering with our mail, and
Richard was hosting research 'cocktail parties' in our hotel room for
every professional criminal Charles had ever consorted with. After
warning us of the danger we were in, the Australian embassy told us
to leave town.

We flew to Bangkok, where we had access to police files and could
track down everyone who had anything to do with Sobhraj and
Kanith House. Herman Knippenberg was now posted to New York
City, but we had access to his 'Knippenberg File' and it was a particular delight to meet the Belgian diplomat Paul Siemons, who with his
no-holds-barred moral compass and sense of humour felt to me like
a human antidote to Sobhraj. We travelled to Chiang Mai, and to all
the murder sites, and met with the local police and witnesses.

On our return to Delhi to continue with the interviews, Charles
announced that he was ready to reveal the details of the murders. These
he always referred to as 'cleanings'. The tapes of these conversations,

remarkable for the matter of fact way in which Charles discussed his crimes, still exist. They make for chilling listening.

We spent almost a year working on the case all over Asia and Europe, speaking to everyone who had known Charles. In Paris we met up with Remy, Nadine and Dominique Rennelleau. Back in New York City we worked with Herman and Angela Knippenberg.

For the next eighteen months, the book was our obsession, much to the consternation of our friends. They were involved in projects such as Rock Against Racism, inventing solar bioshelters and starting indigenous art cooperatives in the Western Desert of Australia.

We were weighed down by the confessions of a multiple murderer. We had arrived back in New York City with two big suitcases of documents and cassette tapes, among them letters that Charles had given us written to him by his co-accused, many of them damning. We had thousands of pages of police reports and court records, like a jigsaw tipped out of a box. And we continued to travel to meet anyone who would speak to us who had been involved in the case.

Putting together a clear narrative and timeline from the puzzle of paperwork required exhaustive attention to detail. Hundreds of international flights, arrests and charges had to be checked for dates, departures and arrivals. Gradually we discovered that, almost always, everything Charles said added up. His memory for dialogue, people and events was astonishing. When we checked what he told us about the murder of André Breugnot, which had been recorded as an accidental death, every detail was correct. We were less successful at finding the body of an unnamed American he said was his first victim, and who he claimed was buried at Pattaya. Charles had drawn Richard a crude map, which we gave to the authorities, but if anyone did bother to look, no body was found.

The question of motive for the sudden battery of killing in Thailand and Kathmandu was the most perplexing aspect of the mystery. Charles' story that he had been hired by a triad as a hit-man to wipe out amateurs in the heroin trade seemed watertight except for a few conundrums we couldn't solve. There were the missing days from when Teresa and Stephanie were last seen and when they were killed. There was the fact that Connie was naked when she was murdered, despite Charles' stated preference for burning people fully clothed. It was very handy that Charles had his now-vanished assistant Ajay to blame when the 'cleanings' got dirty.

It was a moral quandary for us to publish Charles' detailed murder confessions without impugning his young victims. While there was no doubt about the involvement of Vitali Hakim, Stephanie Parry and Connie Joe Bronzich in heroin smuggling, we could never definitively prove that any of the others were involved. We had also travelled the Asian hippie trail and knew that seemingly well-brought-up kids did not think twice about carrying a parcel on a flight from one city to another. In the Rajneeshi cult in Poona where prosperous young Westerners flocked, this was considered a normal way to finance one's spiritual journey.

In 1979 the book was first published as the *Life and Crimes of Charles Sobhraj*.

'It wasn't very sympathetic to me,' Charles complained to the *Bangkok Post*. 'But many of the letters I received about it said they thought the authors didn't like me, and I couldn't be as bad as the book said.'

In Tihar Jail, while still awaiting verdicts in the French tour-group poisoning and Luke Solomon cases, Charles lost no time consolidating his position. He had successfully petitioned the High Court for the removal of the shackles. Using a small hidden tape recorder strapped to his thigh, he began charming jail officials into chatting at length with him about their illegal activities. He recorded them admitting everything from canteen skimming to petty theft and supplying opium. He then took the tape to the superintendent, put it on his desk and announced: 'I am a criminal and you are a criminal, so we should cooperate.' The superintendent could only agree.

He quickly began to turn a profit on the inside. There was 40 per cent commission to be made on all illegal takings. And a fee was

extracted whenever Charles referred new prisoners to one of his battery of lawyers.

In his cell Charles enjoyed the use of a colour television and other
luxuries far beyond the reach of even the most successful, law-
abiding Indians. He had acquired a Canon portable typewriter with
an extensive memory, from which he printed reams of legal reports
at the touch of a button. A disgruntled guard later testified that
Sobhraj and Marie-Andrée Leclerc also had sex twice a week in the
superintendent's office.

In October 1981 the scale of Charles' opulent lifestyle at Tihar
became a scandal which the Indian press enjoyed enormously. To
pre-empt the loss of his privileges Charles' countermove was to send
the incriminating tapes he had made to the High Court. As a result,
the superintendent was sacked and the jail reorganized. But Charles'
lifestyle inside suffered no downgrade.

For many years after our book's publication, Charles maintained
his correspondence with Richard. After the 1981 scandal, he boasted
in a letter that 'due to my incessant complaints against corruption,
the situation has become better for other prisoners'.

In 1983, Marie-Andrée Leclerc was diagnosed with ovarian cancer
and in July of that year the Supreme Court ruled that she should be
'allowed to die in peace in her own country'.

'I'm innocent, but nobody wants to believe it,' she told reporters
before flying home to Quebec. Yes, it was difficult to believe, but not
hard to understand how someone so mentally unstable could have
been reduced to the tragic figure she became.

'Is Charles guilty?' she was asked.

'I never saw him kill anyone,' she said, 'but he is sick.'

Marie-Andrée died in April 1984.

Charles had already been in correspondence with many women
who wanted to come to Delhi and marry him. The syndrome,
called hybristophilia, describes those who experience sexual arousal
from someone who has committed notorious crimes. Consecutively
he accepted two proposals. One was a woman from Perth, Western
Australia, who said she felt sorry for Charles and wanted to change

him. She moved to Delhi, but the romance ended when the reality of acting as his secretary and personal shopper began to lose its appeal. Then came a psychology graduate from UCLA, who succumbed to an 'urge to understand him' and even tried to formalize her betrothal with an esoteric Protestant ceremony in Varanasi when he was there on trial for the murder of Alan Jacobs. She was expelled from India and was said to have left 'kicking and screaming' as she was carried onto the plane.

The women kept coming. Naive helpmates. Ambitious journalists. One young lawyer visited the jail over sixty times for private consultations. She supplied him with tuna, chocolates and an imported wardrobe of shirts and jeans.

Charles also forged alliances with key Indian gangsters inside Tihar, some of whom continued to work for him after their release, as well as siphoning a stream of money from respectful foreign criminals. The Indian press regularly ran profiles on him as 'the man who really runs Tihar'.

Charles had plenty of money for lawyers, but also, having studied Indian law, knew very well how to manipulate the system. 'Indian law favours the accused,' was a favourite saying of his, certainly true in his own case. For the drugging of the French engineering students he was sentenced to only two years.

In the case of Alan Jacobs, the Israeli crane-driver found dead in Varanasi, Charles and Marie-Andrée Leclerc had both been sentenced to life. Evidence showed that Charles had stolen the dead man's passport and cashed his traveller's cheques. And although he had openly discussed this death with Richard, blaming it on Ajay, he did so knowing that the book itself would not stand up in a court of law. This conviction was overturned in the High Court in 1983.

In the case of Luke Solomon, the young Frenchman who had died after Charles had drugged his chicken curry in the Connaught Place restaurant in Delhi – allegedly witnessed by Mary – the wheels of Indian justice finally turned in favour of the defendants, exonerating Sobhraj and Leclerc from an earlier conviction in a lower court.

Then there was the case of the three Frenchmen picked up on a beach near Goa, drugged, robbed and left unconscious in their van with a rock on its accelerator. Eric Damour had produced a holiday snap of himself walking on the sand with Charles. It was published in our book but could never be introduced as evidence because the court insisted that a negative of the photograph must be produced. As no one could find it, the court just refused to look at it, and Charles was never charged.

In 1985, Charles wrote to Richard that he thought his life since his arrest in Delhi warranted another book. It was true. The mayhem he had caused inside the jail microcosm was just as complex as the catastrophes he had created in the macrocosm of the outside world. The betrayals, the extortions, the uncanny control – he had certainly taken to heart a favourite Nietzsche quotation: 'Be robbers and ravagers as long as you cannot be rulers and owners, you men of knowledge.'

After our singular burst of true-crime writing, once was enough. In the years following that adventure, we moved back to our homeland, to an old house in the Australian countryside, and now had two children. For the rest of his life, however, Richard followed the case closely and for years letters from all over the world kept arriving from correspondents who had come across our book and described how they had survived their own travel experiences with Sobhraj. Richard filed them away. A few times when the phone rang it was Charles calling for a chat.

Charles knew that he was safe as long as he was in the Indian judicial system, but the Thai police continued to press for his extradition. Until 1985, Charles had remained confident of legal victory. 'I don't worry much about Thailand,' he wrote to Richard. 'If I don't opt for a "Greece" [his code for a jailbreak], it's because I'm certain to get my freedom by the Indian court.'

In December 1985, however, two High Court judges upheld the magistrate's decision to allow his extradition to Thailand. Charles revised his strategy. 'The Greek stuff has always been at my reach,' he wrote, 'but I pushed the idea aside. Now it is really being forced on me.'

'Thailand is well known for its black laws and its violation of human rights,' Charles had told a reporter. 'If I go there, I will be shot.'

The legal strategy of the Thai police concentrated on two cases. The first was the non-fatal poisoning of the Australian couple at the Railway Hotel in Hua Hin in September 1975. The victims, Russell and Vera Lapthorne, had agreed to return to Bangkok and give evidence against Charles Sobhraj. The second case, the murder of the Dutch couple, Cocky and Henk, was supported by Herman Knippenberg's mountain of evidence and that of the key witness, Nadine Gires, who was willing to testify.

When our book was first published, Charles had told reporters it was 'ninety per cent accurate'. Now with the spectre of Thailand drawing near, he gave interviews which distanced him from the murders and played down the significance of the taped confessions. We had never relied exclusively on his word, however, having used his confessions as a guide to our own investigation.

'I'll be free soon,' he wrote to Richard in April 1985. 'Wherever I'll be, I'll contact you. Keep reading the news.'

One night in March 1986, the wardens in Tihar Jail found a sick cat. It was unconscious but still breathing. The men nursed the animal, and it quickly recovered.

A few days later, in the early afternoon of Sunday 17 March, a white Ambassador car drove to the main gate of Tihar Jail. One of its passengers was David Hall, a suave young Englishman who had briefly resided at Tihar and was now out on bail on charges of heroin smuggling. Like many other prisoners, David Hall had formed a close relationship with Tihar's most celebrated inmate, and since his release had continued to run errands for Charles Sobhraj. 'Today is a special day,' Hall told the two Tamil guards at the gate as he slipped them a 100-rupee note. 'It is Charles Sahib's birthday.'

With Hall was Raju Bhatnagar, another former cellmate of Sobhraj, who remained unrecognized by guards despite his notoriety. Bhatnagar had been 'accidentally' released from Tihar two months before, despite thirty-six charges against him, including seven murders and nineteen abductions.

Piled on the car's back-seat was the 'birthday feast': apples, chocolates, custard puddings, local delicacies and five kilos of grapes. The guards accepted an offer of fruit. Although visits were prohibited on Sunday afternoons, the car was allowed to proceed through the outer gate and along a narrow perimeter road to the precincts of Jail No. 3.

Minutes later, Hall and Bhatnagar carried the boxes of fruit and sweets into the office of the assistant superintendent, Mr S. R. Yadev. Sitting on the desk in animated conversation with Yadev was Sobhraj, still lean and fit after ten years inside, although he was now balding.

The loud exchange of birthday greetings attracted six other wardens into the room, as well as two 'on duty' prisoners. Gatherings of this kind were against prison rules, but the treats were unpacked and passed around. Charles ate some cakes (later thought to have been marked), and then left the room.

'I'll get my friends,' he said.

By the time Charles and his guests had returned, Yadev and the wardens were already groggy, suffering the effects of the chloral hydrate and medazepam which had been injected into the food.

The guards were tied up, their mouths sealed with tape. One of the wardens, Anand Prakash, was taken as a decoy, and the rest were padlocked inside the office. Four of the prisoners joined Sobhraj and his two accomplices as they headed for the car. His forty-second birthday was going according to plan, even though the official date – 6 April – was still three weeks away.

The captured warden was positioned in the front seat of the car, his uniformed arm left dangling out of the window to avert suspicion from the watchtower. The white car was unchallenged at the main gate. The guards who had sampled the feast were now lying oblivious beside their rifles.

Once the crowded car had passed the prison gardens, the warden – bound, gagged and unconscious – was dumped on the road. The seven criminals let out a cheer.

Outside Tihar, it took fifteen minutes for a rickshaw driver to find the warden's bound and comatose body and sound the alarm. Roadblocks were set up at major intersections; airports, bus stands, railway stations and luxury hotels were put under watch.

Delhi's lieutenant governor, H. K. L. Kapoor, posted a reward of 25,000 rupees and angrily suspended the jail officials, six of whom were admitted to hospital at the end of the day, still unconscious.

The world's media seized on the escape, continually rehashing Sobhraj's life and crimes, and taunting the authorities. The prime minister, Rajiv Gandhi, was furious. Once again, using the same techniques that had worked so well so many times before, Charles Sobhraj slid smoothly out of the precincts of the jail and onto the front pages of newspapers around the world. Later, the wardens remembered the ailing cat.

Thousands of miles away on an Australian mountain top, as the mist lifted from a massive valley below in the Blue Mountains National Park, the phone rang early. We were making tea. It was ABC Radio to tell us that Charles Sobhraj had escaped from Tihar Jail. They wanted us to comment.

By now, it was impossible to be surprised by Charles' exploits. Richard told them that South America had always been his plan, and that in recent letters he had mentioned that he had been brushing up his Spanish. But Charles had not risked that final flight. If something had gone wrong, he could have ended up in Thailand.

Early in April, detectives in Bombay received a tip that Charles was in Goa. An elite taskforce of twenty-one police, all posing as tourists, was sent to search the beaches and bars of the tropical tourist mecca. The operation was so secret that colleagues were not told of each other's whereabouts; even the police in Goa were not alerted.

On Sunday 6 April in Panaji, the capital of Goa, the taskforce laid a trap at the well-known restaurant 'O Coqueiro', 'The

Coconut Tree'. The restaurant occupied a gracious historic house, painted white, with wide verandas. On this day it was crowded with a party from an afternoon wedding. Police from the taskforce, wearing the restaurant's uniform of traditional sarongs, served drinks at the bar.

Two men, one tall and elegantly dressed, the other shorter, bearded and carrying a briefcase, strolled through the crowd. Sobhraj and his English accomplice, David Hall, had come to book phone calls to Beirut and Paris. While waiting for the calls, they ordered beers and sat down.

Inspector Madhukar Zende, who had arrested Sobhraj fourteen years before after a drug-mugging at Bombay's Taj Mahal hotel, was sitting at the next table dressed as a tourist. Instantly, he recognized his quarry.

What happened next sounds like a B-grade thriller.

'There you are, Charles! How are you?' shouted Zende from his table, signalling his men to close in. 'I call your bluff. You are under arrest.'

'There seems to be a mix-up,' Charles replied, unruffled. 'I'm Nepalese.'

Pandemonium broke out among the wedding guests and the two criminals were handcuffed and bundled from 'O Coqueiro'. For his forty-second birthday Sobhraj found himself back in custody again. The restaurant still proudly displays a mural on its veranda commemorating this historic event.

Now Charles' life of luxury in Tihar Jail came to an end. He was made to wear fetters and a prominent red uniform. All non-judicial visits were refused, including those of journalists. In court, where he now faced charges of escaping from custody, he still appeared relaxed.

This jailbreak was solely designed to foil his extradition to Thailand, he said, and it did. He knew that an Indian jail was his best protection from the Thai arrest warrant and certain death. He was given another ten years for escaping from jail, and this time Charles stayed in jail.

*

Ten years of imprisonment in Delhi passed. On 17 February 1997, Charles Sobhraj was released from Tihar Jail. There was another media frenzy and more international headlines. Because of the twenty-year statute of limitations, the Thai arrest warrants for the murders of Teresa Knowlton, Vitali Hakim, Stephanie Parry, Cocky Hemker and Henk Bintanja had lapsed. Although he had described each one of these murders in detail, now he could never face trial for them. Aged fifty-two, Charles was free.

Returning to Paris, he posed for photographs praying in Notre Dame Cathedral and charged $5,000 to have lunch with fans. Chantal left her American husband and came back to see him, but Charles had failed to mention he had taken a Chinese wife and that another daughter was on the way. Chantal was moved to a nearby hotel.

The public's continuing fascination kept him busy for the next ten years. He appeared in several documentaries, was befriended by a few Bollywood luminaries, engaged in some petty crime, almost pulled off a big Hollywood film deal, and hinted in letters to Richard that he was involved in high-level dealings with the Taliban, Iran and international arms dealers.

And then in 2003, inexplicably, he travelled back to Nepal, the only country in the world where there was still an outstanding arrest warrant for him. First, a local journalist spotted him on the street and alerted police, and the next day when he was gambling ostentatiously in the casino of the the Yak and Yeti hotel, the police closed in.

Charles claimed he had come to research Nepali handicrafts. This would certainly have been a new and surprisingly wholesome interest for him. Any scenario was possible. He had also hinted at top-secret work for the Chinese government. Or maybe he just felt that it was time for another jail holiday. He was formally charged and found guilty of the murder of Connie Jo Bronzich and finally sentenced to life. The police file of the Carrière case, however, could not be traced by the Nepali authorities until 2008, when it was finally located. In 2014 a further sentence of twenty years' detention was given to Sobhraj for the murder of Laurent Carrière.

At present, Charles remains in jail, where he has enjoyed a relationship, described by them both as a marriage, with a glamourous Nepali translator in her twenties, Nihita Biswas. The daughter of Shakuntala Biswas, his highly respected lawyer, Nihita recently suffered a near nervous breakdown after making the mistake of appearing on an Indian reality TV show on which she was asked what it was like to have sex with a serial killer.

Epilogue

A Visit to Herman

In October 2019, in preparation for this book to be re-published, I went to visit Herman Knippenberg in Wellington, New Zealand, where he is now retired with his second wife Vanessa, also a diplomat.

With Richard gone, Herman was one of the few people with whom I could discuss Charles Sobhraj and his continuing notoriety. The questionable accolade of 'one of the greatest criminals of the twentieth century' has often been bestowed on him. To me, he is nothing so ordinary as a serial killer. The murder spree which brought him to public and police attention only constitutes a brief episode in his criminal career. He was a gangster, a con man, a poisoner, a smuggler of gems, drugs and arms, a seducer, an intellectual, a narcissist ... There was never anyone he met or knew or befriended who he didn't harm. In the life of Sobhraj, there was no such thing as a friend, a lover or business partner. All were prey. Even his brothers and sisters were used and abandoned. Of the one person in his life he seemed at one point to love, his first wife, Chantal, he said recently: 'I didn't really love her, I can only love intelligent women.'

This 'disorder' of psychopathy is currently considered to be a mix of genetic inheritance and learned experience. Charles ticked every box in the Hare Psychopathy Checklist:

Glib and superficial charm; grandiose (exaggeratedly high) estimation of self; need for stimulation; pathological lying; cunning and manipulativeness; lack of remorse or guilt; shallow affect (superficial emotional responsiveness); callousness and lack of empathy; parasitic lifestyle; poor behavioral controls; sexual promiscuity; early behavior problems; lack of realistic long-term goals; impulsivity; irresponsibility; failure to accept responsibility for own actions; many short-term marital relationships; juvenile delinquency ... criminal versatility.

Sobhraj is the perfect psychopath. It was a psychological type that was not as well studied then as it is now.

I had not seen Herman for forty years. Now in his seventies and remarkably fit, he struck me as almost unchanged, displaying the same enthusiasm and energy as when we had spent such intense times together in New York in 1977 while researching the story. In the intervening years his career as a senior diplomat had led him all over the world. But he was still haunted by the case, and had written a paper about it for a master's in leadership theory at Harvard University.

In the peaceful house on a hilltop where Herman and Vanessa now live, we settled side by side in armchairs beneath a bay window. An icy wind was blowing off the bay, nipping around the neighbouring white-painted houses with their neat gardens and picket fences. The steamy Bangkok of the seventies felt very far away. I thought of the Paul Theroux quote: 'As Calcutta smells of death and Bombay of money, Bangkok smells of sex, but this sexual aroma is mingled with the sharper whiffs of death and money.' Herman's living room was adorned with antique lithographs of old Asia and Thai antiques. These objects spoke of the past. And so did we.

Last time we had discussed the case, the shock was still fresh for everyone involved. Now a major television drama series was being shot in Bangkok, telling the story from the point of view of the young Herman. I was curious to know what the older Herman now made of the story.

Since the 1970s, Herman had dealt with every kind of political and criminal situation but he told me that he still considered the

solving of the Sobhraj case to be the most important achievement of
his years in the foreign service.

'Of course, the case appealed to my sense of adventure,' Herman
said. Vanessa placed a tray with coffee and his favourite Dutch
almond biscuits on the low table before us and withdrew. 'My own
travels as a student made it easy to identify with the fate of the young
travellers, and the worries of their families waiting at home for
news,' he continued.

It was the same story for us, I agreed. Although our lives had not
been dull, we had never again had an adventure of such intensity.
Looking at the antique lithographs of Bangkok, of the steamy Chao
Phraya river lined with temples and palms trees, which brought back
memories of exotic consular cocktail parties overlooking the water
and hot afternoons in police stations studying photos of burnt
corpses, I realized how strange it was that this subject, this man
Sobhraj, had stayed on, all this time, as a presence in our lives. After
forty years it was a relief to discuss this with someone else who knew
the territory. I declined a biscuit but then found myself anxiously
nibbling one after another.

Herman said, 'When I saw the bodies of Cocky and Henk in the
morgue and learned that they had been doused with petrol and
ignited while still alive, I had a sense of moral outrage that has never
left me. Now I can see that I was obsessed. I behaved in such a way
that it threatened my career and my marriage. I could have handled
it better.'

Relations between Thailand and the Netherlands might well have
been strained by Herman's involvement in the case, which could easily have been construed as interference in Thai internal affairs. He
had brought into question the proper role of the foreign-service
officer.

I really wanted to know Herman's take on the motive for the murders. At the time of writing the book, I had been repulsed by the
famous Sobhraj line, 'I consider myself a businessman and not a
criminal. I never killed good people.' While reviewing all the research
with the drama producers at Mammoth Screen, I was struck again by

the ring of truth to Charles' story of being a hired killer. To me, the facts added up, and the story hung together. But not to Herman.

'When I speak of the murders,' he told me, 'I'm referring to the string of drownings, burnings, stabbings, the six victims in Thailand and two in Kathmandu. They were all in the period when Sobhraj was running his apartment in Bangkok with a group of young travellers who lived and worked with him. You see, I believe he had created a surrogate family. I think he had a compulsive need to create a family and that Marie-Andrée was brought in to play the mother. Ajay and Marie-Andrée were the true believers in Charles. He was their charismatic leader, and Marie-Andrée was in the thrall of outright subjection and bondage. As for the others, he had surrounded himself with followers who for various reasons were not openly critical of his personality and lifestyle.'

'But,' I said, 'everything Charles told us about being a hit-man seemed so consistent.'

'This claim strikes me as pure cant!' Herman said forcefully. 'For the simple reason that professional hit-men, from what I have seen of them, are skilled soloists who discreetly enter an area of operation. They lead a withdrawn existence in a respectable hotel, and immediately get out or go undercover after doing their thing. It is completely self-evident to me that Sobhraj's flamboyant behaviour meant he would never be hired for a job like that.'

Herman had a point. Amsterdam was a hub for drug-dealing in the 1970s and in the course of his career Herman had become expert in many aspects of the international drug trade. He also had access to reports from drug-enforcement agencies from various countries. None of them, he said, suggested that the Sobhraj murders were drug related.

'As we know,' he continued, 'early on he decided that his Indian father was to blame for his problems and that he should have revenge on him. His real father represented the wealth and privilege he believed was rightfully his. But he also blamed and despised his French stepfather, for being weak, damaged by the war, for being a cuckold, for having only modest financial means. And he believed that the French legal system had cheated him of the many years of his youth and this extended out to a hatred of Europeans in general. We can also look back to the stage of his childhood when the family was living in Dakar and Charles as a boy began his criminal career, surrounded by his admiring siblings.'

'So what do you really think was the motive for the murders, Herman?' I asked. I could tell he had a theory all signed, sealed and delivered. We had checked every possible fact and had never seriously considered the possibility that Charles could have invented his job as a hit-man.

'My theory is that Sobhraj had invited the victims to join him, become part of the family, either as members in residence or as business partners, to smuggle gems or whatever else he was up to. By now he had no doubt he could convince anyone to do anything. As he had Yannick, an ex-policeman, acting as his secretary.'

A passage from the book suddenly came to mind, something I'd never quite resolved. I remembered that Reiner Stein, the young gemologist who went into business with Charles in Bangkok, told us that Charles had asked him what he thought of the Dutch couple. Typical travellers, Reiner had replied. A bit on the hippie side. 'I'm thinking of getting them to do some travelling for me,' Charles had said. Gems, Reiner had thought, because Charles was always asking people to smuggle for him, taking emeralds and rubies to Iran or flying diamonds in from Hong Kong to save the 25 per cent duty. Regarding Hakim, Charles had also talked about 'giving that Turkish fellow a job'.

The pile of almond fingers was dwindling as Herman began building to the climax of his hypothesis.

'What if these kids had declined his offer, they wanted to get home for Christmas and so forth! Imagine the shock of finding out that his powers of persuasion weren't working and that his generous invitations to join his magical world were being turned down!' There were some seconds of silence.

'Sobhraj was a person who grew older, but never grew up,' said Herman with certainty, 'and who, on the basis of stifling his feelings, had merely suppressed his fears of rejection and abandonment. These fears were now being triggered when the kids he was sure would want to join him, refused. And so …' He folded his hands as if the matter was now closed.

In forty years, I had never thought about the story in this way. Herman was suggesting an irrational man out of control. But I had always thought of Charles as chillingly rational. He wanted money and passports so he drugged the people who had them. He was paid to kill amateur drug couriers, so he did. Was Charles' air of perfect control just another of his clever illusions? Could Charles have killed people in a panic because they wounded his ego and wouldn't join his gang?

'He saw these kids as his inferiors,' said Herman. 'He felt cornered by them because he had opened up to them about his illegal activities and was now unable to control them. Also, he was incapable of rational judgment. So these people who were plaguing him with anxiety and imbuing him with self-doubt needed to be destroyed.'

We were both quiet again. I was not convinced but tried to consider the possibility that Sobhraj was not the calculating genius he had presented. Then Herman added, in a very pedantic Herman manner, 'Plus of course we must remember that as a believer in the philosophy of Nietzsche, this man saw himself as a "Superman", an adventurer questing for an experience "beyond good and evil". Or perhaps it was not even that he was "beyond good and evil", but that he had an active preference for the latter!'

It was early afternoon when I finally left Herman and Vanessa, after two intense days of discussing the case. The icy wind was still snapping around the modest capital city of New Zealand. With a couple of hours to pass before my flight home I bought some chai, a beverage I had first discovered on my hippie-trail journey which forty years later was now as ubiquitous as coffee. The scent of cardamom and ginger cheered me as I thought about the meaning of the stories we tell about others, and the stories we tell ourselves. Where was the truth?

Charles had told the story of a rejected child who only wanted to recapture his lost youth and live the life he deserved. Alain Benard, the prison visitor, had told the story of a man of privilege trying to bring justice and opportunity to a brilliant young man damaged by an unfortunate childhood. Herman had told the story of the young diplomat fighting the forces of evil and corruption. Nadine's story was of an innocent girl-next-door who stood up for what she believed was right. Chantal was the beautiful girl who had fallen in love with a superman who was really an evil sorcerer. Marie-Andrée had been destroyed too. And we had told ourselves the story of being journalists who had to do whatever it took to write the book.

I've come to see that these 'hero's journey' stories, which occur in all cultures, are a fascinating tool. We are the hero of our own stories. Setting off in innocence down whatever road we randomly choose when we are too young to know what we are doing, we all meet helpers, and tricksters. We face dangers, find and lose friends and love, trip over cliffs, and usually in one way or another, survive adversity. Through our mistakes and our suffering, most of us slowly learn the lessons of kindness, forgiveness, acceptance, tolerance, gratitude, and of living in the present. As we mature through this process, if we are fortunate, we realize that life is a mixture of light and dark. It's an adventure which 'must be lived forwards but can only be understood backwards,' as Kierkegaard said.

But psychopaths are on a mission to exploit everyone and every situation for their own purposes. Their journey is a different one. They are not pebbles to be smoothed by the ebb and flow of life's currents. They are igneous rock that stay for ever jagged and dangerous, with remorse and empathy unknown emotions. Their journey is one solely of exploitation.

One of the lessons of this cautionary tale should be an awareness that such 'inhuman humans' do live amongst us. Many don't end up in jail, but rather reach the highest level in the corporate and political spheres. By their very existence they can allow us to appreciate what it means to be a flawed, suffering, well-meaning human being.

Acknowledgements

Richard Neville, my husband, best friend and the co-author of this book, died in September 2016. He worked far harder to reach a tight deadline on the first edition of this book than I was capable of doing. We both loved words and adventures. Our two daughters, Lucy Neville and Angelica Neville, are carrying on the family tradition of writing and adventuring.

My thanks go to Matthew Turner at Rogers, Coleridge and White, and the late, legendary Deborah Rogers, who always wanted this book to be republished. Also thanks to Carmen Callil for her help, my patient editor at Penguin Random House, Nick Skidmore, and to my editor in Australia, the wondrous Ruth Naomi Hessey. For their help and hospitality, deepest gratitude to Lissa Coote, Dr Yolande Lucire, Dr Rosalie Chapple and Dr John Merson.

From the time the 'Web of Death' headlines appeared in the *Bangkok Post* in May 1976, a young American living in Thailand became obsessed with tracking down the real story of Charles Sobhraj. He hired a researcher and scoured Asia for clues and additional material. William Heinecke became convinced that the life of Sobhraj had relevance and interest beyond local sensationalism. He flew to India to see Sobhraj and secured from him the rights to his biography. Heinecke then approached an American publisher, David Obst Books, who asked us to write the story.

Bill Heinecke, his wife, Kathy, and the researcher, Lillias Woods, maintained a level of cooperation with us beyond that of a business relationship and we thank them. Without Heinecke's continuing efforts this book could not have been written.

To others in Thailand, particularly Colonel Somphol of Interpol, and the staffs of the embassies of the Netherlands, Belgium, Turkey and the United States, we are also grateful. In Delhi, the criminal lawyers and professional criminals gave us the benefit of their know-ledge, and we especially thank Sobhraj's lawyers, Rupindah Singh, Mr Khaurana and Dr Ghatate, as well as ex-cons Daniel Lytrung and Johann and Houria.

The staffs of several foreign embassies in Delhi were helpful; the Canadians and the Australians especially, and in their private cap-acity, Dr Justin and Mrs Barbara Tiernan. The family of Charles' accomplice, Ajay Chowdury, were kind enough to grant us an interview.

In Nepal the Police Department graciously opened its doors and files to us.

Thanks for help in Holland go to the poet Simon Vinkenoog; to Amsterdam's Detective Commissioner Gerard Toorenaar, Chief of the Serious Crimes Squad; and to old friends who searched for clues in the drug underground.

In Paris we were fortunate to have access to all the family and official papers relating to Charles and we are grateful to the hospital-ity and meticulous filing habits of the Sobhraj archivist and prison visitor who prefers not to have his real name published. Also in Paris we thank Martine Halperin for her translations, and Jim Haynes and Jack Henry Moore who helped, despite a lack of enthusiasm for the subject matter.

In London, Joelle Newman and Andrew Fisher tracked down the work of the French School of Characterologists and digested their theories and charts on our behalf, and David Cowell offered us the insights of a criminologist.

In the United States many people contributed to this project, espe-cially David and Lynda Obst, Carol Realini, Claire Rosen, Phillip Frazer, Anna Wintour and Connie Bessie. The people of Shelter Island, NY, made us welcome, and heartfelt thanks are due to Joan Redmond and Karen Lomuscio.

We are indebted to all the people who appear in this story for their time and memories. Many of the members of Charles' own family, his former friends and lovers, jailmates, surviving victims, enemies and pursuers had more to lose than to gain from their help to us and we thank them all for their generosity.

But it is to the families and friends of the young travellers murdered by Sobhraj to whom we owe the greatest debt. They revived painful memories for our benefit, and the only justification for this addition to their grief might be that the publicity generated by this book could contribute towards ending the inefficiency and apathy that Charles Sobhraj exploited in his career as a killer.

The authors and publishers would like to thank the people listed on the credits page for permission to reproduce the photographs.

Credits

Page xi: Cover of *Across Asia on the Cheap* reproduced by permission of Lonely Planet © 1973.

PHOTO INSERT BETWEEN PAGES 138 AND 139

Page 1 (top left, top right, bottom right): W. Heinecke; (bottom left) the Thai police

Page 2 (top left, bottom): W Heinecke; (top right) © Interpol

Page 3 (top, bottom right): W. Heinecke; (bottom left): Dominique Rennelleau

Page 4 (top left): the Thai police; (top right): Kym Casper; (bottom left and right): the Thai police

Page 5 (top left): the Thai police; (top right): the Indian police; (bottom left and right): the Thai police

Page 6: Eric Damour

Page 7 (top): W. Heinecke; (bottom): Nadine and Remy Gires

Page 8 (top left): the Indian police; (top right, bottom): Gus Photo